Insurance

Other Books by David W. Kennedy
The Condominium & Co-op Apartment Buyer's & Seller's Guide
Perfectly Legal (with Barry Steiner)

Insurance

WHAT DO YOU NEED?
HOW MUCH IS ENOUGH?

David W. Kennedy

Knight-Ridder Press
Tucson, Arizona

Published by Knight-Ridder Press
A Division of HPBooks, Inc.
P.O. Box 5367
Tucson, AZ 85703

Printed in U.S.A.
1st Printing
10   9   8   7   6   5   4   3   2

Library of Congress Cataloging in Publication Data

Kennedy, David W.
   Insurance: what do you need?

   Includes index.
   1. Insurance. 2. Insurance, Life. 3. Insurance,
Disability. 4. Insurance, Health. 5. Insurance,
Automobile. 6. Insurance, Homeowners. I. Title.
HG8051.K42   1986   368   86-33789
ISBN 0-89586-568-8 (hardback)
ISBN 0-89586-436-3 (pbk.)

To Barbara:
This one's for you.

Acknowledgments

This book could not have been written without the assistance of some very special people. Particular mention must be made of Mr. Robert Waldron and his staff at the New York office of The American Council of Life Insurance. Their aid was invaluable.

Also, Harvey Seymour and others at the Insurance Information Institute were of great help.

A good measure of appreciation is also due to Messrs. Norse Blazzard, Esq. and Edward Schlessinger, Esq.

Finally to my wife, Barbara Knispel Kennedy, who spent many extra hours typing the manuscript and who offered many excellent editorial suggestions.

Contents

Introduction

If you are like most Americans, you probably spend nearly $3000 a year on a variety of insurance policies to protect you and your family. But do you really know everything you should about the insurance you are buying? Chances are you don't!

That's unnecessary and dangerous, especially when you consider that insurance protection, especially life insurance, has become a virtual necessity. Plus, in most states, it is *illegal* to drive a car if you don't have auto insurance. And if you own a home, you *must* protect that asset with homeowner's insurance.

Disability and health insurance have become mandatory items for most people as well. In short, almost everyone buys these basic types of insurance policies, keeping them in effect for years.

But because the subject matter of insurance is considered complex, or even boring, most people tend to buy insurance without shopping knowledgeably. Or, they don't re-evaluate their needs when changes occur. This book fills that knowledge gap. It shows you how to evaluate your needs and determine the coverage best for you. In addition to saving money, you'll also end up protecting yourself and your family better. The satisfaction and peace of mind you get from doing that is my reward for writing this book.

D.W.K.
New York City, 1986

1

Insurance Basics

Who needs insurance anyway? There is only one answer: Everyone who could suffer severe financial loss if a certain event should occur. And since that is most of us, I think you'll agree with me that insurance *is* a necessity. We all need it. It protects you or your survivors against severe economic loss.

The function of life insurance is to protect your family from the financial consequences of the breadwinner's premature death. Think about it: If you as the chief income earner should die while your children are still young and you are at the height of your earning power, your family would suffer a terrible economic blow. However, if your children were all grown and your spouse is well provided for as the result of investments and the like, your need for life insurance decreases and may be eliminated altogether.

Or if you and your spouse both work, you can protect your family's lifestyle by each of you purchasing enough life insurance to keep everyone living comfortably if one of you dies. One salary just may not be enough to cover expenses.

Auto insurance is used to protect you against the great costs that may be incurred as the result of an auto accident, especially one where you are at fault and a lawsuit could financially drain you.

The same is true with homeowners insurance. If your home were to burn, it would undoubtedly be an immense economic strain to rebuild that house out of your own funds. To protect against that risk you buy homeowner's insurance.

Disability insurance is purchased so you will have income even if you are unable to work because of a disabling injury or illness. For example, if you were to suffer a heart attack and you couldn't go back to work as a result, how would your family cope financially? Would there be sufficient income to pay your bills?

All insurance then, no matter what type or kind is used to protect against some large economic loss. If there are no accidents or events that could cause you economic loss, you don't need insurance. It's as simple as that. (But most of us can't make such claims, so we do buy insurance.)

The loss should not just be a small one. It should be catastrophic. If, for example, you were to develop a medical problem that required surgery and a necessary period of treatment over many months, the hospital bill for such an occurrence could be $40,000 or more. That would be catastrophic if you had to pay it out of your own pocket.

Or, if the mailman should slip and fall on your front porch because you failed to remove some dangerous condition, you could be sued for hundreds of thousands of dollars. You can insure yourself against that possibility with homeowner's insurance.

On the other hand, a small "fender bender" with damages of $300 will probably not break you financially. Neither would the loss of a small television set to a thief, or the loss of a week's income if you broke your arm. You don't need to insure against these.

In summary, every insurance offering should be evaluated in terms of economic loss if you aren't insured. As a result there may be some kinds of insurance offered to you that you shouldn't buy because the possibility of economic loss is not a fair trade-off for the premium you pay to get it.

One example of that is life insurance for children. Remember that the purpose of life insurance is to protect your family from the economic loss resulting from the death of a family breadwinner. Unless your child is a movie or television star on whom you rely for most of your family's income, there is no good reason for a child to have life insurance.

Also, a single person without dependents, regardless of age, probably doesn't need life insurance either because nobody would suffer economic loss from that person's death. If, however, that single person has children to care for, then life insurance is a must.

In most cases, basic insurance coverage, without "frills," is all you will need. Extra benefits such as accidental death benefits or inflation guards or other riders may not be needed, especially when you realize that you pay extra for them.

Insurance, then, is an economic trade-off. You are paying money to an insurance company to assume a financial risk that you could not otherwise handle yourself. Your job as an insurance consumer is to constantly evaluate whether the trade-off is a good one for you. You must evaluate it from an economic and financial point of view, not an emotional one. In other words, make a "hard-headed-consumer" decision. Don't let a salesperson "bully" you into buying insurance by appealing to emotions that have nothing to do with your finances.

Shopping for Insurance

The average American family spends nearly $3000 a year, or more, on complete insurance coverage. Since most people have life insurance, auto and homeowner's coverage at minimum, insurance costs constitute a large financial outlay. Yet most of us are *sold* insurance. We don't *buy* it.

Typically, an insurance agent convinces us that we need a certain amount of coverage and that the cost of the policy will be a certain amount. Few of us really shop around and compare the costs of policies, much less the benefits that we can get from one policy as compared to another.

People who will haggle with other salespeople over potential purchases will not shop around for insurance. That's a big mistake. Few insurance policies are exactly the same, and certainly there may be one policy that is perfectly suited to your needs and your budget. But if you don't look for it, you may end up buying an expensive policy that doesn't cover you the way it should.

It's not the fault of insurance salespeople, either. Remember, they are in business to sell policies. Many of them are affiliated exclusively with one company and they will, of course, try to sell you only the policies of that company.

Your watchword when buying insurance should be the same as when you make any substantial purchase: *caveat emptor,* which means "let the buyer beware." *You* are responsible for what you buy, and if you make a mistake, it's your problem, and potentially a big one.

To stay competitive and to distinguish their products from the other insurance companies, an insurer will often load up his particular policy with what are known as "bells and whistles." An example is a life insurance policy that gives you the option of adding children to your plan. As you'll soon learn, children don't need life insurance coverage, and this needless coverage is an unnecessary expense. Such coverages may have no relevance to your particular situation, but may appeal to somebody. Be wary of the bells and whistles. They are expensive.

Shopping around means making choices among policies based not only on price but whether the policy fits your needs and your family situation. Finding the right policy may take a while, but by judiciously applying the principles of this book, you will undoubtedly find the policy that is right for you, whether it be for life, health, disability, auto or homeowners insurance.

Price is not the only consideration you should consider when you shop around. Other factors, such as service, are important too. If you make a claim, can you expect fair and prompt treatment? What do you think of the company's agents and representatives? Do they seem to be empathetic and understanding?

Sources of Information

Although there are no easy answers to these questions, there are sources of information available. For example, most local libraries will have a copy of the insurance rating guides of A.M. Best and Co. These guides not only provide information on premiums and statistics on the financial viability of all insurers, but they also measure service and rates of customer complaints.

Another excellent source of information is your state insurance department. In many states, that department has a consumer division whose main purpose is to help consumers with insurance company complaints and resolution of conflicts.

Local better business bureaus may also have information on certain insurance companies, particularly if a pattern of complaints has developed.

Finally, you should consider the reputation of the company from experiences related by your friends and relatives, particularly as they regard claims and service. A company's reputation, good or bad, is usually based on more fact than fiction—a good or bad reputation is generally earned.

Insurance Agents

Insurance agents are essentially salespeople. They exist to sell a product, and as in any profession, there are good practitioners and bad ones.

There is a distinction made in the insurance industry between insurance *agents* and insurance *brokers*. Agents normally sell the products of one company. Brokers offer and sell insurance from a number of different insurance companies.

Whether agents are better than brokers, or vice versa, is a debate that will probably never be resolved. But, as an insurance consumer you should take into consideration a number of factors before selecting an agent or broker. And remember, if you are dissatisfied with a particular agent or broker, you can always change.

Consider the following:

□ An agent or broker has two main functions. He or she should be a source of information about what is available in the marketplace, and be able to tell you what is suitable for you in your circumstances.

□ The second function is the real crux of the customer/seller relationship—service. For example, if the agent or broker fails to return your calls or is slow in filling your claims requests, look for a new insurance representative.

◻ Being salespeople, agents or brokers will try to sell you as much insurance as possible because typically their pay is a commission based on the volume of insurance sold. Therefore, don't let yourself get talked into purchasing more insurance than you actually need. *You* should make the decision of how much insurance you need, not an agent or broker.

◻ Similarly, don't take everything that an agent (in particular) tells you at full face value. Some facts about a particular policy may be glossed over or ignored altogether. Be skeptical and ask for proof of statements made about such items as investment return or dividend amounts.

◻ Finally, deal with somebody with years of experience in the field. There is a high turnover of insurance salespeople every year. People seem to float in and out of these sales positions quite freely. A simple order taker will do you no good. An experienced person who can guide you and give you some worthwhile advice is a definite asset.

How Insurance Companies Operate

To fully understand insurance you should have some basic knowledge of how insurance companies make and use their money. Insurance companies are in the business of taking on risks for a fee. That is, you as an individual face a number of uncertainties in your life, such as the possibility of getting in an auto accident or of your house burning down.

Because all of these events could, if they occur, wipe you out financially, you have the choice of keeping that risk or transferring it. Buying insurance then, is transferring that risk.

When you buy an insurance policy, or contract, you determine that you would rather pay a small amount now to protect you against the possible future risk actually happening later on. The premium you pay is the cost of transferring the risk.

About Deductibles

All types of insurance except life, have *deductibles*. A deductible is the amount that you will be responsible for paying out of pocket before your insurance pays anything.

For example, car insurance typically involves a deductible. If you were unlucky enough to have three small accidents within one year and the costs to repair your car were $250, $300 and $225 respectively, you might want to pay for those repairs yourself for two main reasons.

1) From the insurance company's point of view, these claims are relatively small, and the paperwork involved would be out of proportion to the claims. As a result, your premiums might be raised.

2) If you have a series of small claims, the company could cancel your insurance. They have a right to.

Also, insurance is supposed to protect you against *large,* financially draining circumstances. Small claims such as these are not in the large category, although they still do amount to significant cash outlay.

If, though, you ruined your new $15,000 car, that would take a huge bite out of your finances if you chose to replace it.

Therefore, in each case where deductibles are available you will have to determine how much you will pay out of your own pocket and at what point the loss becomes significant.

Some people feel comfortable with auto, homeowners and health deductibles around $500. Some may prefer to absorb less. Others more.

How Deductibles Work

Suppose you have a $500 deductible on your auto policy and cause an auto accident totaling $1200 worth of damage. You must pay the deductible—$500. The insurance company will pay $700 of the bill. The amount of the deductible is always subtracted from the total amount of damage. The insurance company pays the rest.

Many medical insurance plans provide for a 20% deductible in addition to the personal deductible. That is, the insurance company will pay 80% of all bills above the personal deductible—let's say $1000. Given a $3000 hospital bill, you would have to pay $1000 plus 20% of the remaining $2000. That's $400 more, or $1400. The insurance company would then be responsible for paying the remaining $1600, if the policy covers the illness or injury being claimed.

When you think about it, that makes sense because the less the insurance company is at risk for, the less you should have to pay in premiums for that risk transfer.

Every time you buy insurance other than life insurance you have to decide how much of a deductible you want to assume. The term used by financial professionals is how much do you want to *self-insure?* You may decide that you need a $500 deductible on your auto, a $1,000 deductible on your homeowners and a $750 on your health insurance. Or you may have the same deductible for each. The higher your deductible, the less you will pay for the insurance covering that risk.

No matter what size deductible you choose or the type of insurance involved, there is one truism with regard to deductibles: *The higher the deductible, the lower the premium.*

In my opinion, the best way to cut down on your entire insurance bill is by raising deductibles. When you review a policy that you have, consider whether you should raise the deductible to save money.

Maximum savings are achievable when you raise your deductibles and discover every discount you qualify for. That, together with a safety-conscious attitude in everything you do, will enable you to pay as little as possible for the most insurance coverage.

Part of the premium you pay goes into a reserve that the company keeps toward paying off those risks that actually happen. Part of the money goes toward operating the business, and a portion goes toward investments that the insurance company buys to add to its profit.

An insurance company picks and chooses what risks it wants to take on. For instance, life insurers normally sell life, health and disability insurance only. Other insurers, known as *P & C (Property and Casualty) carriers*, insure against property-related risks such as automobile and homeowners insurance.

An insurance company could sell all kinds of insurance, but very few do because a different expertise and way of doing business are required to sell life or health insurance, as opposed to property insurance.

Insurers also select the policyholders whom they want to deal with and the particular environments that they wish to insure. This is known as *managing risk,* or *underwriting.* It means that an insurance company operates within certain guidelines that it sets for itself, such as whether or not to insure a certain type of car or driver. It then quantifies that risk by putting a premium cost, or value, on the risk. Then it proceeds to sell the contract, or policy.

Of course, some people who buy the insurance (except for life insurance) never make a claim. As a result, the insurance company gets to keep and use all the premium money paid in without having to pay anything out.

Ideally, all insurance companies would like to have that happen, but of course it doesn't. Valid claims are paid out all of the time. In essence, when you take out insurance you are making a bet with the insurance company. You are betting that a certain event will occur. The company is saying it won't. But you are paying for the privilege of making that bet.

The most successful insurance companies are those who not only win more bets than they lose, but also run their businesses efficiently and invest the funds wisely.

The insurance company hopes that investment income

alone will offset any losses incurred in paying out claims. An insurance company with a good investment record will probably make money. If the investment performance is poor, chances are the company will lose money.

Insurance companies use statistical mathematicians called *actuaries* whose job it is to calculate the odds on a certain event happening within a certain time frame. For example, they have figured out the odds are for a 40-year-old non-smoking male to live to be 65 years old. In many ways that is the easiest part of the insurance business because actuaries have a good record managing risk statistically.

It is in the other two aspects where insurance companies can have trouble and end up losing money. These are the business and the investment sides of the enterprise. A poorly managed company, one with too many employees and otherwise operated in an inefficient manner, can have the best risk management program imaginable and still lose money. And if the company loses money due to poor management, it will raise premiums to stay in business. If you have a policy with that company, you'll pay more for insurance coverage.

Investing is also an uncertain business for insurers. They have to invest. The only way they can expand the pool of money that policyholders pay is by investing. And as very large investors they invest in everything from stocks and bonds to real estate and business venturing. A good deal of money can be made or lost depending on how savvy the insurance company is in this area.

The best companies are successful at operating all three aspects of the business. Those are the ones you want to deal with. If a company has been around for a number of years, and it has a good reputation, then it probably is a good company. Since a lot of companies fall into that category, you'll have to make your choice of which company or companies to go with based on other factors. As mentioned earlier, these include the quality of service or the kinds of people they hire to sell their product.

State Regulation of Insurance Companies

Insurance companies perform what's called a *fiduciary function*. In other words, they take in and dispense money under the terms of certain legal contracts. These contracts involve an element of trust. This element means the insurance companies are subject to regulation by the states in which they do business.

Every state regulates the sale of insurance policies and the procedures for responding to a claim. A few states, most notably, New York, California and Pennsylvania have very strict insurance laws. Those laws are written to protect the state residents against the insurance companies. As a result, some companies will not do business in those states. But since these three states are consumer-oriented and are trying to protect the consumer, the companies operating in these states are the ones you should be interested in dealing with.

The state of New York has the strictest insurance laws. Yet even if you don't live in New York, you can take advantage of the laws. To do so, make sure that the insurance company you want to do business with is qualified to sell policies in New York. If it isn't, find a company that is.

Insurance Review

Your entire insurance package should be reviewed at least once a year. Carefully study each policy and rethink it 60 days prior to renewal. I recommend a two-month advance review because most insurance policies are billed on an annual basis, beginning and ending on a specific date.

If, however, there is a drastic change in your circumstances, such as the birth of a child or a sudden change in your financial situation, then you should review the affected policies right away.

For instance, the birth of a child might prompt you to change the beneficiary on your life insurance policy. Or you may wish to purchase more. Similarly, the purchase of a second car should cause you to review your auto insurance coverage. And buying a house should prompt a new look at your homeowner's insurance.

In summary, you should be on the lookout for changes in your life that might change your insurance needs.

Determining How Much Insurance You Need

Unfortunately, there are no absolute rules or guidelines that tell you exactly what your insurance needs are. Since each individual's requirements are so personal and unique, and each family's financial circumstances are so different, you must work it out for yourself with your agent.

However, here is a good approach that can get you started:

First, figure out how much insurance coverage you already have that is provided by others. If, for instance, your employer gives you $200,000 worth of life insurance as a fringe benefit, that may be all the life insurance you need. Or, your spouse's employer may cover your family with health insurance. In this case you may need little or no additional health coverage. The same can be true with auto insurance if you are a travelling salesperson.

Once you determine how much insurance others provide for you (whether you have to pay for all or part of that coverage is unimportant at this point) then you can get a fuller picture of how much insurance coverage you need.

Second, you'll have to determine what insurance coverage is most valuable to you. If you have just moved into a new house, a homeowners policy may take precedence over a disability policy at this point. Or, if you just became a parent, protecting your family through the purchase of life insurance may take precedence in your mind.

Third, you must rank your insurance needs in order of priority according to your own situation. Obviously, the needs that appear near the top of the list are those you should spend the most on. But, if you are like most people, you'll want to have some of all of the major insurance types—life, health, auto, homeowners and disability—and not do without any completely.

Then of course, you must look at your own budget and decide how much you can spend on your entire insurance package. If you take advantage of discounts (more about that later) and deductibles (also to be discussed) you can probably meet all your insurance needs affordably.

A good insurance agent or broker should be of some assistance in helping you determine your insurance needs and allocating your available funds. You should discuss your needs and desires with an articulate insurance professional who has helped others plan their total insurance programs.

The Insurance Buyer's 13 Commandments

The following "commandments" are discussed in greater depth throughout this book. They are summarized here to give you a flavor of what lies ahead.

I. Thou shalt know exactly at all times how much you have paid for all forms of insurance coverage. By knowing how much you have spent, you can determine whether you can save money by buying a different policy.

II. Thou shalt not trust everything an insurance company or insurance agent tells you. After all, insurance companies are in business to make a profit, and agents make their living by selling policies.

14

III. Thou shalt always shop around for the best insurance buys available. This may require patience and hard work.

IV. Thou shalt never buy more insurance than needed. This requires a constant evaluation of insurance needs on an ongoing basis.

V. Thou shalt always, whenever possible, take advantage of other people's insurance coverage. For example, if you are employed and your employer provides health insurance for your family, use it. Or if a fraternal lodge offers you life or disability insurance at a substantial discount, consider it very carefully.

VI. Thou shalt always take the maximum available deductible affordable. This is the best way to save the most on your total insurance bill.

VII. Thou shalt always know what discounts are available and to take them whenever possible. Discounts save you money.

VIII. Thou shalt evaluate the entire insurance package regularly, to avoid purchasing duplicate or overlapping coverage.

IX. Thou shalt conduct an annual review of insurance needs. Because your family and economic circumstances and need for insurance are constantly changing, a yearly insurance check-up is a smart way to look after your insurance program. For example, if you are over 65, you probably don't need a disability insurance policy. You may not need life insurance any more, either.

X. Thou shalt never buy insurance from a company not licensed in your state.

XI. Thou shalt not cancel any policy without first having a good reason for doing so. Finding a cheaper policy that offers the same benefits would be an example of a good reason.

XII. Thou shalt not buy unnecessary insurance policies. Examples are, travel insurance, mugging insurance and credit card insurance.

XIII. Thou shalt realize that insurance coverage is an important part of one's overall financial planning. Therefore, you must give it due importance.

Read Your Insurance Policies

Most people buy an insurance policy, stick a copy of it in a drawer, and don't read it until they have to make a claim. That's unwise.

Read the policy as soon as you receive it. As soon as your agent sells you a policy, ask for a duplicate that you can read and study before you receive the actual policy. It may be heavy going, but it may not. Some states now require that insurance policies be written in plain English. Three examples of such policies are reproduced in this book.

If you don't understand something when you read it, mark it. When you have finished reading the entire policy, call your agent (if sold by an agent) or the company (if sold directly to you by a company representative) and get the answers to your questions. Make sure you understand the policy. You may want to make notes to yourself on your copy of the policy.

Pay particular attention to how to make a claim in the case of auto, homeowner's and health insurance, and how to change beneficiaries in the case of life insurance.

Many people photocopy their policies in full and give

copies to their attorney or relatives to keep in case of an emergency. That's a smart thing to do. It's also a good idea to keep your policies in a fireproof safe deposit box or strong box. And be sure to tell your immediate family members where the copies are kept in case you are unable to get them yourself.

An insurance policy defines the rights and responsibilities of the insurer (the company) as well as the insured (the policyholder). A thorough knowledge of its contents will help you to act efficiently if and when you have to make a claim or you want to change your policy.

Applying for Insurance

The effective date of your insurance policy can be very important because this is the date that the policy actually begins. You can't make a claim before that date, just as you can't make a claim after the policy has expires. With many types of life insurance, for example, you must pass a physical examination to receive the insurance. Because different states have different rules regarding the timing of when a life insurance policy goes into effect, find out from the agent or company employee who sold you the policy when the policy begins. It could be when you turn over the initial premium to the salesperson, or it may not be until you have the policy in your hands.

Timing is also crucial with regard to auto and homeowner's insurance as well. It is quite possible that an auto accident could occur or your house could burn down immediately after you apply for the appropriate insurance. Therefore, you need to know exactly when your policy goes into effect.

One other very important thing about life insurance: In most states, you have the option of cancelling a life insurance purchase within 10 days of signing the contract.

имеет право

This is called the *second look provision*. You are entitled to get any premiums back you have paid if you cancel. This second look provision is normally available only with life, health and disability policies.

2

Life Insurance

Life insurance is very different from auto and homeowner's insurance. In auto and homeowner's insurance, you effectively make a bet with the insurance company that you won't get in a crash or your house won't burn down. If those events do happen, the insurance company "loses" the bet and has to pay the claim. In most cases, the event doesn't occur. As a policyholder, you know that and hope it won't occur, but there is a risk that it will. And if the event does occur, it could be very costly to you. So, for a fee you transfer that risk to the insurance company.

Life insurance is different. Both you and the insurance company know that the insured event—your death—will occur. The risk involved is *when you will die*. It could be 40 years from now, or it could be tomorrow. The *when,* not the *if* is being insured against. Life insurance is therefore a time-oriented product. The insurance company plays the odds that you won't die before "your" time.

Insurance companies have turned these odds into amazingly accurate predictability. Actuarial science determines for example, the odds that a 35-year-old man will die within one, five or ten years—or will live to age 80. Because the odds of that particular event occurring are quite small, insurance companies feel quite confident in selling a life insurance policy to any healthy 35-year-old man. Some 35-year-old men do die within a short period of time, but most don't. The premiums that all 35-year-olds pay are mathematically determined by the insurance company based on the odds.

As you grow older, the odds of your dying increase, and that is why with *term* insurance (explained on page 28) you must pay more as you get older.

Of course, insurance carriers structure the odds in their favor. If you are in poor health, the chances are that an insurance company will not insure your life because they could lose the bet and have to pay off early.

Insurance companies call the choosing of customers *underwriting*. And in underwriting, life insurance is no different from auto and homeowners insurance: *An insurance company can pick and choose its customers.* If it feels that because of your health, it doesn't want to sell you a policy, you can't make the company insure you.

Specialized insurers do insure high-risk individuals, but these policies can be expensive. And even these insurers are under no obligation to accept everybody.

What Is Life Insurance?

Life insurance has many uses. Its main use is to protect a dependent or a family from the premature death of the breadwinner. Life insurance can also be used as an estate-planning tool or as a means of saving for retirement. It can be used to make a charitable gift, or it can be borrowed against for present needs.

If you were to use the services of a financial planner, one of the first questions he or she would ask you would be what type and how much life insurance you have. That's because life insurance is the most basic of all the financial instruments planners use to evaluate and plan the financial programs of their clients.

In short, life insurance has become a financial and estate-planning necessity for many people. Yet, few individuals who buy life insurance really know what they are buying, much less how much is appropriate.

The old saying "Life insurance is not bought, it's sold." tells a sorry tale. People are usually convinced to buy insurance by a salesperson who may end up selling you more or less life insurance than actually needed or wanted.

It doesn't make sense for people to spend hundreds or thousands of dollars a year on a product that they know little or nothing about. Because the subject of life insurance has all the sex appeal of a sea slug, they find it hard to understand.

But it is not difficult at all. Fundamentally, life insurance has one basic function: To provide income for a family whose breadwinner has died prematurely. The income that breadwinner brought in enabled the family to buy a house, feed and clothe itself, and save money for the children's educations. If, because of death, that income is suddenly cut off, the family would suddenly be in a financial bind. Life insurance plugs the gap, and as a result is a necessity for most families.

Who Needs Life Insurance?

But not *everybody* needs life insurance. Life insurance is designed for protecting those individuals who are dependent on the earnings of someone else. If nobody depends on you, you don't need life insurance.

Children certainly don't need life insurance because they aren't earning a living, and nobody is depending on their earning power. Similarly, single individuals who have no responsibilities do not need life insurance. But, a single parent or a single person who is supporting an aged parent or relative should be insured.

Similarly, most retired couples probably don't need life insurance if their family responsibilities are behind them. By cashing in their life insurance, however, they may be able to provide a nice nest egg for their retirement years. That will be discussed later.

Even though life insurance has many uses and is flexible, it should only be purchased in the first instance as an instrument that affords financial protection to those people who are dependent on the insured's income.

Naturally, as the circumstances of your life change, you should reassess your need for life insurance. If you become single with no dependents, you don't need life insurance. If you get married and have children, your life insurance needs increase. Then you should purchase as much life insurance as your family would need if you should die. Suppose that you suddenly become quite wealthy, and your family was well provided for through investments, savings and other income sources. Then you probably wouldn't need life insurance.

In short, your particular need for life insurance and the amount necessary should be reviewed regularly. If you are employed and you have group life coverage as a fringe benefit, or if your spouse gets a job where life insurance is part of the employment package, your need for individual coverage may disappear altogether. For example, if you and your spouse work and both of your employers provide you with a total of $300,000 worth of life insurance as a fringe benefit, that may be sufficient to meet all your life insurance needs.

How Much Life Insurance Do You Need?

Before you can determine how much insurance you need, you have to figure out what the proceeds of a life insurance policy will be used for after your death.

You've already learned that the most important function of life insurance is to replace income lost because of your death. That's the most important need of all.

In the event of your death, your life insurance should also pay enough money to take care of your burial, final debts and any estate taxes that might be due. Hospital and doctor bills may also result from a final illness. Of course, the exact amount of these figures is unknowable, but you should select a figure that is on the high side just to be safe.

In addition, if you should die prematurely, your spouse and your family will probably need some interim money to readjust their lives. For example, your family might have to move from their expensive house, or your spouse might

Personal Financial Statement

CURRENT NET WORTH

Assets

Real Estate

    Home (full market value) $ _____

    Business $ _____

    Other $ _____

Life Insurance

    Cash value of your life insurance $ _____

    Cash value of family member's life insurance $ _____

Cash or equivalent funds

    Cash in bank $ _____

    Emergency fund $ _____

    Permanent savings $ _____

    Checking account $ _____

    Money market/Certificates $ _____

    Pension plan $ _____

Investments

    Bonds $ _____

    Stocks $ _____

    Mutual Funds $ _____

Personal Property

    Home furnishings $ _____

    Automobile $ _____

    Jewelry, clothes, silver, china, furs, art, etc. $ _____

    Miscellaneous $ _____

Total Assets $ _____

Liabilities
   Mortgages $ _____
   Installment loans $ _____
   Educations loans $ _____
   Other loans $ _____
   Charge accounts $ _____
   Other debts $ _____

Total Liabilities $ _____

Total Assets $ _____
minus Total Liabilities $ _____
Net Worth $ _____

ESTIMATE OF FAMILY RESOURCES
AFTER POLICYHOLDER'S DEATH

Annual Income
   Survivor's salary $ _____
   Interest $ _____
   Dividends or savings $ _____
   Real estate rent received $ _____
Benefits
   Annuity income $ _____
   Social Security $ _____
   Veterans' $ _____
   Life insurance $ _____
   Pension $ _____
   Trust income $ _____
   Other income $ _____

Total Annual Income $ _____

Estimated Annual Expenses

Housing

    Rent $ _____

    Mortgage $ _____

    Utilities $ _____

    Other $ _____

    Food $ _____

    Home $ _____

    Away $ _____

Clothing/upkeep $ _____

Transportation $ _____

Education $ _____

Entertainment and recreation $ _____

Medical and dental expenses $ _____

Insurance premiums

    Life $ _____

    Health $ _____

    Disability $ _____

    Auto $ _____

    Other $ _____

Payments

    Loan $ _____

    Installment $ _____

Taxes

    Local $ _____

    State $ _____

    Property $ _____

    Income $ _____

    Other $ _____

Total Annual Income minus $ _____
Total Annual Expenses $ _____
Net Resources $ _____

Typical Events That Should Trigger
Re-Evaluation of Your Life Insurance Plan

- Marriage.
- Birth of a child.
- Death of a child.
- Death of a spouse.
- Adoption of a child.
- A dependent relative coming to live with you permanently.
- Commencing a financial obligation for an aged parent, handicapped relative or disabled child.
- Taking on any large financial obligation.
- The permanent disability of a child or aged parent that you are responsible for.
- Ending of that financial obligation.
- Purchase of a house.
- Retirement.
- Change in jobs.
- A spouse's job change.
- Children getting married and going out on their own.
- A sudden change in your economic fortunes.
- Starting a business.
- Ending a business.
- Divorce.
- Remarriage.

have to get a job. All of this must be provided for as well.

Life insurance salespeople have a tendency to be rather glib, and as a rule of thumb they usually say that your total insurance needs should equal five times your annual income. However, like most generalizations this one is probably wrong for you. For example, if you have five children who are still young, and you want to provide for their educations, five times your annual salary may not be enough. On the other hand, if you have just one child and a working spouse who also has insurance coverage, five times your income may be too much.

It comes down to working out your own numbers the best way you can. The accompanying Personal Financial Statement is a guide for you to estimate your family's financial picture. You need to determine two things: 1) How much income your family will have in the event of your death. 2) And how much income will be needed by your family to continue the same lifestyle after your death. Although not perfect, it is an excellent worksheet to help you approximate your life insurance needs. You should recalculate these numbers annually so you can adjust your life insurance needs as your financial and family situations change.

Types of Life Insurance

In recent years there have been a number of new life insurance products introduced. All of them are a variation of one or more of four basic types, *term, whole life (cash value), universal and variable life* insurance. To evaluate your life insurance needs properly, you need to thoroughly understand each type.

Term Insurance

This type of insurance is aptly named. It provides life

insurance protection for a specified term of years. One, three or five years are common periods. Few last longer than five years.

Initially, term insurance is quite cheap. That's the best thing about it. However, after each period expires, the cost of the policy rises for the next period. Suppose you bought term insurance as a very young person, say 21 years old. Then you renewed it up to age 65. By that time you would probably be paying more for it than you would be for other types of life insurance.

Term insurance is sometimes considered "pure insurance" because it doesn't provide you with anything other than insurance protection. If you die while your term policy is in effect, your beneficiary gets the face amount of your policy. It's is a very simple and understandable concept.

If, however, you live through the term of the policy, the policy expires, and your life insurance protection ends unless you renew.

Term insurance is available both as an individual product and through a group. Group term insurance is usually offered or given to you by an employer as part of your fringe benefits package. A typical group term amount for an employee is $50,000.

Because term insurance is relatively inexpensive, it is probably most suitable for young families who have limited funds to spend on life insurance. Whether it will be suitable for the rest of that policyholder's life is for the policyholder to decide.

If you buy term insurance and are expecting to renew it, you must insist on a *guaranteed renewable* term. Remember that when a term policy expires, you lose your life insurance protection. Suppose your health deteriorated since you last purchased term. The insurance company could refuse to renew your policy, and you might be unable to get coverage anywhere.

With a guaranteed renewable policy, however, the company cannot deny your right to renew no matter what your physical condition might be. To limit their risk, most companies won't renew you past age 70. Some policies may even be non-renewable at 55. If you still need life insurance coverage after that expiration age, most policies provide for a conversion of the term policy to a cash value policy.

Whole Life, or Cash Value, Policies

In contrast to term insurance, which expires and must be renewed periodically, whole life has no term of years. There is no need to renew it. As long as you pay the premium as due, your policy lasts your whole lifetime. If you live past age 65 or 70 or whatever, good for you. If you have paid the premiums, your policy remains in force and your beneficiaries collect the face amount of the policy upon your death. (Because of these principles, another name for whole life is *straight life.*)

Even so, there's more to whole life than just that. There is an added element called the *cash value.* This is how it works. Every time you pay your premium, the insurance company does two things. It puts a portion of that money into a fund to cover the possibility that you will die soon, requiring a payout. The other portion is put into a separate "savings" account that you can take advantage of. This is often called *forced savings,* and it's just that.

The cash value serves two main purposes. If you decide at a later age—say 65 when you are retiring—that you no longer need life insurance coverage, you can cash the policy in and receive a nice nest egg for your retirement. Because only a portion of your premium has been set aside for the cash value, the cash value will normally not equal the face amount of the policy. (It would if you lived to a ripe old age of 95 or so.)

Nevertheless, the amount could very easily be about 50% of the face amount. So, if you had a $100,000 policy, you might be able to cash it in for about $50,000.

You can also use the cash value as an account to borrow from. Assume, for example, that you want to send your first child to college, but you don't have the funds readily available to do that. A personal loan from a bank might do, but the interest might be very high.

Alternatively, you could borrow from the cash value of your life insurance policy. The insurance company will usually lend you the money at an interest rate that is two or three points lower than the bank rate.

One of the beauties of this loan is that you don't even have to pay it back. If you don't and you should die, the amount of the loan will be deducted from the proceeds of the policy when it is paid to your beneficiary. If you borrowed $10,000 from your $100,000 face amount policy, for example, and you don't pay it back, your beneficiary would receive $90,000 upon your death.

Cash value, to sum up, is a feature of whole life that you can use *during your lifetime*. With term policies you get no such benefit.

Because it costs more money to fund a cash value policy, whole life premiums are considerably higher than term premiums or a policy of a similar face amount. Initially, whole life costs 4 to 5 times as much!

Another difference is that term premiums increase, while whole life premiums are the same every month you hold the policy. So, if when you first buy the policy, it costs you $500 a year, that's what you'll pay as long as you keep it in effect.

Because the first few years of whole life premiums will be higher than term premiums for a policy of the same face amount, you should plan to keep a whole life policy for your whole life—hence the name. The longer you keep a whole life policy, the less it costs compared to a term policy.

Financial planners usually argue that because term insurance is cheaper, it is better. Actually they believe that everyone should buy term insurance and invest the difference between what the term policy costs and the cost of a comparable cash value policy. That argument assumes two things: 1) Everyone will invest the difference. 2) The cash value is a worthless addition to an insurance policy.

Many people do, however, need a forced savings vehicle. If they use the cash value to take a loan or to cash in when they retire, that is something that they should be permitted to do if they so choose. But with IRA's, Keoghs and corporate pension plans available, there may be less need for life insurance as a retirement tool.

You will, of course, have to determine for yourself whether or not you have saved enough for your own retirement through IRA's, Keoghs and savings. A cash value policy can be used to supplement your retirement account quite substantially, and some cash value buyers purchase these policies for just that purpose.

Whole life insurance has been sold for many years, and far more Americans are owners of such policies than term. So it seems that Americans are comfortable with it and find it useful.

Another argument against whole life does have some merit to it. That is, that since salespeople make a much larger commission on whole life rather than term, they would rather sell you a whole life policy. At least 55% of your first year's premium goes toward paying the salesperson's commission. With a term policy, it is about 35%. But, if you decide that whole life is what you need, that's what you should buy.

Borrowing on a Whole Life Policy. As mentioned, you can borrow against the policy. However, you should do it as a loan of last resort. True, the loan is normally given at an interest rate cheaper than prevailing bank rates. But since you want to protect your beneficiaries to the fullest extent possible, you should only borrow from a policy out of absolute necessity. Remember, if you die before paying back the loan, any remaining amount due on the loan will be subtracted from the death benefit given to your beneficiary.

To determine exactly how much you can borrow, look up the table of cash values on your policy. You can usually borrow any sum up to the full cash value available.

It's much easier than getting a bank loan. If you own a

cash value policy that you have been paying on and you are totally up to date on your premiums, you automatically qualify. *You cannot be rejected for a cash value loan.* No other collateral need be put up to get the loan.

Each insurer will have its own rules and regulations with regard to how you can pay back the loan, but as long as you are paying the interest according to schedule, your policy will not be in jeopardy. If you make no payments of either principal or interest before you renew your policy, the company can cancel the policy. Therefore be sure you understand the payback schedule thoroughly before you take out a policy loan.

Universal Life

Universal life is the "hot" new insurance product. If you haven't received a solicitation for it, you probably will soon. In many ways it looks like a whole life policy, but it is more flexible. Here's how it works:

After you make a required initial premium payment, you can make future premium payments at any time and in any amount, subject to a built-in minimum. For example, if your first required payment was $600, you need not pay that amount again. You may, if you wish, make a payment of $500 or $450 or $1,000 as you see fit. You can even designate how much of your payment should be applied to the insurance part of the policy and how much to the cash value. You can even skip payments if you like and the insurance company will pay for the insurance part of your policy out of the cash value.

You have the flexibility of raising or lowering the amount in your insurance portion and your cash value as your insurance needs change. There is no need to buy another policy. Universal life is a kind of all-in-one policy. Thus you save money on commissions and other fees associated with the purchase of a new life insurance policy.

Because cash values build up tax-free, you may want to make a large premium payment and designate that the extra amount be allocated to the cash value portion of the policy. That way later on you can borrow on that cash value. And since you don't pay taxes on the amount borrowed, you are getting a double tax break. That is, you get a tax break because the cash builds up tax-free in the cash value portion of the policy. In addition, you don't pay any taxes on any amount you borrow from the policy.

Another feature of Universal life is that the insurance company doesn't just sit on the savings portion of your account. They invest that money and try to earn as much from it as possible. For example, with a rising stock market, many insurance companies can realize 10% gains on these accounts. Usually they guarantee a rate of 4% or 5%.

When agents sell universal life, many of them will talk in terms of the highest gains achievable, not the much lower *guaranteed rates*. Because the amount of money actually earned will probably be closer to the guaranteed rate than the higher rate, you may get a distorted picture of the policy's true benefits.

Also, because the insurance company invests your money for you, they charge high investment fees back to you. This is an annual fee similar to a brokerage commission you would pay to a stockbroker who invested your money for you. In addition, there are some other fees and commissions that have to be paid that you don't pay with a term or cash value policy.

Most universal policies also impose a surrender charge if you decide to cash in the policy. Oftentimes all these fees and charges are not mentioned by the salesperson.

With investment assumptions based on an interest rate that is not guaranteed and a heavy burden of fees and charges, the ultimate death benefit going to your beneficiary could be far less than the salesperson promised when you were sold the policy.

Even so, many insurance companies are good investors, and you may come close to what the salesperson promised. Remember, however, that *there is no guarantee of investment performance in a universal policy above what a bank would give you on a savings account.*

Variable Life

A new product that puts the onus of investing on you is called *variable life*. With variable life the cash value is affected by investments, while the death benefit is a fixed, minimum amount.

With a variable life policy, the insurance company offers you the option of investing the cash value portion of your account in stocks, bonds, mutual funds or a combination of all of them. You can mix and match any way you like. And with most variable policies, you can borrow against the cash value.

Variable life insurance is not for the investment novice. *If you pick the wrong investments, you could wipe out your total cash value.* Therefore, variable life insurance can be a risky investment. Remember, if you consider a high cash value important, variable life may not be right for you.

Although fees and commissions with variable life are not as large as they are with universal life, they are substantial nevertheless.

There are also some other types of policies. With *adjustable life* you can increase or decrease your insurance coverage by adjusting your premium payments. There's even a *variable-universal life* policy that combines the features variable and universal coverage options into one policy.

With all these different types of variable life policies, there appears to be a life insurance product available to suit the needs of just about everyone. Your best bet is to sit down with a knowledgeable insurance broker, go over the options, and with his or her assistance pick the policy that most suits your family's needs.

Endowment Policies

Another kind of life insurance should be mentioned,

mainly so you will stay away from it. It's called *endowment insurance,* and it's one of the worst buys in life insurance today. There is no reason to buy it because other policies perform the same function at a cheaper price.

An endowment policy emphasizes the cash value aspects of life insurance. It provides a death benefit, but not one that is permanently endowed.

Here's how it works. You would buy an endowment policy that matures or "endows" after a set number of years or when you reach a certain age. For example, if you were to buy an endowment policy today that endows in 20 years, at the end of that time you would get the face amount of the policy.

If you died before the 20 years was up, and you had been paying your premium regularly, your beneficiary would receive the face amount of the policy. But, if you live the 20 years and collect on the policy, there will be no death benefit paid, because there is nothing left in the policy.

As mentioned earlier, premiums for endowment policies are higher than for whole life insurance. The shorter the endowment period, the higher the premium.

Endowment policies are often sold by agents as an ideal vehicle to use to send your children to college. Because you get a set amount of money at a certain guaranteed time, the idea sounds good. The only problem is that such a policy doesn't take into account the vagaries of inflation. Nor does it prove to be a good "investment" either. You can undoubtedly make your money compound faster and save for your children's education by using real investment vehicles such as stocks, bonds or mutual funds to better benefit.

A term policy will, in most cases, do the same job as an endowment policy and at a much cheaper price. Most financial planners and insurance experts counsel against purchasing an endowment policy. It is a product that has outlived any usefulness it might have once had.

Limited Payment Policies

Limited payment policies, or as they are sometimes called *vanishing premium* life insurance policies, are becoming heavily advertised these days. You make premium payments for a set number of years such as six, eight or ten years. Then you need not make any more payments after that period. When you finish paying, you have fully paid the policy.

There's only one problem with these policies. There is no guarantee as to exactly how long you will have to make payments. That's because what they hide in the fine print of the policies is something to this effect: "If we continue crediting interest at the same rate we are right now, the policy will be paid off in six years."

Interest is credited to the policies as the result of excess investment earnings, and of course, no one can guarantee investment results. If an agent or advertisement or anyone else "guarantees" that you will only have to pay premiums, for say five years, be wary.

Also, remember that a limited payment policy is being paid off much more quickly than a conventional life policy, so your premium will naturally be higher for the limited number of years. So unless you are sure that you can make these high payments each year, you should opt for a more conventional policy.

Few people feel secure enough in their job or career to be absolutely sure they will be doing better each year. And if you don't keep up with the payments, you might have to surrender the policy. When you apply for insurance again you will be older and your health may have deteriorated, so a new policy will obviously cost you more.

Single Premium Life Insurance

Another new product getting a lot of play these days is the single premium policy. As its name implies, you make just one premium payment for this policy. That premium, however, is usually very large—for example, $20,000 is not uncommon.

"Single premium" isn't really life insurance. It's really just a cash-value product that looks like life insurance. You do get death benefits from the product, but they are considerably less than if you spent the same amount for a term policy. Upon payment of the premium, you get a fully paid up policy.

The main selling point of this product is the tax-free buildup of the cash value. The insurance company normally guarantees that you will earn a specific interest rate, such as 9%.

Since the whole point here is to build up the cash value as quickly as possible, most buyers purchase single premium life so they can borrow that money at some later time for such things as their children's education. The cash value build-up occurs much faster than with a regular cash value policy, and you can start borrowing usually after you have had the policy for two years.

Of course, if you do take out a loan or loans, the amount you take out is deducted from the ultimate amount that your beneficiary will get at your death. But, and this is important, any money remaining in the cash value that has not been borrowed is added to the face amount of the policy. And your beneficiary gets the full amount.

For example, if you buy a $50,000 face amount single premium whole life policy and over your life time you only borrow $15,000 from it, your beneficiary would get the $50,000 (since the policy is paid up already) and any money remaining in the cash value account minus $15,000.

Besides the heavy lump sum premium that you must pay, these policies have a number of other drawbacks.

☐ If you cash in the policy, all of the money that you invested in it, as well as the accumulated build-up will be fully taxable.

☐ The insurance company will charge you a loan fee each

and every time you borrow. Those fees are taken out of your cash value, so your return from the policy may be less than you anticipated or were led to believe by the salesperson.

□ Although you earn a guaranteed interest rate, if inflation should happen to jump up into the double digits as it did in the late 1970's and early 1980's, you would, in effect, be losing money. That's because that interest rate never changes and if the guaranteed rate is 8% and inflation is 11%, you would be losing 3% on your money.

□ If you have to give up the policy within the first few years of your purchase, you will have to pay a hefty surrender charge based on a percentage of the cash value.

Because of all these disadvantages, once you buy a single premium policy you will probably be stuck with it for life, so be very careful before you plunk down the huge single premium these policies require.

Shopping for Life Insurance

With the myriad of policies available and over 2000 companies offering life insurance, shopping for the proper policy can be a chore. But if you use the following procedure, you may be able to find the right policy in a very short time. Here's what you can do:

First, go to three different insurance agents and ask each to make you a proposal for life insurance. You must, of course, give all three the exact same information about your needs and financial resources. Then, once you have the three proposals in hand, circulate them to all three of the agents. Have them criticize the other proposals in a written reply to you. You will want them to particularly note the advantages and disadvantages of the other agents' proposals.

Don't use more than three agents because the process will get too complicated. And do put a time limit on their replies so that you can make your choice expeditiously. If you can do this with three "independent" agents—that is agents who represent more than one insurer—your chances of finding the right policy will undoubtedly be enhanced.

If you are totally honest with the three agents involved, and you let them know from the beginning what you are doing, you will probably get the agents' competitive juices flowing. All should give you the best proposal possible. Eliminate any agent who doesn't want to play this game, and find another one.

Once you have studied the proposals and the criticisms of each proposal, you will have a better understanding of what you need. Then you can then make an informed decision.

If you are still unsure of which insurance company to pick, there are some other things you might want to check out. The best way to do that, of course, is to check with your state's insurance department. They will be able to tell you which companies meet these criteria and which don't.

□ How stable is the company? Is it financially able to meet its debts on a regular basis? Will the company still be there when I die so that the insurance will be paid to my beneficiaries? Stick to a better known company rather than a fly-by-night.

□ Does the company have a balanced investment portfolio? If not, it may be putting all of its eggs in one basket, and if the investment turns sour the company could end up bankrupt.

□ If the company is a *mutual company,* find out if it has always met its dividend projections. If it has, you can be fairly sure that it is financially solid.

□ Go to the A. M. Best series of insurance analyzers and look for the expense-to-premium ratio reported for the company you are interested in doing business with. If that ratio is above 20, find another company. The lower the number, the better.

Here are some other important questions you might want to ask:

□ Do you really know the company you are dealing with?

If it is not licensed to do business in New York State (the toughest of all states to be registered in) don't do business with it.

☐ Will the person who sold you the policy be there when you may need service on it? There is a huge turnover in insurance agents. Remember, service is a vital part of the insurance transaction.

☐ If you have to change beneficiaries or borrow money, will your needs be dealt with quickly and efficiently? If not, go elsewhere.

Life Insurance As Fringe Benefit

Most employers in this country, no matter what their size, usually offer term life insurance to their employees as a fringe benefit at little or no cost to the employee. This is *group coverage*. The employer acts as policyholder and all eligible employees are entitled to the same group benefits.

Employees may receive $50,000 worth of life insurance as a tax-free fringe benefit. If your employer pays for your premiums for coverage above $50,000, tax law says the premiums paid for the amount above $50,000 is considered part of your taxable income. Tax law also says that if you pay the premiums entirely, any amount above $50,000 is fully taxable to you as well.

Many employers do allow their employees to purchase supplemental life insurance coverage above the $50,000 mark. In many cases, this coverage can be bought at the group rate, which is typically cheaper than an individually purchased policy. For exact information on rates and more details, contact your employer's benefits office.

Also, most plans provide for a conversion privilege. That allows an employee who leaves the firm to convert his or her group policy to an individual policy. The applicable rate is determined by his or her age at the time. Normally, this is done without the former employee having to furnish any further evidence of insurability. That means you don't have to have a medical examination. There is usually a time limit on the conversion privilege, usually 31 days from leaving employment.

Many people find that they can satisfy their life insurance needs almost exclusively through employer paid group and supplemental coverages. The cost is almost always cheaper than an individual policy with the same benefit. Run your own cost comparison to be sure you are getting the most for your money this way.

Remember that this is term coverage. If you need whole life or any other cash-value product, you will have to buy it on your own.

In summary, the employer's group policy is an excellent fringe benefit that all employees can use to partially satisfy their life insurance needs. I strongly urge you to take advantage of it.

Life Insurance and Your Estate

Estate planning is the process by which you decide how to dispose of your property both while you are alive and after your death. Your property is called your *estate*. As you would expect, life insurance must become an integral part of your estate planning. Besides providing a lump sum amount of money for your beneficiary on your death, life insurance has a number of advantages as far as your estate is concerned:

□ Because insurance proceeds are usually paid within one month from the death of the insured, a policy gives your heirs *liquidity*. This means having cash to pay off outstanding debts, hospital bills and other expenses. A life insurance policy must also supply money to live on now that the breadwinner is gone.

□ Life insurance allows you to give money to your beneficiary without it having to go through *probate*. This is the legal proceeding that recognizes the validity of an individual's last will and testament. As you may know, probate proceedings often take months to complete. Heirs who are left property in a will have to wait until the probate process is completed before they can legally receive the property.

☐ With some people, estate tax can be very large. Taxes are paid on the assets left in your "estate" at your death. The fewer assets the less the tax bill. Therefore, many savvy individuals use life insurance as a way of avoiding estate taxes. They do it by making a gift of a policy to an individual or charity prior to their death. And, of course, the recipient of the policy gets the proceeds of the policy tax-free at your death because the proceeds of life insurance policies are obtained tax-free.

Women and Life Insurance

Female breadwinners, or single women who have someone dependent on them for support, should have life insurance. And, the good news is that it will cost women about 10% less to buy a policy than it would men of the same age. The reason why is determined through actuarial insight: women live longer than men. As a result, the life insurance company doesn't have to pay off on the policy as soon.

This price difference is reflected across the board. It's the same for term, whole life, universal and variable policies. Women non-smokers probably get the best rate. Women smokers have to pay a bit higher rate. Then come male non-smokers. The highest rate of all is paid by male smokers.

Life insurance is one of the few insurance products where women come out ahead. As a rule, women have to pay more for health and disability insurance than their male counterparts. Young women usually pay less for auto insurance than men of the same age.

But this isn't the whole of the story about women and life

insurance. There is a movement afoot on the federal government level and by some state legislatures to equalize life insurance premiums for men and women. The so-called "unisex insurance movement" would raise the amount that women are paying for premiums and lower the amount that men are now paying. Rates would be figured without regard to the insured's sex.

Montana presently requires this kind of rate pricing on life insurance. More states are expected to jump on the bandwagon sometime soon.

If you are a woman who needs life insurance, you had better buy a policy now before your rates go up. The chances for passage of a national unisex life insurance bill are about even right now. Once such a bill goes into effect, women nationwide will have to pay more for life insurance.

How Life Insurance Starts

When you tell an insurance agent you want to buy insurance, the agent will ask you to fill out an application. After filling out the application, you may be required to undergo a complete health physical. Assuming that you are then considered to be an acceptable risk, you will usually be asked to pay for all or part of the annual premium. Some policies cover you as soon as you pay this amount. Should you die the next day, your beneficiary would receive the face amount of the policy. That amount is called the *death benefit*.

With other policies, however, there may be a short waiting period before the policy goes into effect. Find out from your agent when your policy will start. If you need immediate protection, you can get it by asking for a *conditional receipt*. Your insurance is not in force unless you are given a conditional receipt. And you can't get a conditional receipt unless you pay the proper premium.

The receipt is "conditional" because you must be found to be insurable under the company's underwriting guidelines as of that date. Once the insurance is in effect, it makes no difference what you die from or when you die. The insurance will pay off unless you lied in your application or you commit suicide within two years from acquiring the policy or die through an act of war. You may die from an accident, illness, injury, as the result of a criminal act or simply from natural causes and your beneficiary will collect.

Naming a beneficiary is critically important. It may not always be wise to name one's spouse and/or children as the beneficiaries of your policy. There are a great many legal, estate planning and tax ramifications involved in the naming of a beneficiary. It is important enough that you should discuss it with your financial advisor or attorney. The naming of a beneficiary should not be taken lightly. Consult an expert if you are unsure of what to do.

You would also be wise to name a contingent or back-up beneficiary. That way if something should happen to your primary beneficiary, the contingent beneficiary would automatically be substituted.

While you own the policy, you can and should be able to change the beneficiary on the policy as your needs change. Possibly, your original beneficiary will predecease you, or you may decide that somebody else should be the object of your bounty. Regardless, be sure you know the procedure for changing beneficiaries. It usually requires nothing more than a phone call to your insurance agent or company and then filling out a simple form.

Premiums

Life insurance premiums are a mystery to most people, including some life insurance professionals. How companies arrive at the premiums they charge seems to be a combination of higher mathematics, probability theory and pure guesswork. Because no two companies produce exactly the same life insurance policy and since there are over

2000 companies selling life insurance, there are 2000 different pricing methods.

That's why comparing policies by price is difficult. Even term policies, which are relatively straightforward, provide pricing comparison problems. The accompanying sample from Insurance Information Inc. of Lowell, Massachusetts is a computer printout of premiums for five different companies for the same individual.

Even this sample can't show the complexities involved in term. Whole life or universal life policies are even more difficult to compare. Best's Insurance Rating Service, which does an excellent job of rating policies, has not come up with a foolproof method for comparing premiums either.

Perhaps the simplest thing you can do is to find a reliable insurance broker who will shop the market for you. Rely on that person to get the best deal he or she can find to fit your needs.

Traditionally, life insurance premiums are quoted as annual premiums. You should pay your premium once a year if you can. By paying once a year instead of monthly, quarterly or semi-annually, you will avoid the service charges and interest payments that companies charge to their policyholders who don't pay once a year.

The larger the face amount of the policy, the lower the unit cost. Therefore, try to buy as much coverage as you can. If you need $250,000 worth of coverage, it will cost you less to buy it in one policy than buying two $125,000 policies.

Lowering Your Premium After Purchase

Life insurance premiums can be lowered if you show evidence that you are trying to improve your health. For example, if you join a health club and work out regularly or you go on a strict diet and lose weight, you can ask the insurance company to re-evaluate you. Many will lower

INSURANCE INFORMATION, INC.
45 Palmer Street
Lowell, Massachusetts 01852
****
TEL: (617) 453-2557
04/10/86

Insurance illustration for:
    JOHN SAMPLE

Birthdate: 04/10/48
Male
Non-smoker, Preferred Risk
Account #: 123-45-6

Company:	WM PENN	BNKRS NATL	SCRTY MUTL	METROPLTN	BNKRS SEC
Policy:	EXE-U-TERM	PART	SECURITY80	1 YR TERM	5 YR TERM
Insurance Age:	38	38	38	38	38
Face amount:	100,000	100,000	100,000	100,000	100,000

Year   Annual Premiums
                          (Including all fees and discounts)

Year	WM PENN	BNKRS NATL	SCRTY MUTL	METROPLTN	BNKRS SEC
1	109	140	125	136	154
2	175	90	130	142	154
3	205	109	155	152	154
3 Year Total	489	339	410	430	462
3 Yr Int Adj Prem	462	325	389	409	440
4	248	124	169	162	154
5	276	139	182	173	154
5 Year Total	1,013	602	761	765	770
5 Yr Int Adj Prem	903	546	685	691	700

Additional Information

	WM PENN	BNKRS NATL	SCRTY MUTL	METROPLTN	BNKRS SEC
Policy Fee	20			25	
First Year Fee			25		
Reentry Year	7				5
Yrs Prems Guaranteed	7	1	1	5	5
Minimum Face Amount	100,000	50,000	100,000	50,000	10,000

The interest adjusted premium assumes an opportunity rate of 5% after tax. Premiums are assumed to be paid in full at the start of each policy year. Due to rounding, the figures shown may vary slightly from actual values.

This is an illustration based on dated material and not a contract. For further information, see your insurance agent or contact one of the insurance companies listed on the next page.

We believe the rates shown to be accurate as of the above date. Because term insurance rates are very volatile, we suggest you use this information promptly.

*** SEE ENCLOSED DISCLAIMER ***

Company and Policy Information

WILLIAM PENN LIFE INSURANCE COMPANY   Tel: (516) 328-6000
2 CORPORATE PLACE SOUTH   (ask for Agency Department)
PISCATAWAY, NEW JERSEY 08854
EXEC-U-TERM: Annual Renewable & Convertible Plan. Re-start end of 7th yr to
new low prem if qualified.
BEST'S RATING: A

BANKERS NATIONAL LIFE INSURANCE COMPANY   Tel: 1-800-631-0099
1599 LITTTLETON ROAD   (ask for Agency Department)
PARSIPPANY, NEW JERSEY 07054
PART: Participating Annual Renewable Term - Renewable to age 100 and
convertible prior to age 65.
BEST'S RATING: A

METROPOLITAN LIFE INSURANCE COMPANY   Tel: (212) 578-2211
ONE MADISON AVENUE   (ask for Agency Department)
NEW YORK, NEW YORK 10010
ONE YEAR TERM WITH PREMIUM ADJUSTMENT: Annual Renewable/Convertible
Participating to 100 (70 in NY)
BEST'S RATING: A+

BANKERS SECURITY LIFE INSURANCE SOCIETY   Tel: (202) 298-6225
1701 PENNSYLVANIA AVE., N.W.   (ask for Agency Department)
WASHINGTON, D.C.   20006
FIVE YEAR TERM: Five Year Renewable and Convertible Term - Renewable to Age 70
Non-participating Plan
BEST'S RATING: A+

your premium after giving you a new physical examination.

If you stop skydiving, or change a hazardous occupation to a less dangerous one, make sure your agent or your insurance company knows this. Your premium could be lowered substantially. Or, if you were a smoker and you have now quit, ask for a re-evaluation.

Don't assume that your premium can't be lowered. It can. But *you* must take the initiative in getting it lowered. Keep your insurance company informed of those things that may lessen their risk of carrying you as an insurable individual.

Too many people buy a life insurance policy and promptly forget about it other than to pay the premium when it comes due. If you interact with your insurance company on a regular basis, whether through your agent or with a representative of the company, you may find you can lower your premium and hear of any changes that the company may make in your coverage from time to time.

Once You Make the Purchase

Since life insurance is such an important and expensive item, most states allow life insurance purchasers a 10-day "second look." This allows the life insurance purchaser to cancel the policy within 10 days of its purchase. "Second look" is state, not federal, law. Check with your state to determine how long you have to cancel.

If you should decide you made a mistake, you will get all of your money back. If your agent or company refuses to refund your money, immediately contact your state insurance department. A list of state insurance commissioners, with their addresses and phone numbers, is included in the appendix of this book.

Many insurance experts counsel that you should give photocopies of your policy to your beneficiaries and your attorney. This is a good idea because if you die and your policy is locked away in a safe or safety deposit box, and nobody knows where to find it, the beneficiary or attorney could produce it quickly. This way claims procedures can be started right away.

You might also want to keep a separate record of your policy number, the name of the company and the amount for which you are insured for each policy you have. Keep this record in a separate place. A fireproof safe deposit box or strong box are good choices. And don't forget to include all of your policies. If you are covered by some group life insurance through your employer or other organization, that information should be available to your beneficiaries and attorney as well.

If You Stop Paying Premiums

For various reasons, such as financial reverses, some people have to "give up" their insurance policies. This can be unfortunate, especially with certain types of policies. If you stop paying the premiums on a term policy, your policy will run out and your beneficiary will no longer be protected.

With a cash value policy, however, you have some options. You can, of course, ask for the cash value of your policy to be paid to you. The insurance company is required to give it. But you must ask for the cash. It won't be given to you automatically.

Since it is unwise to be totally without life insurance if you need it, you may be able to effectively "trade-in" your cash value policy for another kid of coverage. You might choose a term policy or a paid-up (a policy in which no further premiums are due) of a smaller amount. Technically, these are known as *non-forfeiture options*. For instance, if you were originally paying on a $100,000 policy, you may have paid in enough to buy a paid up $25,000 policy.

If your financial problems are temporary ones, you may want to reinstate your original policy. Most companies allow you to do that upon full payment of all missed premiums, plus interest. You may also have to requalify by taking a new medical exam. If the company thinks your health has deteriorated, and you are no longer a good risk, they can turn you down.

All life insurance carriers provide a *grace period* for you to pay a late premium. Usually that period is 31 days. The length of the grace period depends on company policy. Obviously, you should endeavor to pay your premium as close to its due date as possible. If you should experience a temporary problem, you can rely on the grace period.

Many cash value policies provide for automatic premium loans. These are provisions that help you pay a premium if you are temporarily strapped for money and can't pay your premium. The provision says that if there is sufficient money in the cash value portion of the policy and a premium is not paid by the end of the grace period, the premium is paid from the cash value. This payment is a *loan*. The loan reduces the cash value of the policy if it is not paid back. It therefore reduces the proceeds of the policy at your death.

Participating vs. Non-Participating Policies

One of the problems in comparing premiums is that some policies, both term and cash value, are issued by mutual insurance companies. Mutual insurance companies pay dividends to their policyholders. The amount of the dividend depends on the profit earned by the company during the year.

A policy that pays a dividend is called a *participating policy*. One that doesn't is called *non-participating*. In participating policies the dividends are tied to the performance of the company over a specified period, such as one year. Therefore the exact amount varies from year to year in many cases. If a dividend is paid, it can be paid directly to the policyholder in the form of a check. There is no guarantee that a dividend will be paid. But mutual companies that issue participating policies usually do pay a dividend each and every year.

By the way, instead of companies using the term *participating,* the word is often shortened to just *par.* There are par and non-par policies.

Getting a check directly from the insurance company is the most common way of receiving a dividend. You also have other options. You can often use dividends to pay part of your premiums. Or you can, if you like, buy more insurance with them.

Another option you have is to leave the dividends with the insurance company to accumulate interest. If you do, however, you will be taxed on that interest just as you would if you allowed it to build up interest in a savings account.

Any sums left on deposit with an insurance company can be withdrawn. If your insurance company is paying a higher interest rate than other investments would yield, then you'd be wise to keep the money there. If you can earn more elsewhere, you should withdraw the accumulated dividends and invest there. For example, if money market funds are paying 7% and your insurance company is paying 8%, stick with the insurance company.

Usually, because par policies *do* pay dividends, they are a bit more expensive than non-par policies. However, when you take the dividend into account, par policy premiums cost about the same as non-par policies.

Underwriting Standards

As explained earlier, underwriting is the act of deciding who an insurance company will insure and who they won't. Most companies use three general standards in making those decisions. Each company may apply those standards differently. That's why you might be able to get insurance from one company when you can't get it from another.

The three standards looked at are, your health, your lifestyle and your occupation.

First, consider your health. If you are in poor health, you may have difficulty getting coverage at all. Some companies may, however, for a high price, insure you no matter what the state of your health.

If you suffer from one of the following maladies, you will run into some problems getting insurance.

☐ Diabetes.

☐ High blood pressure.

☐ Heart trouble.

☐ Excessive weight.

☐ Cancer.

☐ AIDS.

Depending on your age, when you initially apply for life insurance you may have to undergo a physical examination. In most cases, that examination will determine whether you qualify for insurance. Some companies also require a physical examination if you wish to renew a policy. That's why it's wise for people with health problems to try to get a guaranteed renewable type of policy. A guaranteed renewable policy means no medical exam is required to renew.

The second standard that life insurers look at is your lifestyle. Do you smoke? Do you drink heavily? Are you sedentary? Do you have a history of drug abuse? Do you have a stressful job? Do you race automobiles as a hobby? These and other factors may be taken into consideration by certain companies. What weight they put on different factors is a matter of each company's particular choice.

The third standard is your occupation. Some occupations are considered more dangerous than others. Life insurance will cost you more if you are in a dangerous occupation, less if you are in a less dangerous occupation.

Some examples of dangerous occupations include:

☐ Underground coal miners.

☐ Deep sea divers.

☐ Experimental test pilots (not airline pilots).

☐ Oil field fire fighters (not ordinary fire fighters).
☐ Motorcycle police officers.
☐ Astronauts.

If you find it difficult to get insurance from a regular insurance carrier because of your health, your lifestyle or your occupation, you should go to insurance companies specializing in "rated" risks. Look for a life insurance agent that specializes in this area. You will probably have to pay more for life insurance coverage but, in most cases, you can find an insurer who will cover you.

Your age at the time you apply for a life insurance policy also has a great bearing on how much the policy will cost you. No matter what type of life insurance you are interested in, *the older you are when you buy a life insurance policy, the more expensive it will be.*

Obviously, that's because as you grow older, the chances of your dying increase. And because of that risk, you must pay the insurance company more.

Preferred Risks

There are no "discounts" available with life insurance. But you may qualify as a *preferred risk* if you are in top physical condition, don't smoke and work in a non-stressful environment. A person who qualifies as a preferred risk is charged about 5% less. Oftentimes, a non-smoker will be given an additional discount on life insurance.

If you buy a policy and then get back into shape, stop smoking and maintain a more healthful and less stressful lifestyle, your company may cut your premium. You are now a better risk, and the chances of your living longer have improved. Remember, selling life insurance is like gambling. If you can increase the odds of your living longer, the carrier will lower your premium in most cases.

Again, shopping around for an appropriate policy is vital. Life insurance is a competitive business. And preferred risks are desirable clients. So if you are a preferred risk, you may be able to find a company that will give you a lot of coverage for a relatively small premium.

"Rated" Policyholders

Individuals who can't get life insurance because of health problems are known as "rated" risks. If you are unable to get life insurance yourself, don't despair. Look for an agent who specializes in placing *rated risks*. There are a few around, and they can usually find a policy for you.

A rated term policy is still significantly cheaper than a regular whole life policy, so shop for a rated term policy if a term policy is what you want and need. One or more company's underwriting standards may make you an insurable risk under one of their term policies.

Of course, you will have to pay more for that policy, but you should be able to get coverage somehow. If your health problems are so bad that you cannot get life insurance coverage anywhere, you might be able to get in on some group coverage.

If the group coverage is offered by a union, fraternal organization or religious group, you may be able to be covered without undergoing a physical or even answering any questions about your medical history.

"Guaranteed issue" policies might also be available. These are special policies that cover "rated" risks. If you die within the first two or three years of taking out one of these policies, your beneficiary does not receive the death benefit or face amount of the policy.Instead, the beneficiary receives all the premiums that were paid, plus interest. If you outlive that limited period, your beneficiary receives the full death benefit, as if the policy was a regular term policy.

Important Policy Provisions

While there are no standard life insurance policies, most of them do have some things in common. For instance, if you look at the sample term life insurance policy at the end of this chapter (page 67) you will notice a section entitled "The Contract." That section contains provisions common to most types of life insurance policies.

For example, there is the *incontestability clause*. When you apply for a life insurance policy, you make certain representations as to your health and other information. That application then becomes part of the policy. If you lied about your health or other important pieces of information, the company can legally deny any or all of a claim made under the policy. However, they can only do that during the first two years the policy is in effect.

Suppose, for instance, you lied on your application for a life policy and answered "no" to a question concerning cancer, when in fact you had cancer 10 years ago. That lie would be grounds for denying a claim within two years from the date the policy was issued. But if a claim is made to collect on the policy five years later and the policy has not been cancelled, the insurance company must pay the claim.

The suicide clause is another important clause. Contrary to popular belief, a life insurance policy will pay if a policyholder commits suicide, but not within two years after the policy was issued. Again, if five years pass between the issuing of the policy and the suicide, the insurer must pay.

Any misstatement with regard to age or sex will not cause a claim to be denied. Most policies would be "adjusted." Why would anybody misstate his age or sex? To get a lower premium. The lower your age, the lower your premium. And women pay less for life insurance than men do.

A "policy settlement clause" is another common provision found in most insurance policies. The clause usually says that the proceeds of the policy will not be paid to the beneficiary until proof of death is received by the insurance company. That means a Certificate of Death is required.

There is no time limit imposed on presenting that certificate. Proceeds are paid with interest from the week of death.

Life Insurance Riders

A *rider* is an additional coverage that you can purchase. It's an "extra" or "option" that doesn't appear in the company's basic insurance contract. The availability of many riders is common to most insurers.

Insurance agents tend to push these riders hard with certain clients, but they may not always be needed. In fact, these options are called "riders" because the majority of policyholders *don't* need them. Be sure to assess your need for them very carefully before purchasing any.

Common riders include the following:

Double Indemnity

This rider doubles the face amount of the policy if the policyholder dies as a result of an accident. If you have a $50,000 policy with the double indemnity rider, and you die as a result of an accident (as defined in the rider), your beneficiary receives a double death benefit—$100,000, not $50,000.

The chances of your dying as a result of an accident are quite a bit less than your dying of an illness, so the additional premium that you pay for the accidental death benefit is probably not worth the extra expense. By the way, the cost of this rider increases as you get older, so there is probably less reason to carry the rider as you get older.

Guaranteed Insurability

It is available only to policyholders under 40 years old.

Usually its cost is high. Essentially, it allows the policyholder to purchase additional coverage at stated ages such as 25, 28, 31, 35 and 40. The hook to get you to buy this rider is the guarantee that you can purchase this extra coverage regardless of your future physical condition.

Although you may need additional insurance as you reach your peak earning years around age 40, you can probably get a term policy for less than the amount of this rider. That policy will give you all the extra needed coverage more inexpensively.

Cost-of-Living

This is similar to guaranteed insurability. Again, you can increase the amount of your insurance without having to take a physical exam, but the amount you can buy is tied to increases in the cost of living.

This rider makes some sense for people who need extra coverage, but it is still overpriced. And you may be able to accomplish the same objective by purchasing a small term policy at a cheaper price.

Waiver of Premium

If you purchase disability insurance (which I highly recommended) you don't need this rider because this rider frees you from the necessity of paying any more premiums if you become "totally" disabled. This is another expensive option that is not worth what you pay for it, especially if the insurer interprets total disability strictly. You are much better off buying disability insurance (see Chapter 3) that will provide you with broader coverage.

Disability Income Rider

This is similar to the waiver of premium option. It provides for a certain amount of monthly income if the policyholder becomes fully disabled. This rider usually is only included if there is a waiver of premium available. It is very expensive. Your best bet is to purchase a separate disability policy.

Family Rider

It is another common rider that many insurers try to sell. Usually this entails covering your non-working spouse and your children at an additional premium. Avoid it. Children need not be covered by life insurance, especially when they are quite young. And a non-working spouse is not the breadwinner in the home, so coverage is not needed there, either.

All riders, no matter what they promise, should be analyzed on a cost-benefit relationship. Riders on an insurance policy are similar to a fully equipped car. Some of the fancy gadgets might seem nice to have, but you might not use them and they cost a bundle, so are they really worth it?

Some Tax Consequences of Life Insurance

It was mentioned earlier that life insurance is a very flexible product. Nowhere is that more evident than in taxes. The most important fact about life insurance and taxes is that your beneficiary gets the proceeds of your life insurance totally tax-free. So if you leave your beneficiary $100,000 in insurance, that individual will not have to pay any taxes on that money.

So for estate planning purposes, this is very important. The more life insurance you have, the more your family will collect tax-free when you die.

Furthermore, if you have the policy set up properly by not making it payable to your estate and not retaining the right to change beneficiaries, it isn't taxed as part of your estate upon your death. If this is what you prefer, tell your insurance agent. He or she can help you set it up.

With a cash value policy, your cash value grows each year until the policy endows. That build-up within the cash value portion of the account is not subject to taxes, either. Should you cash in the policy before it matures, however, you *are* taxed on that portion of the cash value that exceeds the premiums you paid.

Group life insurance given to you as a fringe benefit by your employer also has some important and different tax consequences from a whole life policy. As far as the beneficiary is concerned, there is no difference between a group or individual policy. All proceeds are received tax free. With a group policy furnished by an employer, for estate tax purposes, the proceeds of the policy must be included in the employee's final gross estate. Any interest earned on those proceeds is taxable.

However, the entire face amount of the policy need not be included in the gross estate. There is a $5000 exemption that applies.

As a final bit of advice, don't put your only copy of your life insurance policy in a bank safety deposit box or vault. Sometimes, those boxes are sealed upon the owner's death. If that were to happen in your case, your beneficiaries might be delayed from getting the insurance proceeds. That money could be very important for your family immediately after your death.

Settlement Options

One way or another, a life insurance policy always pays benefits. If you die and you are insured, your beneficiary gets the benefits. If you have an endowment policy and it matures, you get the proceeds. Or, if you surrender a cash value policy before it matures, you are entitled to the cash value. The benefits, however, don't always have to be taken in a lump sum by you or your beneficiary.

There are some *settlement options* that you or your beneficiary can take advantage of. These options can be selected by you at the time your policy is issued, at anytime after the policy has been issued, or by your beneficiary when the death benefit is payable.

Among the options are the following:

Lump Sum

You or your beneficiary can choose to get a lump sum payout. Unless it is a death benefit payout, there will probably be some tax consequence involved. If you are, for instance, thinking about taking the $30,000 cash value buildup out of your policy, you would have to pay taxes on the net gain, so it might not be a wise choice.

Your beneficiary might not be wise to take a lump sum payment either. That's especially true if the beneficiary might be prone to "spending" the money all at once

Interest Income

Under this option, the insurance company holds the benefit proceeds and pays interest on the money to the appropriate individual (either you or your beneficiary). The interest can be paid for one's entire lifetime or for an agreed upon number of years. Arrangements are also made to pay out the principal and any remaining interest at the request of you or your beneficiary. The interest rate at which payments are made under this option are at a rate guaranteed in the policy when you buy it, but the actual rate could be higher.

Fixed Amount

Here the insurer pays the money out in equal installments until the total amount is exhausted. Interest at a guaranteed-or-better rate is paid on the unpaid balance.

Fixed Period

Compared to the fixed amount option, this one differs in that the amount of the equal installments are determined so the proceeds and the guaranteed interest will be paid out over a predetermined length of time.

Life Income

Again, equal installments are paid out, but the amount of the installment depends on the age and sex of the person being paid.

Once you decide on the settlement option, many companies will prohibit you from making a change in the strategy. And you often can pick an option for your beneficiary. So if you make a choice for your beneficiary, be aware whether it can be changed or not.

Your beneficiary is not totally locked into your decision if you give him or her the right to change the settlement option. If your policy offers you that choice, it is probably the best way to go because circumstances may change and your beneficiary may need the money in a form other than the one you originally planned for.

Making a Gift of a Life Insurance Policy

Many individuals, to fulfill charitable obligations, will give a life insurance policy to a well-regarded charity. You can get a present charitable tax deduction for such a gift. The exact amount of the deduction depends on the present value of the policy. Determining that value involves making a determination as to the age, and the type of policy being given.

Because ascertaining the value can be tricky, you should seek the advice of a competent attorney before making the gift. There are some complications involved, but for the most part, the insurance company should be able to value the policy for you for federal tax purposes.

Don't make a gift of a brand new policy. Some legal cases have held that the gift of a newly acquired policy can be null and void, so play it safe and give a policy that is fully paid up, or one that you have been paying on for a number of years.

An insurance policy can also be given to an individual, not just a charity. Again there are some legal complications involved, so be sure that you get good legal advice before you make such a gift.

Why make a gift of an insurance policy? Because you can probably give much more that way than if you had to make a cash gift. For example, if you want to give $100,000 to your favorite charity on your death, by giving them a life insurance policy with that face amount, that $100,000 policy may have only cost you $15,000 or so in premiums.

If you wanted to leave $100,000 in cash, that cash would actually have to be in your estate. Or, some of your assets intended for someone else might have to be sold to make up the $100,000.

Leaving an insurance policy is certainly better than leaving stocks and bonds because the value of those items can fluctuate. The face value of an insurance policy doesn't.

Switching Policies

Exchanging one life insurance policy for another, especially one that you have been paying the premiums on for more than three years, is not a good idea.

There are a number of realities you might not be aware of before you change policies. When you switch policies:

□ You will have to pay a new commission to the agent who sold you the new policy. Although you don't pay the commission directly, it does come out of your first year premium payments, so not as much goes to pay for the insurance itself.

□ There are many other expenses and costs that have to be paid as well. These will all come out of the first few years of premium payments.

□ Because of your health, you may not be insurable any more. If you give up a policy, especially one that was guaranteed renewable, you start out fresh and are evaluated just as any new policyholder would be.

□ You will probably have to undergo a new physical examination to check on your health. If your health has deteriorated, you could conceivably be turned down.

□ You are older than you were when you bought the original policy. Now you want to change policies. The new one will, therefore, cost you more.

□ If the policy you want to give up is more than 10 years old, it may have some desirable features, such as a low interest rate for borrowing. A new policy might not have these features.

Switching policies is not something to be taken lightly. If an agent or company representative convinces you to switch, make sure that the reasons for the switch are clear to you. Be sure you understand all the advantages and disadvantages involved.

Don't make the switch totally on the basis of cost. True, a cash value policy costs about five times what a term policy costs, but that's only initially. The cost of a regular term policy rises as you renew it. Switching from a cash value to a term policy will save you money in the short run, but do you need the forced savings that come about with a cash value policy? Think about such things before making a switch.

Exchanging one policy for another may have some tax consequences. Before you make a switch, be sure you check with your tax advisor and your insurance agent. This is especially advisable before changing an endowment policy for another different type of policy.

In short, don't make a switch just because somebody tells you to. Demand a good, clear presentation that convinces you it's in your best interests to make a change.

Mail Order Life Insurance

Many companies sell life insurance through the mail. You may have gotten a solicitation yourself. Before you buy such a policy, investigate it very thoroughly.

First, don't assume that since the offer to buy came through the mail, the insurance will be cheaper. That may not be true. You may be able to find an identical policy offered by a local insurance agent or company that is less expensive.

Second, you may have trouble determining exactly what you are buying. When you can talk to a company agent or representative, you can question him about various parts of the policy and get answers. It is almost impossible to get good answers from a mail order insurance company.

Finally, you probably know little about the company and the quality of service you'll get after you buy the policy.

In short, when you buy life insurance through the mail, you are "buying a pig in a poke." Unless you thoroughly investigate the policy and take the offering to an insurance advisor or agent to analyze it for you, you shouldn't buy, even if it looks like a good deal. If you do ask your broker or agent to look at the mail order insurance, find out if he can match the policy in terms of price and coverage.

Savings Bank Life Insurance

Undoubtedly, the best deal available in life insurance today is *savings bank life insurance (SBLI)*. Unfortunately, it is only available in three states: New York, Connecticut and Massachusetts.

Typically, you can buy an excellent term insurance product for a premium significantly less than the same policy available through any other insurer.

An inexpensive cash value policy and now group life policies can also be obtained at a reduced rate. They are only available through savings banks in the three states mentioned.

A 45-year-old male non-smoker, for instance, can obtain $100,000 worth of group annual renewable term for $150 the first year. And, in most cases, a physical exam is not even required. Waiver of premium and double indemnity are also available as riders on those policies at an additional premium.

If you live or work in New York, Connecticut or Massachusetts, you should certainly look into SBLI. It could be your best buy. At some point other states may also adopt a similar scheme, but only these three states offer SBLI right now.

Questions to Ask
When Buying Life Insurance

1) Do I need life insurance at all?

2) If so, do I need term, whole life, universal or variable?

3) Have I determined the proper amount of coverage by ascertaining the needs of my family if I were to die tomorrow?

4) Have I thoroughly shopped the market for the best buy that most suits my needs?

5) Are some of my life insurance needs already met by insurance provided by my employer or through a group policy issued by a club, fraternal organization or labor union?

6) Have I checked out the financial viability of the company I want to buy from?

7) Do I, in fact, qualify for life insurance coverage? Is my health good enough?

8) If I already own life insurance, have I re-evaluated needs lately?

9) Do I need any riders on my insurance?

10) Has my life insurance become an integral part of my overall financial and estate plan?

Sample Life Insurance Policies

Immediately following are two sample policies supplied by the Education Services of the American Council of Life Insurance. These policies are typical of the "easy-to-understand" type that have become prevalent in the past few years. You'll notice that they are written in plain English.

The first policy is for term insurance. The second is a whole life agreement.

SAMPLE

COUNCIL LIFE INSURANCE COMPANY
WASHINGTON, D.C.

INSURED	DENNIS SMITH	$40,000 SUM INSURED
ORIGINAL TERM EXPIRY DATE	AUG 09, 1983	
POLICY DATE	AUG 09, 1982 062201 0000001	POLICY NUMBER

TERM LIFE INSURANCE POLICY

OUR INSURING AGREEMENT

If the Insured dies while this policy is in full force and prior to the Original Term Expiry Date or prior to any Term Expiry Date after that, we will pay the Sum Insured to the Beneficiary.

We, Council Life Insurance Company, issue this policy in consideration of your application and the payment of premiums.

Our Company and you, the Owner, are bound by the conditions and provisions of the policy.

YOUR RIGHT TO RETURN YOUR POLICY

We want you to be satisifed with your policy. If you aren't, return it to us within 10 days of the date you receive it. Return it to our Home Office or to your agent. We will refund any premium you have paid. We will consider your policy as if it had never existed.

If you have any questions or problems with your policy, we will be ready to help you. You may call upon your agent or our Home Office for assistance at any time.

Signed at our Home Office, Washington, D.C.

W. Prescott Smith

Secretary

John E. Wells III

President

POLICY HIGHLIGHTS:

■ YEARLY RENEWABLE LEVEL TERM LIFE INSURANCE TO AGE 98

■ CONVERTIBLE

■ CONVERSION PRIVILEGE TERMINATES AT AGE 80

■ PREMIUMS PAYABLE DURING INSURED'S LIFETIME TO END OF PREMIUM PAYMENT PERIOD

■ NONPARTICIPATING— NO DIVIDENDS PAID

1

POLICY INDEX

Additional Benefit Provisions, if any, Election of Settlement Options and a copy of the application follow Page 14.

ENDORSEMENTS

2

Life Insurance

POLICY SPECIFICATIONS

PLAN OF INSURANCE—YEARLY RENEWABLE AND CONVERTIBLE TERM

INSURED— DENNIS SMITH $40,000 —SUM INSURED

ORIGINAL TERM—
EXPIRY DATE— AUG 09, 1983

POLICY DATE— AUG 09, 1982 062201 0000001 —POLICY NUMBER

DATE OF ISSUE— AUG 09, 1982 29—MALE —ISSUE AGE AND SEX

PREMIUM CLASS— STANDARD MONTHLY —PREMIUM INTERVAL

OWNER, BENEFICIARY—AS DESIGNATED IN THE APPLICATION SUBJECT TO THE PROVISIONS OF THIS POLICY

BENEFIT AND PREMIUM SCHEDULE

FORM NO.	BENEFIT	PREMIUM	PAYMENT PERIOD
BC38F	TERM LIFE INSURANCE FOR 1 YEAR, RENEWABLE EVERY YEAR AS SHOWN IN THE TABLE OF RENEWAL PREMIUMS. CONVERTIBLE ON OR BEFORE AUG 08, 2033. CONVERSION CREDIT OF UP TO $90.00 AVAILABLE IF CONVERTED ON OR BEFORE AUG 08, 1987.	$9.50	1 YEAR
BC63F	PREMIUM WAIVER	$.40	1 YEAR

TOTAL PREMIUM ON POLICY DATE

ANNUAL	SEMIANNUAL	QUARTERLY	B-O-M MONTHLY
$109.80	$56.40	$29.80	$9.90

3

062201   0000001—POLICY NUMBER

TABLE OF RENEWAL PREMIUMS

POLICY YEAR	ATTAINED AGE	MONTHLY PREMIUMS		
		LIFE INSURANCE	PREMIUM WAIVER	TOTAL
2	30	$ 9.50	$ .40	$ 9.90
3	31	9.50	.40	9.90
4	32	9.90	.40	10.30
5	33	9.90	.40	10.30
6	34	10.30	.40	10.70
7	35	10.30	.40	10.70
8	36	10.70	.40	11.10
9	37	11.50	.80	12.30
10	38	11.90	.80	12.70
11	39	12.70	.80	13.50
12	40	13.90	.80	14.70
13	41	14.70	.80	15.50
14	42	15.90	.80	16.70
15	43	16.70	1.20	17.90
16	44	17.90	1.20	19.10
17	45	19.50	1.20	20.70
18	46	21.10	1.60	22.70
19	47	22.70	1.60	24.30
20	48	24.70	2.00	26.70
21	49	26.70	2.00	28.70
22	50	28.70	2.80	31.50
23	51	31.50	3.20	34.70
24	52	33.90	4.00	37.90
25	53	37.10	5.20	42.30
26	54	40.30	6.00	46.30
27	55	43.90	7.20	51.10
28	56	47.50	8.40	55.90
29	57	51.90	10.00	61.90
30	58	56.70	11.20	67.90
31	59	61.90	12.40	74.30
32	60	67.50	4.40	71.90
33	61	73.90	4.00	77.90
34	62	80.70	3.60	84.30
35	63	88.30	3.20	91.50
36	64	97.10	3.60	100.70
37	65	106.70		106.70
38	66	117.50		117.50
39	67	129.90		129.90
40	68	143.50		143.50

4

062201   0000001—POLICY NUMBER

TABLE OF RENEWAL PREMIUMS

| POLICY YEAR | ATTAINED AGE | MONTHLY PREMIUMS | | |
		LIFE INSURANCE	PREMIUM WAIVER	TOTAL
41	69	158.30		158.30
42	70	174.70		174.70
43	71	191.90		191.90
44	72	209.90		209.90
45	73	229.50		229.50
46	74	250.70		250.70
47	75	273.90		273.90
48	76	300.70		300.70
49	77	330.70		330.70
50	78	365.10		365.10
51	79	402.70		402.70
52	80	443.90		443.90
53	81	487.50		487.50
54	82	533.90		533.90
55	83	581.90		581.90
56	84	631.90		631.90
57	85	683.90		683.90
58	86	737.50		737.50
59	87	793.50		793.50
60	88	852.30		852.30
61	89	915.90		915.90
62	90	985.90		985.90
63	91	1,063.90		1,063.00
64	92	1,160.50		1,153.50
65	93	1,257.50		1,257.50
66	94	1,383.50		1,383.50
67	95	1,509.10		1,509.10
68	96	1,635.10		1,635.10
69	97	1,760.70		1,760.70

5

DEFINITIONS

This section contains the standard meaning of terms used in your policy.

You

"You" means the Owner of this policy. "Your" and "yours" also refer to the Owner.

We

"We" means our company. "Us," "our" and "ours" also refer to our company.

Insured

"The Insured" is the person whose life is covered by this insurance policy.

Beneficiary

"The Beneficiary" is the person or persons to whom this policy's Sum Insured is paid when the Insured dies.

Sum Insured

"The Sum Insured" is the amount payable under your policy when the Insured dies. It may also be thought of as the death benefit or the face amount.

In Full Force

"In full force" means that each premium has been paid either by its Due Date or within the grace period.

Issue Age and Attained Age

"Issue Age" is the Insured's age on the last birthday before the Policy Date. It is shown on the Policy Specifications Page. We use it for each benefit of your policy, unless a different age is stated. "Attained Age" is the Issue Age plus the number of years and months since your policy was issued.

Written Notice

"Written Notice" is a request or notice in writing by you to us at our Home Office. It is how you let us know any requests you have, or changes you want to make to your policy.

Policy Date

The Policy Date is shown on the Policy Specifications Page. We use it to set premium Due Dates, policy years and policy anniversaries.

Date of Issue

The Date of Issue is shown on the Policy Specifications Page. We use it to interpret the Incontestability and Suicide provisions.

Policy Specifications Page

The Policy Specifications Page starts on Page 3 of your policy and gives basic information about your policy. This includes important items such as Date of Issue and Table of Renewal Premiums.

6

THE CONTRACT

Your insurance policy is a legal contract between you and us. Certain provisions are standard. This section gives these provisions and explains how they can affect your policy.

The Entire Contract

The entire contract is made up of this policy and your written application. We attached a copy of your application at issue.

All statements you made in the application, in the absence of fraud, are considered representations and not warranties. Only the statements made in your written application can be used by us to defend a claim or void this policy.

Changes to this policy are not valid unless we make them in writing. They must be signed by one of our Executive Officers.

Incontestability

We cannot contest your policy after it has been in force during the Insured's lifetime for two years from its Date of Issue, except for nonpayment of premiums.

Suicide

We will not pay the Sum Insured if the Insured commits suicide while sane or insane within two years after the Date of Issue. Instead, we will pay a sum equal to the total amount of premiums paid to that date.

Misstatement of Age or Sex

We will make adjustments if the Insured's age or sex was misstated in the application. The Sum Insured, and any other benefits, will be what the premiums paid would have bought at the correct age and sex.

Policy Settlement

We will pay the Sum Insured to the Beneficiary when we receive proof of the Insured's death. We will refund the part of any premium which has been paid for a period beyond the policy month in which the Insured died.

We may ask that this policy be returned to us at the time of settlement.

Nonparticipating

Your policy is nonparticipating. The premium does not include a charge for participating in surplus. This means we do not pay dividends on your policy.

PREMIUMS

You must pay your premiums on time to keep your policy in full force. You have certain rights if you do not. This section explains how and when your premiums are to be paid. It also gives some of your rights if a premium is not paid.

Payment

Your first premium is due on the Policy Date. It must be paid on or before delivery of your policy.

All premiums are to be paid in advance either at our Home Office or to one of our agents authorized to collect premiums The amount of premium is shown on the Policy Specifications Page. If you request a receipt, we will give you one. It will be signed by an Executive Officer and countersigned by the agent.

Frequency

Premiums are to be paid on the first day of each Premium Interval. This is the "Due Date" of a premium. The Premium Interval is shown on the Policy Specifications Page.

You may change the Premium Interval by Written Notice. The change has to be made in accordance with our published rates and payment rules. No change to a less frequent Premium Interval can be made during the first policy year.

Grace Period

You have 31 days from Due Date to pay a premium. This is called "the grace period." The policy will continue in full force. No interest will be charged. But, if the Insured dies during the grace period, we will subtract the unpaid premium for those 31 days. (There is no grace period for the first premium.)

Default

If a premium is not paid by the end of the grace period, your policy will be in default. It will cease to be in full force. It will have no futher value. The date of default is the Due Date of the unpaid premium.

Reinstatement

You have the right to put your policy back in full force any time within five years of the date of default. You would then resume paying premiums.

We will require you to:

1. Give us evidence the Insured is still insurable according to our rules;

2. Pay the applicable renewal premium for the term period from the date of reinstatement to the next Term Expiry Date; and

3. Pay the unpaid premium for the 31-day grace period following the Due Date of the last premium in default, with compound interest at 6% per year from that Due Date.

8

OWNERSHIP AND BENEFICIARY

This section describes the Owner and the Beneficiary: who they are and what their rights in this policy are.

Ownership

You, the Owner, are named in the application. You may make use of all rights of this policy while the Insured is living. These rights are subject to the rights of any assignee or living irrevocable beneficiary. "Irrevocable" means that you have given up your right to change the Beneficiary named.

If you die, the Contingent Owner, if one is named, will become the Owner. If there is no named Owner then living, the rights of ownership will vest in the executors, administrators or assigns of the Owner

Beneficiary

The Beneficiary is named in the application. More than one beneficiary may be named. The rights of any beneificiary who dies before the Insured will pass to the surviving beneficiary or beneficiaries unless you provide otherwise.

If no beneficiary is living at the Insured's death, we will pay the Sum Insured to you, your legal representatives or assigns.

The rights of any beneficiary will be subject to all the provisions of this policy. You may impose other limitations with our consent.

Change of Ownership or Beneficiary

You may change the Owner or the Beneficiary, unless an irrevocable one has been named, while the Insured is living. Change is made by Written Notice. The change takes effect on the date the notice was signed, if we acknowledge receipt of your notice in writing.

Any change is subject to any of our actions made before the date your notice was acknowledged. We may require return of this policy for endorsement before making a change.

Assignment and Assignee

Only you may make an assignment of this policy. You must notify us if you assign this policy. We are not responsible for the validity or effect of an assignment. Any change you make is subject to any action we made before the date the notice was received.

9

RENEWAL

Your policy is renewable each year. This section explains what you have to do.

Yearly Renewal

You may renew your policy each year, without evidence of insurability, until the policy anniversary at the Insured's Attained Age 98. A Table of Renewal Premiums showing the premium payable for each policy year is on the Policy Specifications Page. You must pay the renewal premium shown when due to keep your policy in full force. The renewal of your policy becomes effective when we receive the renewal premium, subject to the grace period provision.

When Renewal Premium Due

Your policy has an Original Term Expiry Date which is the end of the first term period. This is the first policy anniversary. Your first renewal premium is due on this date. Each time you renew your policy, you establish a new Term Expiry Date which will be the policy anniversary following the previous expiry date. Your renewal premium for the next term period is due on this new Term Expiry Date.

Effect of Total Disability on Renewal

We will waive any premium coming due and automatically renew your policy for you if:

1. A Premium Waiver Benefit is in your policy;

2. The Insured meets the conditions to qualify for waiver of premiums;

3. The Insured is disabled on any Term Expiry Date; and

4. You have not converted this policy.

10

CONVERSION

You may convert this policy to a different type of life insurance policy. This section explains how this is done.

Conversion Election

You may convert this policy, without evidence of insurability, to a nonparticipating life insurance policy. You must make this election prior to the date shown on the Policy Specifications Page for this and while your policy is in full force. The Sum Insured of the new policy may not be greater than the Sum Insured of this policy on the date of conversion. However, it may be less, subject to our then minimum amount requirements.

Conditions of Conversion

We will issue your new policy subject to the following conditions:

1. The premium during the first year must be as great as the premium for a Whole Life insurance policy with the same initial death benefit.

2. The Sum Insured must be level.

3. Your new policy will be issued on a restricted basis or in a class other than standard if we issued this policy in that way.

4. Your new policy may have a Premium Waiver Benefit if this policy has one. It will be the one we are then issuing. However, you cannot enlarge the Premium Waiver Benefit in this policy, and you must give us proof that the Insured is not disabled on the date of conversion.

   You may do this without evidence of insurability if this term insurance is converted to a Whole Life policy. But, you must have our consent if the Premium Waiver Benefit is to be included in a policy that is not Whole Life.

5. Your new policy may include benefits for loss from accident if these benefits are in this policy. The benefits will be those we are then issuing. However, you cannot enlarge the benefits in this policy

6. Your new policy may include a Guaranteed Insurability Benefit if this policy has one. It will be the one we are then issuing.

7. You may have our consent to continue any other benefits which are part of this policy.

Issue Age of New Policy

The Issue Age of the new policy may be:

(a) The Insured's Attained Age on the date of conversion; or

(b) The Issue Age of the Insured on the Policy Date of this policy.

If you choose (a), the premium rate will be the one we are using on the date of conversion. Your new policy will become effective when we receive your application and first premium payment.

If you choose (b), the premium rate will be the one we were using on the Policy Date of this policy. Your new policy will become effective when you pay the greater of:

(1) The difference between the premiums you have paid for this policy and the premiums you would have paid for the new policy, plus 6% interest compounded annually; and

(2) The Cash Value of the new policy on the date of conversion.

Conversion Credit

A Conversion Credit is available to you if you convert this policy before the date shown on the Policy Specifications Page for this. The amount of Conversion Credit is also shown there. This amount is multiplied by the ratio of (a) the amount of insurance converted to (b) the Sum Insured on the Date of Issue.

If you convert during the first policy year, the Conversion Credit will be the amount determined above further multiplied by the ratio of (1) the premiums you have paid for this policy to (2) the premiums you would have paid for the new policy.

11

DECREASING TERM INSURANCE OPTION

Your policy is a level term insurance policy. This means the Sum Insured remains the same but the amount of your premium increases each policy year. You may change this and pay the same premium each year and have the Sum Insured decrease. This section explains how this is done.

Election of Option

You may elect this Decreasing Term Insurance Option on any policy anniversary prior to the Insured's Attained Age 80.

You must make this election by Written Notice.

If you do this, you would continue to pay the Life Insurance Premium payable during the prior policy year. You pay this premium instead of the premiums shown in the Table of Renewal Premiums on the Policy Specifications Page.

If you elect this option, the Sum Insured for the next policy year and all policy years after that will be determined from the table on the next page. This amount is based on the premium payable and the Attained Age of the Insured at the beginning of each policy year. Changes in the Sum Insured will occur each year on the policy anniversary.

You determine the Sum Insured from the table by first determining the annual life premium payable. To do this, take the Life Insurance Premium shown on the Policy Specifications Page for the policy year preceding the year in which you elect this option. Then adjust it as follows:

1. If you pay your premiums annually, deduct $15;

2. If you pay your premiums semiannually, multiply by 1.961 and then deduct $15;

3. If you pay your premiums quarterly, multiply by 3.846 and then deduct $15; or

4. If you pay your premiums by Bank-O-Matic (monthly), multiply by 11.494 and then deduct $15.

5. If you pay your premiums by Monthly Account, multiply by 10.417 and then deduct $15.

If your policy has a Premium Waiver Benefit, we will automatically continue the coverage at the premium rate shown on the next page. But, you may terminate this coverage by giving us Written Notice.

You must have our consent to continue any other benefits which are part of your policy.

If you elect this option, your policy must be returned to us for our endorsement. We will return the policy to you with a new Specifications Page showing the Table of Decreasing Sums Insured and the level premium payable.

12

TABLE FOR DECREASING TERM OPTION

Age Last Birthday Male and Female	Sum Insured Per $100 Annual Life Premium*	
	Male	Female
16	45,870	49,260
17	45,870	49,260
18	45,870	49,260
19	45,870	49,260
20	45,870	49,260
21	45,870	49,260
22	45,870	49,260
23	45,870	49,260
24	45,870	49,260
25	45,870	49,260
26	45,870	49,260
27	45,660	49,260
28	45,050	48,780
29	44,440	48,310
30	43,860	47,620
31	43,290	46,950
32	42,370	46,080
33	41,490	45,250
34	40,320	44,440
35	38,910	43,670
36	37,170	42,190
37	35,210	40,490
38	32,890	38,610
39	30,670	37,040
40	28,490	34,970
41	26,390	32,890
42	24,450	30,490
43	22,680	28,740
44	21,010	26,670
45	19,420	25,000
46	17,890	23,420
47	16,470	21,880
48	15,130	20,410
49	13,890	19,050
50	12,720	17,480
51	11,660	15,770
52	10,680	14,470
53	9,790	13,090
54	8,980	12,020
55	8,230	10,850

Age Last Birthday Male and Female	Sum Insured Per $100 Annual Life Premium*	
	Male	Female
56	7,540	9,940
57	6,900	9,100
58	6,310	8,210
59	5,770	7,510
60	5,270	6,860
61	4,820	6,170
62	4,400	5,630
63	4,010	5,130
64	3,650	4,660
65	3,310	4,220
66	3,000	3,820
67	2,710	3,400
68	2,450	3,060
69	2,220	2,760
70	2,010	2,500
71	1,830	2,260
72	1,670	2,030
73	1,530	1,850
74	1,400	1,690
75	1,280	1,540
76	1,160	1,390
77	1,060	1,250
78	960	1,130
79	870	1,010
80	790	920
81	720	830
82	650	750
83	600	680
84	550	620
85	510	570
86	470	520
87	440	480
88	410	440
89	380	410
90	350	380
91	330	350
92	300	320
93	280	290
94	250	260
95	230	240
96	200	210
97	160	160

ANNUAL PREMIUM FOR PREMIUM WAIVER BENEFIT PER $100 ANNUAL LIFE INSURANCE PREMIUM

Age Last Birthday at Time Option is Selected— Male and Female	Premium**
16-39	$5.00
41-49	7.00
50-59	8.00
60-64	5.00

**Premiums shown will be adjusted for policies in a class other than standard.

*Amounts shown will be adjusted for policies in a class other than standard.

13

SETTLEMENT OPTIONS

This section describes the ways the proceeds of this policy can be paid other than in one lump sum payment.

All or any part of the proceeds may be left with us and paid under one of the following options.

Option 1

Interest Income: Proceeds left with us with interest paid at regular times as elected. Interest on each $1,000 of proceeds with be: $30.00 if paid yearly; $14.89 if paid two times a year; $7.42 if paid four times a year; or $2.47 if paid monthly. Payments are made at equal intervals.

Option 2

Installments for Fixed Period: Proceeds paid in equal payments one, two, four or twelve times a year, from one to thirty years. The amount of payment for each $1,000 of proceeds is shown in the Table for Option 2. Payments are made at equal intervals.

Option 3A

Life Income—Guaranteed Period: Proceeds paid in equal payments for as long as the payee lives. This option has guaranteed payment periods of not less than 10 or 20 years as elected.

Option 3B

Life Income—Guaranteed Return of Proceeds: Proceeds paid in equal payments for as long as the payee lives. In addition, a cash refund will be paid at the death of the payee for an amount, if any, equal to the original proceeds less the sum of all installments paid.

The amount of each payment will be in accordance with the Table for Option 3. It will be determined by the payee's sex and age last birthday on the date the first payment is due.

Option 4

Installments for Fixed Amount: Proceeds paid in equal payments one, two, four or twelve times a year. At least 5% of the original proceeds must be paid each year until the entire proceeds and interest are paid. Payments are made at equal intervals.

Option 5

Alternate Life Income: Proceeds paid as a life income. The amount of each payment will be based on our single premium annuity rates on the date of the option. These rates will be furnished on request.

14

ELECTION OF SETTLEMENT OPTIONS

This section tells you how to elect a settlement option.

Election

You may elect a settlement option in the application or by Written Notice. During the Insured's lifetime, only you may make or change any election.

If there is no option in effect when the Insured dies, the payee may elect one. The payee may also name a contingent payee to receive any final payment.

The payee may change an option in effect when the Insured dies only if the option elected does not provide otherwise. However, if a life income option is in effect, that election may not be changed after payments have begun.

Availability

The options are available only with our consent if the payee is other than a natural person acting in his or her own right. Other settlement options can be arranged with our consent.

Guaranteed Interest and Excess Interest

We guarantee an interest rate of 3% per year, compounded yearly, under Options 1, 2 and 4. We will pay or credit additional interest under these options if our Board of Directors votes to do so.

Minimum Amounts

If the proceeds for one payee are less than $1,000, we have the right to pay that amount in a lump sum. No option is available under which the amount of proceeds would not be enough to make payments of at least $25.

Death of Payee

If a payee dies, we will pay any remaining amounts to the payee's legal representatives, unless other arrangements have been made with us. We will pay:

1. Under Options 1 and 4, the unpaid amount plus accrued interest; and

2. Under Options 2 and 3A, the commuted value of the remaining payments.

The commuted value is based on compound interest at 3% per year.

Rights to Commute and Withdraw

Unless other arrangements have been made with us, a payee will have the right to:

1. Withdraw proceeds left under Option 1 or 4; and

2. Withdraw the commuted value of the remaining payments under Option 2.

Proof of Age and Sex

We may require proof of the payee's age and sex before making any payment. If age or sex has been misstated, adjustments will be made.

Operative Date

We put an option into effect on the date the proceeds become payable, or on the date of election, if later. This means the first payment under Option 1 is made at the end of the interest period elected. Under Options 2, 3, 4 and 5, the first payment is made on the date we put the option into effect.

15

TABLE FOR SETTLEMENT OPTIONS

Monthly Payments Per $1000 of Proceeds Applied

OPTION 2			OPTION 3A				OPTION 3B	
				10 Years Certain & Life		20 Years Certain & Life	Cash Refund	
Period of Years	Monthly Payments	Age of Payee	Male	Female	Male	Female	Male	Female
1	$84.47	25 & under	$3.23	$3.09	$3.22	$3.08	$3.19	$3.07
2	42.86	26	3.26	3.11	3.24	3.10	3.22	3.09
3	28.99	27	3.29	3.13	3.27	3.12	3.25	3.11
4	22.06	28	3.32	3.16	3.30	3.15	3.28	3.13
5	17.91	29	3.35	3.18	3.33	3.17	3.30	3.16
6	$15.14	30	3.38	3.21	3.36	3.20	3.33	3.18
7	13.16	31	3.42	3.24	3.40	3.22	3.36	3.21
8	11.68	32	3.46	3.26	3.43	3.25	3.40	3.23
9	10.53	33	3.50	3.30	3.47	3.28	3.43	3.26
10	9.61	34	3.53	3.33	3.50	3.31	3.46	3.29
11	$8.86	35	3.58	3.36	3.54	3.34	3.50	3.32
12	8.24	36	3.62	3.40	3.58	3.38	3.54	3.35
13	7.71	37	3.67	3.43	3.62	3.41	3.58	3.38
14	7.26	38	3.72	3.47	3.66	3.45	3.62	3.42
15	6.87	39	3.77	3.51	3.71	3.48	3.66	3.45
16	$6.53	40	3.82	3.55	3.75	3.52	3.70	3.49
17	6.23	41	3.88	3.60	3.80	3.56	3.75	3.53
18	5.96	42	3.94	3.64	3.85	3.60	3.79	3.57
19	5.73	43	4.00	3.69	3.90	3.65	3.84	3.61
20	5.51	44	4.06	3.74	3.95	3.69	3.89	3.65
21	$5.32	45	4.13	3.79	4.00	3.74	3.94	3.70
22	5.15	46	4.20	3.85	4.05	3.79	4.00	3.75
23	4.99	47	4.27	3.91	4.11	3.84	4.05	3.80
24	4.84	48	4.35	3.97	4.16	3.89	4.11	3.85
25	4.71	49	4.42	4.04	4.22	3.95	4.17	3.90
26	$4.59	50	4.50	4.10	4.28	4.00	4.24	3.96
27	4.47	51	4.59	4.18	4.34	4.06	4.30	4.02
28	4.37	52	4.68	4.25	4.40	4.12	4.37	4.08
29	4.27	53	4.77	4.33	4.46	4.19	4.45	4.15
30	4.18	54	4.87	4.41	4.54	4.25	4.52	4.22
		55	$4.97	$4.50	$4.59	$4.32	$4.60	$4.29
		56	5.07	4.59	4.65	4.39	4.69	4.37
		57	5.18	4.69	4.71	4.46	4.77	4.45
		58	5.30	4.79	4.78	4.53	4.86	4.53
		59	5.41	4.89	4.84	4.60	4.96	4.62
		60	5.54	5.01	4.90	4.67	5.06	4.72
		61	5.67	5.13	4.96	4.74	5.17	4.81
		62	5.81	5.25	5.02	4.82	5.28	4.92
		63	5.95	5.39	5.08	4.89	5.40	5.03
		64	6.10	5.52	5.13	4.96	5.52	5.15
		65	6.25	5.68	5.18	5.03	5.65	5.27
		66	6.41	5.83	5.23	5.09	5.79	5.41
		67	6.57	6.00	5.28	5.15	5.94	5.54
		68	6.75	6.18	5.32	5.21	6.09	5.69
		69	6.93	6.36	5.35	5.26	6.25	5.85
		70	7.10	6.55	5.39	5.31	6.42	6.02
		71	7.28	6.75	5.41	5.35	6.61	6.20
		72	7.47	6.96	5.44	5.38	6.80	6.38
		73	7.65	7.17	5.46	5.41	7.00	6.58
		74	7.84	7.38	5.47	5.43	7.22	6.79
		75	8.02	7.59	5.49	5 45	7.44	7.01
		76	8.20	7.81	5.49	5.47	7.69	7.25
		77	8.38	8.01	5.50	5.48	7.95	7.49
		78	8.54	8.21	5.51	5.49	8.22	7.76
		79	8.70	8.40	5.51	5.49	8.52	8.04
		80	8.85	8.58	5.51	5.50	8.84	8.32
		81	8.99	8.74	5.51	5.50	9.17	8.62
		82	9.12	8.88	5.51	5.51	9.54	8.94
		83	9.23	9.01	5.51	5.51	9.94	9.26
		84	9.31	9.12	5.51	5.51	10.35	9.60
		85 & over	9.39	9.21	5.51	5.51	10.81	9.94

Annual, semiannual or quarterly payments under Option 2 are 11.839, 5.963 and 2.993 respectively times the monthly payments.

16

PART I   Life Insurance Application To *The COUNCIL Life Insurance Company*

IMPORTANT NOTICE—This application is subject to approval by the Company's Home Office. Be sure all questions in all parts of the application are answered completely and accurately, since the application is the basis of the insurance contract and will become part of any policy issued.

1. Insured's Full Name (Please Print-Give title as Mr., Dr., Rev., etc.)

	Mo., Day, Yr. of Birth	Ins. Age	Sex	Place of Birth	Social Security No.
MR. DENNIS SMITH	8/25/53	29	M	TULSA, OKLA.	001-30-0000

Single ☑ Married ☐ Widowed ☐ Divorced ☐ Separated ☐

2. Addresses last 5 yrs.

		Number Street	City	State	Zip Code	County	Yrs.
Mail to ☑ Home:	Present	711 SUNSET DRIVE	WASH.	D.C.	20000	U.S.A	3
	Former						
☐ Business:	Present						
	Former						

3. Occupation

	Title	Describe Exact Duties	Yrs.
Present	COMPUTER SPECIALIST	DEVELOP PROGRAMS FOR CLIENTS	3
Former	COMPUTER ANALYST	DEVELOP SOFTWARE PACKAGES	6

4. a) Employer ABC COMPUTER CONSULTANTS
b) Any change contemplated? Yes ☐ (Explain in Remarks) No ☑

5. Have you ever   Yes   No
  a) been rejected, deferred or discharged by the Armed Forces for medical reasons or applied for a government disability rating?   ☐ ☑
  b) applied for insurance or for reinstatement which was declined, postponed, modified or rated?   ☐ ☑
  c) used LSD, heroin, cocaine or methadone?   ☐ ☑

6. a) In the past 3 years have you
  (i) had your driver's license suspended or revoked or been convicted of more than one speeding violation?   ☐ ☑
  (ii) operated, been a crew member of, or had any duties aboard any kind of aircraft?   ☐ ☑
  (iii) engaged in underwater diving below 40 feet, parachuting, or motor vehicle racing?   ☐ ☑
  b) In the future, do you intend to engage in any activities mentioned in (ii) and (iii) of a) above?   ☐ ☑
  (If "Yes" to 5a or any of 6, complete Supplemental Form 3375)

7. Have you smoked one or more cigarettes within the past 12 months?   ☑ ☐

8. Are other insurance applications pending or contemplated?   ☐ ☑

9. Do you intend to go to any foreign country?   ☐ ☑

10. Will coverage applied for replace or change any life insurance or annuities? (If "Yes", submit Replacement Form)   ☐ ☑

11. Total Life Insurance in force $_____   None ☑

12. Face Amount $ 40,000   Plan TERM
  Accidental Death ☐   Waiver of Premium ☐
  Purchase Option—Regular ☐   Preferred ☐ PEP ☐ GOR ☐
  ____ units of Wife's Term—name: ____
  $____ initial amount Decreasing Term, _____ Years
  (Joint ☐)   (Mot. Pro. ☐)   (Straight Line ☐)
  Children's Term ☐   Other: ____

13. Auto. Prem. Loan provision operative if available? Yes ☑ No ☐

14. Dividend Option
  Additions (for other than Term policies) ☐   Deposits ☐
  Reduce premium, if applicable, otherwise cash ☐
  Supplemental Protection (Keyman only) ☐
  I Year Term—any balance to ____
  Deposits ☐ Additions ☐ Reduce prem. (cash if mo.) ☐

15. Beneficiary—for children's, wife's or joint insurance as provided in contract; for other insurance as follows, subject to policy's beneficiary provisions:

	(Name)	(Relationship to Insured)	
1st	KARYN SMITH	MOTHER	If living. If not
2nd	RONALD R. SMITH	FATHER	If living. If not
3rd	JEAN SMITH	SISTER	If living. If not

the executors or administrators of: Insured   Other (use Remarks) ☐
(Joint beneficiaries will receive equally or survivor, unless otherwise specified.)

16. Flexible Plan settlement (personal beneficiary only)   ☑

17. Rights—During Insured's lifetime all rights belong to
  Insured ☑   Other: ____
  Trustee ☐
  (attach Trust)
  (After Insured's death as provided in contract w/ wife's insurance.)

18. Premium—Frequency MO. Amt. Paid $ 109.80 None ☐
  Have you received a Conditional Receipt? Yes ☑ No ☐

REMARKS [Include details (company, date, amt., etc.) for all "Yes" answers to questions 4b, 5b, 5c, 8, 9 and 10]

SMOKES ONE PACK A DAY

I agree that: (1) No one but the Company's President, a Vice-President or Secretary has authority to accept information not contained in the application, to modify or enlarge any contract, or to waive any requirement. (2) Except as otherwise provided in any conditional receipt issued, any policy issued shall take effect upon its delivery and payment of the first premium during the lifetime of each person to be insured. Due dates of later premiums shall be as specified in the policy.

Dated at WASH., D.C. on AUG. 9 19 82   Signature of Insured *Dennis Smith*

Signature of Applicant (if other than Insured) who agrees to be bound by the representations and agreements in this and any other part of this application N/A
(Name)   (Relationship)   (Complete address of Applicant)

Countersigned by *Michael C. Baker*
Field Underwriter (Licensed Resident Agent)

17

Life Insurance

PART 1A Statements Forming Part Of Application To *The COUNCIL Life Insurance Company*
[Complete this Part if any Non-Medical or Family Insurance is Applied For]

1. Name of Insured **DENNIS SMITH** Ins. Age **29** Height **5** ft **10** in. Weight **165** lbs.

2. If Family, Children's, Wife's or Joint Insurance desired, other family members proposed for insurance:

Wife (include maiden name)	Ins. Age	Mo., Day, Yr. of Birth	Height ft. in.	Weight lbs.	Life in Force $	Place of Birth

Children	Sex	Ins. Age	Mo., Day, Yr. of Birth	Children	Sex	Ins. Age	Mo., Day, Yr. of Birth

3. Has any eligible dependent (a) been omitted from 2? Yes ☐ No ☑ (b) applied for insurance or for reinstatement which was declined, postponed, modified or rated or had a policy cancelled or renewal refused? Yes ☐ No ☑ (Give name, date, company in 8)

4. Have you or anyone else been proposed for insurance, so far as you know, ever been treated for or had indication of (underline applicable item) **Yes No**
   a) high blood pressure? (If "Yes", list drugs prescribed and dates taken.) ☐ ☑
   b) chest pain, heart attack, rheumatic fever, heart murmur, irregular pulse or other disorder of the heart or blood vessels? ☐ ☑
   c) cancer, tumor, cyst, or any disorder of the thyroid, skin, or lymph glands? ☐ ☑
   d) diabetes or anemia or other blood disorder? ☐ ☑
   e) sugar, albumin, blood or pus in the urine, or venereal disease? ☐ ☑
   f) any disorder of the kidney, bladder, prostate, breast or reproductive organs? ☐ ☑
   g) ulcer, intestinal bleeding, hepatitis, colitis, or other disorder of the stomach, intestine, spleen, pancreas, liver or gall bladder? ☐ ☑
   h) asthma, tuberculosis, bronchitis, emphysema or other disorder of the lungs? ☑ ☐
   i) fainting, convulsions, migraine headache, paralysis, epilepsy or any mental or nervous disorder? ☐ ☑
   j) arthritis, gout, amputation, sciatica, back pain or other disorder of the muscles, bones or joints? ☐ ☑
   k) disorder of the eyes, ears, nose, throat or sinuses? ☑ ☐
   l) varicose veins, hemorrhoids, hernia or rectal disorder? ☐ ☑
   m) alcoholism or drug habit? ☐ ☑

5. Have you or anyone else proposed for insurance, so far as you know, (underline applicable item) **Yes No**
   a) consulted or been examined or treated by any physician or practitioner in the past 5 years? ☑ ☐
   b) had, or been advised to have, an x-ray, cardiogram, blood or other diagnostic test in the past 5 years? ☐ ☑
   c) been a patient in a hospital, clinic, or other medical facility in the past 5 years? ☐ ☑
   d) ever had a surgical operation performed or advised? ☐ ☑
   e) ever made claim for disability or applied for compensation or retirement based on accident or sickness? ☐ ☑

6. Are you or any other person proposed for insurance, so far as you know, in impaired physical or mental health, or under any kind of medication? ☐ ☑

7. Weight change in last 6 months of adults proposed for insurance:

Name	Gain	Loss	Cause
N/A			

8. Details of all "Yes" answers. For any checkup or routine examination, indicate what symptoms, if any, prompted it and include results of the examination and any special tests. Include clinic number if applicable.

Question No.	Name of Person	Illness & Treatment	No. of Attacks	Dates: Onset-Recovery	Doctor, Clinic or Hospital and Complete Address
4H	DENNIS SMITH	BRONCHITIS	6	1960-1967	DR. WILLIAM BILLS 29 QUEBEC ST. TULSA, OKLA.
4K	DENNIS SMITH	CONJUNCTIVITIS	1	1981	DR. J.L. MARSHALL
5B	DENNIS SMITH	CHEST X-RAY-JOB	1		99 ELM ST, WASH, D.C.
5D	DENNIS SMITH	BROKEN KNEECAP	1	1972-1973	DR. WILLIAM BILLS

So far as may be lawful, I waive for myself and all persons claiming an interest in any insurance issued on this application, all provisions of law forbidding any physician or other person who has attended or examined, or who may attend or examine, me or any other person covered by such insurance, from disclosing any knowledge or information which he thereby acquired.

I represent the statements and answers in this and in any other part of this application to be true and complete to the best of my knowledge and belief, and offer them to the Company for the purpose of inducing it to issue the policy or policies and to accept the payment of premiums thereunder. I also agree that payment of the first premium (if after this date) shall be a representation by me that such statements and answers would be the same if made at the time of such payment.

Dated at **WASH., D.C.** on **AUG. 9** 19**82** Signature of Insured **Dennis Smith**

Witnessed by **Michael C. Baker** Signature of Wife (if insured) **N/A**
Field Underwriter (Licensed Resident Agent)

AUTHORIZATION

For purposes of determining my eligibility for insurance, I hereby authorize any physician, practitioner, hospital, clinic, institution, insurance company, Medical Information Bureau, or other organization or person that has records or knowledge of me or my health to give any such information to the Council Life Insurance Company.

If application is made to The Council Life Insurance Company for insurance on any member of my family, this authorization also applies to such member. A photostatic copy of this authorization shall be as valid as the original.

Signed on **Aug. 9** 19**82** **Dennis Smith**
Signature of Insured

152 18

SAMPLE

THE COUNCIL LIFE INSURANCE COMPANY

The Council Life Insurance Company agrees to pay the benefits
provided in this policy, subject to its terms and conditions.
Executed at New York, New York on the Date of Issue.

David Olson

Secretary

Barbara Sloan

President

Life Policy — Participating

Amount payable at death of Insured $10,000.

Premiums payable to age 90.

Schedule of benefits and premiums page 2.

Right to Examine Policy—Please examine this policy carefully. The Owner may return
the policy for any reason within ten days after receiving it. If returned, the policy will be
considered void from the beginning and any premium paid will be refunded.

A GUIDE TO THE PROVISIONS OF THIS POLICY

Accidental Death Benefit	12
Beneficiaries	7
Cash Value, Extended Term and Paid-Up Insurance	5
Change of Policy	6
Contract	3
Dividends	4
Loans	6
Ownership	3
Premiums and Reinstatement	4
Specification	2
Waiver of Premium Right	11

Endorsements Made At Issue Appear After "General Provisions." Additional Benefits, If
Any, Are Provided By Rider.

1

─── Specifications ───

Plan and Additional Benefits	Amount	Premium	Years Payable
Whole Life (Premiums payable to age 90)	$10,000	$229.50	55
Waiver of Premium (To age 65)		4.30	30
Accidental Death (To age 70)	10,000	7.80	35

A premium is payable on the policy date and every 12 policy months thereafter. The first premium is $241.60.

TABLE OF GUARANTEED VALUES

END OF POLICY YEAR	CASH OR LOAN VALUE	PAID-UP. INSURANCE	EXTENDED TERM INSURANCE YEARS	DAYS
1	$ 14	$ 30	0	152
2	174	450	4	182
3	338	860	8	65
4	506	1,250	10	344
5	676	1,640	12	360
6	879	2,070	14	335
7	1,084	2,500	16	147
8	1,293	2,910	17	207
9	1,504	3,300	18	177
10	1,719	3,690	19	78
11	1,908	4,000	19	209
12	2,099	4,300	19	306
13	2,294	4,590	20	8
14	2,490	4,870	20	47
15	2,690	5,140	20	65
16	2,891	5,410	20	66
17	3,095	5,660	20	52
18	3,301	5,910	20	27
19	3,508	6,150	19	358
20	3,718	6,390	19	317
AGE 60	4,620	7,200	18	111
AGE 65	5,504	7,860	16	147

Paid-up additions and dividend accumulations increase the cash values; indebtedness decreases them.

The percentage referred to in section 5.6 is 83.000%.

Direct Beneficiary	Helen M. Benson, wife of the insured
Owner	Thomas A. Benson, the insured

Insured	Thomas A. Benson	**Age and Sex**	37 Male
Policy Date	November 1, 1980	**Policy Number**	000/00
Date of Issue	November 1, 1980		

2

SECTION 1. THE CONTRACT

1.1 LIFE INSURANCE BENEFIT

The Council Life Insurance Company agrees, subject to the terms and conditions of this policy, to pay the Amount shown on page 2 to the beneficiary upon receipt at its Home Office of proof of the death of the Insured.

1.2 INCONTESTABILITY

This policy shall be incontestable after it has been in force during the lifetime of the Insured for two years from the Date of Issue.

1.3 SUICIDE

If within two years from the Date of Issue the Insured dies by suicide, the amount payable by the Company shall be limited to the premiums paid.

1.4 DATES

The contestable and suicide periods commence with the Date of Issue. Policy months, years and anniversaries are computed from the Policy Date. Both dates are shown on page 2 of this policy.

1.5 MISSTATEMENT OF AGE

If the age of the Insured has been misstated, the amount payable shall be the amount which the premiums paid would have purchased at the correct age.

1.6 GENERAL

This policy and the application, a copy of which is attached when the policy is issued, constitute the entire contract. All statements in the application are representations and not warranties. No statement shall void this policy or be used in defense of a claim under it unless contained in the application.

Only an officer of the Company is authorized to alter this policy or to waive any of the Company's rights or requirements.

All payments by the Company under this policy are payable at its Home Office.

SECTION 2. OWNERSHIP

2.1 THE OWNER

The Owner is as shown on page 2, or his successor or transferee. All policy rights and privileges may be exercised by the Owner without the consent of any beneficiary. Such rights and privileges may be exercised only during the lifetime of the Insured and thereafter to the extent permitted by Sections 8 and 9.

2.2 TRANSFER OF OWNERSHIP

The Owner may transfer the ownership of this policy by filing written evidence of transfer satisfactory to the Company at its Home Office and, unless waived by the Company, submitting the policy for endorsement to show the transfer.

2.3 COLLATERAL ASSIGNMENT

The Owner may assign this policy as collateral security. The Company assumes no responsibility for the validity or effect of any collateral assignment of this policy. The Company shall not be charged with notice of any assignment unless the assignment is in writing and filed at its Home Office before payment is made.

The interest of any beneficiary shall be subordinate to any collateral assignment made either before or after the beneficiary designation.

A collateral assignee is not an Owner and a collateral assignment is not a transfer of ownership.

3

SECTION 3. PREMIUMS AND REINSTATEMENT

3.1 PREMIUMS

(a) Payment. All premiums after the first are payable at the Home Office or to an authorized agent. A receipt signed by an officer of the Company will be provided upon request.

(b) Frequency. Premiums may be paid annually, semiannually, or quarterly at the published rates for this policy. A change to any such frequency shall be effective upon acceptance by the Company of the premium for the changed frequency. Premiums may be paid on any other frequency approved by the Company.

(c) Default. If a premium is not paid on or before its due date, this policy shall terminate on the due date except as provided in Sections 3.1(d), 5.3 and 5.4.

(d) Grace Period. A grace period of 31 days shall be allowed for payment of a premium not paid on its due date. The policy shall continue in full force during this period. If the Insured dies during the grace period, the overdue premium shall be paid from the proceeds of the policy.

(e) Premium Refund at Death. The portion of any premium paid which applies to a period beyond the policy month in which the Insured died shall be refunded as part of the proceeds of this policy.

3.2 REINSTATEMENT

If the policy has not been surrendered for its cash value, it may be reinstated within five years after the due date of the unpaid premium provided the following conditions are satisfied:

(a) Within 31 days following expiration of the grace period, reinstatement may be made without evidence of insurability during the lifetime of the Insured by payment of the overdue premium.

(b) After 31 days following expiration of the grace period, reinstatement is subject to:

(i) receipt of evidence of insurability of the Insured satisfactory to the Company;

(ii) payment of all overdue premiums with interest from the due date of each at the rate of 6% compounded annually; or any lower rate established by the Company.

Any policy indebtedness existing on the due date of the unpaid premium, together with interest from that date, must be repaid or reinstated.

SECTION 4. DIVIDENDS

4.1 ANNUAL DIVIDENDS

This policy shall share in the divisible surplus, if any, of the Company. This policy's share shall be determined annually and credited as a dividend. Payment of the first dividend is contingent upon payment of the premium or premiums for the second policy year and shall be credited proportionately as each premium is paid. Thereafter, each dividend shall be payable on the policy anniversary.

4.2 USE OF DIVIDENDS

As directed by the Owner, dividends may be paid in cash or applied under one of the following:

(a) Paid-Up Additions. Dividends may be applied to purchase fully paid-up additional insurance. Paid-up additions will also share in the divisible surplus.

(b) Dividend Accumulations. Dividends may be left to accumulate at interest. Interest is credited at a rate of 3% compounded annually, or any higher rate established by the Company.

(c) Premium Payment. Dividends may be applied toward payment of any premium due within one year, if the balance of the premium is paid. If the balance is not paid, or if this policy is in force as paid-up insurance, the dividend will be applied to purchase paid-up additions.

If no direction is given by the Owner, dividends will be applied to purchase paid-up additions.

4.3 USE OF ADDITIONS AND ACCUMULATIONS

Paid-up additions and dividend accumulations increase the policy's cash value and loan value and are payable as part of the policy proceeds. Additions may be surrendered and accumulations withdrawn unless required under the Loan, Extended Term Insurance, or Paid-up Insurance provisions.

4.4 DIVIDEND AT DEATH

A dividend for the period from the beginning of the policy year to the end of the policy month in which the Insured dies shall be paid as part of the policy proceeds.

4

SECTION 5. CASH VALUE, EXTENDED TERM AND PAID-UP INSURANCE

5.1 CASH VALUE

The cash value, when all premiums due have been paid, shall be the reserve on this policy less the deduction described in Section 5.5, plus the reserve for any paid-up additions and the amount of any dividend accumulations.

The cash value within three months after the due date of any unpaid premium shall be the cash value on the due date reduced by any subsequent surrender of paid-up additions or withdrawal of dividend accumulations. The cash value at any time after such three months shall be the reserve on the form of insurance then in force, plus the reserve for any paid-up additions and the amount of any dividend accumulations.

If this policy is surrendered within 31 days after a policy anniversary, the cash value shall be not less than the cash value on that anniversary.

5.2 CASH SURRENDER

The Owner may surrender this policy for its cash value less any indebtedness. The policy shall terminate upon receipt at the Home Office of this policy and a written surrender of all claims. Receipt of the policy may be waived by the Company.

The Company may defer paying the cash value for a period not exceeding six months from the date of surrender. If payment is deferred 30 days or more, interest shall be paid on the cash value less any indebtedness at the rate of 3% compounded annually from the date of surrender to the date of payment.

5.3 EXTENDED TERM INSURANCE

If any premium remains unpaid at the end of the grace period, this policy shall continue in force as nonparticipating extended term insurance. The amount of insurance shall be the amount of this policy, plus any paid-up additions and dividend accumulations, less any indebtedness. The term insurance shall begin as of the due date of the unpaid premium and its duration shall be determined by applying the cash value less any indebtedness as a net single premium at the attained age of the Insured. If the term insurance would extend to or beyond attained age 100, paid-up insurance under Section 5.4 below will be provided instead.

5.4 PAID-UP INSURANCE

In lieu of extended term insurance this policy may be continued in force as participating paid-up life insurance.

Paid-up insurance may be requested by written notice filed at the Home Office before, or within three months after, the due date of the unpaid premium. The insurance will be for the amount that the cash value will purchase as a net single premium at the attained age of the Insured. Any indebtedness shall remain outstanding.

5.5 TABLE OF GUARANTEED VALUES

The cash values, paid-up insurance, and extended term insurance shown on page 2 are for the end of the policy year indicated. These values are based on the assumption that premiums have been paid for the number of years stated and are exclusive of any paid-up additions, dividend accumulations, or indebtedness. During the policy year allowance shall be made for any portion of a year's premium paid and for the time elapsed in that year. Values for policy years not shown are calculated on the same basis as this table and will be furnished on request. All values are equal to or greater than those required by the State in which this policy is delivered.

In determining cash values a deduction is made from the reserve. During the first five policy years, the deduction for each $1,000 of Amount is $9 plus $.15 for each year of the Insured's issue age. After the fifth policy year, the deduction decreases yearly by one-fifth of the initial deduction until there is no deduction in the tenth and subsequent policy years. If the premium paying period is less than ten years, there is no deduction in the last two policy years of the premium paying period or thereafter.

5.6 RESERVES AND NET PREMIUMS

Reserves, net premiums and present values are determined in accordance with the Commissioners 1958 Standard Ordinary Mortality Table and 3% interest, except that for the first five years of any extended term insurance, the Commissioners 1958 Extended Term Insurance Table is used. All reserves are based on continuous payment of premiums and immediate payment of claims. Net annual premiums are the same in each policy year, except that if premiums are payable for more than 20 years, the net annual premium in the 21st and subsequent policy years is determined by applying the percentage shown on page 2 to the net annual premium for the 20th policy year. On the Policy Date, the present value of all future guaranteed benefits equals the present value of all future net annual premiums. The reserve at the end of any policy year is the excess of the present value of all future guaranteed benefits over the present value of all future net annual premiums. The reserve is exclusive of any additional benefits.

5

SECTION 6. LOANS

6.1 POLICY LOAN

The Owner may obtain a policy loan by assignment of this policy to the Company. The amount of the loan, plus any existing indebtedness, shall not exceed the loan value. No loan shall be granted if the policy is in force as extended term insurance. The Company may defer making a loan for six months unless the loan is to be used to pay premiums on policies issued by the Company.

6.2 PREMIUM LOAN

A premium loan shall be granted to pay an overdue premium if the premium loan option is in effect. If the loan value, less any indebtedness, is insufficient to pay the overdue premium, a premium will be paid for any other frequency permitted by this policy for which the loan value less any indebtedness is sufficient. The premium loan option may be elected or revoked by written notice filed at the Home Office.

6.3 LOAN VALUE

The loan value is the largest amount which, with accrued interest, does not exceed the cash value either on the next premium due date or at the end of one year from the date of the loan.

6.4 LOAN INTEREST

Interest is payable at the rate of 8% compounded annually, or at any lower rate established by the Company for any period during which the loan is outstanding.

The Company shall provide at least 30 days written notice to the Owner (or any other party designated by the Owner to receive notice under this policy) and any assignee recorded at the Home Office of any increase in interest rate on loans outstanding 40 or more days prior to the effective date of the increase.

Interest accrues on a daily basis from the date of the loan on policy loans and from the premium due date on premium loans, and is compounded annually. Interest unpaid on a loan anniversary is added to and becomes part of the loan principal and bears interest on the same terms.

6.5 INDEBTEDNESS

Indebtedness consists of unpaid policy and premium loans on the policy including accrued interest. Indebtedness may be repaid at any time. Any unpaid indebtedness will be deducted from the policy proceeds.

If indebtedness equals or exceeds the cash value, this policy shall terminate. Termination shall occur 31 days after a notice has been mailed to the address of record of the Owner and of any assignee recorded at the Home Office.

SECTION 7. CHANGE OF POLICY

7 CHANGE OF PLAN

The Owner may change this policy to any permanent life or endowment plan offered by the Company on the Date of Issue of this policy. The change may be made upon payment of any cost and subject to the conditions determined by the Company. For a change made after the first year to a plan having a higher reserve, the cost shall not exceed the difference in cash values or the difference in reserves, whichever is greater, plus 3½% of such difference.

6

SECTION 8. BENEFICIARIES

8.1 DESIGNATION AND CHANGE OF BENEFICIARIES

(a) By Owner. The Owner may designate and change direct and contingent beneficiaries and further payees of death proceeds:

(1) during the lifetime of the Insured.

(2) during the 60 days following the date of death of the Insured, if the Insured immediately before his death was not the Owner. Any such designation of direct beneficiary may not be changed. If the Owner is the direct beneficiary and elects a payment plan, any such designation of contingent beneficiaries and further payees may be changed.

(b) By Direct Beneficiary. The direct beneficiary may designate and change contingent beneficiaries and further payees if:

(1) the direct beneficiary is the Owner.

(2) at any time after the death of the Insured, no contingent beneficiary or further payee is living, and no designation is made by the Owner under Section 8.1 (a) (2).

(3) the direct beneficiary elects a payment plan after the death of the Insured, in which case the interest in the share of such direct beneficiary or any other payee designated by the Owner shall terminate.

(c) By Spouse (Marital Deduction Provision). Notwithstanding any provision of Section 8 or 9 of this policy to the contrary, if the Insured immediately before death was the Owner and if the direct beneficiary is the spouse of the Insured and survives the Insured, such direct beneficiary shall have the power to appoint all amounts payable under the policy either to the executors or administrators of the direct beneficiary's estate or to such other contingent beneficiaries and further payees as he may designate. The exercise of that power shall revoke any then existing designation of contingent beneficiaries and further payees and any election of a payment plan applying to them.

(d) Effective Date. Any designation or change of beneficiary shall be made by the filing and recording at the Home Office of a written request satisfactory to the Company. Unless waived by the Company, the request must be endorsed on the policy. Upon the recording, the request will take effect as of the date it was signed. The Company will not be held responsible for any payment or other action taken by it before the recording of the request.

8.2 SUCCESSION IN INTEREST OF BENEFICIARIES

(a) Direct Beneficiaries. The proceeds of this policy shall be payable in equal shares to the direct beneficiaries who survive to receive payment. The unpaid share of any direct beneficiary who dies while receiving payment shall be payable in equal shares to the direct beneficiaries who survive to receive payment.

(b) Contingent Beneficiaries. At the death of the last surviving direct beneficiary, payments due or to become due shall be payable in equal shares to the contingent beneficiaries who survive to receive payment. The unpaid share of any contingent beneficiary who dies while receiving payment shall be payable in equal shares to the contingent beneficiaries who survive to receive payment.

(c) Further Payees. At the death of the last to survive of the direct and contingent beneficiaries, the proceeds, or the withdrawal value of any payments due or to become due if a payment plan is in effect, shall be paid in one sum:

(1) in equal shares to the further payees who survive to receive payment; or
(2) if no further payees survive to receive payment, to the executors or administrators of the last to survive of the direct and contingent beneficiaries.

(d) Estate of Owner. If no direct or contingent beneficiaries or further payees survive the Insured, the proceeds shall be paid to the Owner or the executors or administrators of the Owner.

8.3 GENERAL

(a) Transfer of Ownership. A transfer of ownership will not change the interest of any beneficiary.

(b) Claims of Creditors. So far as permitted by law, no amount payable under this policy shall be subject to the claims of creditors of the payee.

(c) Succession under Payment Plans. A direct or contingent beneficiary succeeding to an interest in a payment plan shall continue under such plan subject to its terms, with the rights of transfer between plans and of withdrawal under plans as provided in this policy.

7

SECTION 9. PAYMENT OF POLICY BENEFITS

9.1 PAYMENT

Payment of policy benefits upon surrender or maturity will be made in cash or under one of the payment plans described in Section 9.2, if elected.

If policy benefits become payable by reason of the Insured's death, payment will be made under any payment plan then in effect. If no election of a payment plan is in effect, the proceeds will be held under the Interest Income Plan (Option A) with interest accumulating from the date of death until an election or cash withdrawal is made.

9.2 PAYMENT PLANS

(a) Interest Income Plan (Option A). The proceeds will earn interest which may be received in monthly payments or accumulated. The first interest payment is due one month after the plan becomes effective. Withdrawal of accumulated interest as well as full or partial proceeds may be made at any time.

(b) Installment Income Plans. Monthly installment income payments will be made as provided by the plan elected. The first payment is due on the date the plan becomes effective.

(1) Specified Period (Option B). Monthly installment income payments will be made providing for payment of the proceeds with interest over a specified period of one to 30 years. Withdrawal of the present value of any unpaid installments may be made at any time.

(2) Specified Amount (Option D). Monthly installment income payments will be made for a specified amount of not less than $5 per $1,000 of proceeds. Payments will continue until the entire proceeds with interest are paid, with the final payment not exceeding the unpaid balance. Withdrawal of the unpaid balance may be made at any time.

(c) Life Income Plans. Monthly life income payments will be made as provided by the plan elected. The first payment is due on the date the plan becomes effective. Proof of date of birth satisfactory to the Company must be furnished for any individual upon whose life income payments depend.

(1) Single Life Income (Option C). Monthly payments will be made for the selected certain period, if any, and thereafter during the remaining lifetime of the individual upon whose life income payments depend. The selections available are:

  (i) no certain period,
  (ii) a certain period of 10 or 20 years, or
  (iii) a refund certain period such that the sum of the income payments during the certain period will be equal to the proceeds applied under the plan, with the final payment not exceeding the unpaid balance.

(2) Joint and Survivor Life Income (Option E). Monthly payments will be made for a 10 year certain period and thereafter during the joint lifetime of the two individuals upon whose lives income payments depend and continuing during the remaining lifetime of the survivor.

(3) Withdrawal. Withdrawal of the present value of any unpaid income payments which were to be made during a certain period may be made at any time after the death of all individuals upon whose lives income payments depend.

(d) Payment Frequency. In lieu of monthly payments a quarterly, semiannual or annual frequency may be selected.

9.3 PAYMENT PLAN RATES

(a) Interest Income and Installment Income Plans. Proceeds under the Interest Income and Installment Income plans will earn interest at rates declared annually by the Company, but not less than a rate of 3% compounded annually. Interest in excess of 3% will increase payments, except that for the Installment Income Specified Amount Plan (Option D), excess interest will be applied to lengthen the period during which payments are made.

The present value for withdrawal purposes will be based on a rate of 3% compounded annually.

The Company may from time to time also make available higher guaranteed interest rates under the Interest Income and Installment Income plans, with certain conditions on withdrawal as then published by the Company for those plans.

(b) Life Income Plans. Life Income Plan payments will be based on rates declared by the Company. These rates will provide not less than 104% of the income provided by the Company's Immediate Annuities being offered on the date the plan becomes effective. The rates are based on the sex and age nearest birthday of any individual upon whose life income payments depend, and adjusted for any certain period and the immediate payment of the first income payment. In no event will payments under these rates be less than the minimums described in Section 9.3(c).

(c) Minimum Income Payments. Minimum monthly income payments for the Installment Income Plans (Options B and D) and the Life Income Plans (Options C and E) are shown in the Minimum Income Table. The minimum Life Income payments are determined as of the date the payment plan becomes effective and depend on the age nearest birthday adjusted for policy duration.

The adjusted age is equal to the age nearest birthday decreased by one year if more than 25 years have elapsed since the Policy Date, two years if more than 35 years have elapsed, three years if more than 40 years have elapsed, four years if more than 45 years have elapsed or five years if more than 50 years have elapsed.

8

9.4 ELECTION OF PAYMENT PLANS

(a) Effective Date. Election of payment plans for death proceeds made by the Owner and filed at the Home Office during the Insured's lifetime will be effective on the date of death of the Insured. All other elections of payment plans will be effective when filed at the Home Office, or later if specified.

(b) Death Proceeds. Payment plans for death proceeds may be elected:

(1) by the Owner during the lifetime of the Insured.

(2) by the Owner during the 60 days following the date of death of the Insured, if the Insured immediately before his death was not the Owner. Any such election may not be changed by the Owner.

(3) by a direct or contingent beneficiary to whom such proceeds become payable, if no election is then in effect and no election is made by the Owner under Section 9.4(b) (2).

(c) Surrender or Maturity Proceeds. Payment plans for surrender or maturity proceeds may be elected by the Owner for himself as direct beneficiary.

(d) Transfers Between Payment Plans. A direct or contingent beneficiary receiving payment under a payment plan with the right to withdraw may elect to transfer the withdrawal value to any other payment plan then available.

(e) Life Income Plan Limitations. An individual beneficiary may receive payments under a Life Income Plan only if the payments depend upon his life. A corporation may receive payments under a Life Income Plan only if the payments depend upon the life of the Insured, or a surviving spouse or dependent of the Insured.

(f) Minimum Amounts. Proceeds of less than $5,000 may not be applied without the Company's approval under any payment plan except the Interest Income Plan (Option A) with interest accumulated. The Company retains the right to change the payment frequency or pay the withdrawal value if payments under a payment plan are or become less than $25.

9.5 INCREASE OF MONTHLY INCOME

The direct beneficiary who is to receive the proceeds of this policy under a payment plan may increase the total monthly income by payment of an annuity premium to the Company. The premium, after deduction of charges not exceeding 2% and any applicable premium tax, shall be applied under the payment plan at the same rates as the policy proceeds. The net amount so applied may not exceed twice the proceeds payable under this policy.

MINIMUM INCOME TABLE

Minimum Monthly Income Payments Per $1,000 Proceeds

INSTALLMENT INCOME PLANS (Options B and D)

PERIOD (YEARS)	MONTHLY PAYMENT	PERIOD (YEARS)	MONTHLY PAYMENT	PERIOD (YEARS)	MONTHLY PAYMENT
1	$84.50	11	$8.86	21	$5.32
2	42.87	12	8.24	22	5.15
3	29.00	13	7.71	23	4.99
4	22.07	14	7.26	24	4.84
5	17.91	15	6.87	25	4.71
6	15.14	16	6.53	26	4.59
7	13.17	17	6.23	27	4.48
8	11.69	18	5.96	28	4.37
9	10.54	19	5.73	29	4.27
10	9.62	20	5.51	30	4.18

9

MINIMUM INCOME TABLE

Minimum Monthly Income Payments Per $1,000 Proceeds

LIFE INCOME PLANS

SINGLE LIFE MONTHLY PAYMENTS (Option C)					
ADJUSTED AGE		CERTAIN PERIOD			
MALE	FEMALE	NONE	10 YEARS	20 YEARS	REFUND
50	55	$ 4.62	$4.56	$4.34	$4.36
51	56	4.72	4.65	4.40	4.44
52	57	4.83	4.75	4.46	4.52
53	58	4.94	4.85	4.53	4.61
54	59	5.07	4.96	4.59	4.69
55	60	5.20	5.07	4.66	4.79
56	61	5.33	5.19	4.72	4.88
57	62	5.48	5.31	4.78	4.99
58	63	5.64	5.43	4.84	5.09
59	64	5.80	5.57	4.90	5.20
60	65	5.98	5.70	4.96	5.32
61	66	6.16	5.85	5.02	5.44
62	67	6.36	5.99	5.07	5.57
63	68	6.57	6.14	5.13	5.71
64	69	6.79	6.30	5.17	5.85
65	70	7.03	6.45	5.22	6.00
66	71	7.28	6.62	5.26	6.15
67	72	7.54	6.78	5.30	6.31
68	73	7.83	6.95	5.33	6.48
69	74	8.13	7.11	5.36	6.66
70	75	8.45	7.28	5.39	6.85
71	76	8.79	7.45	5.41	7.05
72	77	9.16	7.62	5.43	7.26
73	78	9.55	7.79	5.45	7.48
74	79	9.96	7.95	5.46	7.71
75	80	10.41	8.11	5.48	7.95

JOINT AND SURVIVOR MONTHLY PAYMENTS (Option E)

ADJUSTED AGE   JOINT PAYEE ADJUSTED AGE

MALE		45	50	55	60	65	70	75
	FEMALE	50	55	60	65	70	75	80
45	50	$3.68	$3.80	$3.90	$3.97	$4.02	$4.06	$4.10
50	55	3.80	3.97	4.13	4.25	4.34	4.41	4.46
55	60	3.90	4.13	4.35	4.56	4.72	4.84	4.92
60	65	3.97	4.25	4.56	4.86	5.13	5.33	5.48
65	70	4.02	4.34	4.72	5.13	5.51	5.85	6.10
70	75	4.06	4.41	4.84	5.33	5.85	6.33	6.73
75	80	4.10	4.46	4.92	5.48	6.10	6.73	7.28

10

WAIVER OF PREMIUM BENEFIT

1. THE BENEFIT

If total disability of the Insured commences before the policy anniversary nearest his 60th birthday, the Company will waive the payment of premiums becoming due during total disability of the Insured.

If total disability of the Insured commences on or after the policy anniversary nearest his 60th birthday but before the policy anniversary nearest his 65th birthday, the Company will waive the payment of premiums becoming due during total disability of the Insured and before the policy anniversary nearest his 65th birthday.

The Company will refund that portion of any premium paid which applies to a period of total disability beyond the policy month in which the disability began.

The premium for this benefit is shown on page 2.

2. DEFINITION OF TOTAL DISABILITY

Total disability means disability which:

(a) resulted from bodily injury or disease;
(b) began after the Date of Issue of this policy and before the policy anniversary nearest the Insured's 65th birthday;
(c) has existed continuously for at least six months; and
(d) prevents the Insured from engaging in an occupation. During the first 24 months of disability, occupation means the occupation of the Insured at the time such disability began; thereafter it means any occupation for which he is reasonably fitted by education, training or experience, with due regard to his vocation and earnings prior to disability.

The total and irrecoverable loss of the sight of both eyes, or of speech or hearing, or of the use of both hands, or of both feet, or of one hand and one foot, shall be considered total disability, even if the Insured shall engage in an occupation.

3. PROOF OF DISABILITY

Before any premium is waived, proof of total disability must be received by the Company at its Home Office.

(a) during the lifetime of the Insured;
(b) during the continuance of total disability; and
(c) not later than one year after the policy anniversary nearest the Insured's 65th birthday.

Premiums will be waived although proof of total disability was not given within the time specified, if it is shown that it was given as soon as reasonably possible, but not later than one year after recovery.

4. PROOF OF CONTINUANCE OF DISABILITY

Proof of the continuance of total disability may be required once a year. If such proof is not furnished, no further premiums shall be waived. Further proof of continuance of disability will no longer be required if, on the policy anniversary nearest the Insured's 65th birthday, the Insured is then and has been totally and continuously disabled for five or more years.

5. PREMIUMS

Any premium becoming due during disability and before receipt of proof of total disability is payable and should be paid. Any such premiums paid shall be refunded by the Company upon acceptance of proof of total disability. If such premiums are not paid, this benefit shall be allowed if total disability is shown to have begun before the end of the grace period of the first unpaid premium.

If on any policy anniversary following the date of disablement the Insured continues to be disabled and this benefit has not terminated, an annual premium will be waived.

6. TERMINATION

This benefit shall be in effect while this policy is in force, but shall terminate on the policy anniversary nearest the Insured's 65th birthday unless the Insured is then totally disabled and such disability occurred prior to the policy anniversary nearest the Insured's 60th birthday. It may also be terminated within 31 days of a premium due date upon receipt at the Home Office of the Owner's written request.

11

ACCIDENTAL DEATH BENEFIT

1. THE BENEFIT

The Company agrees to pay an Accidental Death Benefit upon receipt at its Home Office of proof that the death of the Insured resulted, directly and independently of all other causes, from accidental bodily injury, provided that death occurred while this benefit was in effect.

2. PREMIUM AND AMOUNT OF BENEFIT

The premium for and the amount of this benefit are shown on page 2. This benefit shall be payable as part of the policy proceeds.

3. RISKS NOT ASSUMED

This benefit shall not be payable for death of the Insured resulting from suicide, for death resulting from or contributed to by bodily or mental infirmity or disease, or for any other death which did not result, directly and independently of all other causes, from accidental bodily injury.

Even though death resulted directly and independently of all other causes from accidental bodily injury, this benefit shall not be payable if the death of the Insured resulted from:

(a) Any act or incident of war. The word "war" includes any war, declared or undeclared, and armed aggression resisted by the armed forces of any country or combination of countries.

(b) Riding in any kind of aircraft, unless the Insured was riding solely as a passenger in an aircraft not operated by or for the Armed Forces, or descent from any kind of aircraft while in flight. An Insured who had any duties whatsoever at any time on the flight or any leg of the flight with respect to any purpose of the flight or to the aircraft or who was participating in training shall not be considered a passenger.

4. TERMINATION

This benefit shall be in effect while this policy is in force other than under the Extended Term Insurance or Paid-up Insurance provisions, but shall terminate on the policy anniversary nearest the Insured's 70th birthday. It may also be terminated within 31 days of a premium due date upon receipt at the Home Office of the Owner's written request.

David Olson
Secretary

THE COUNCIL LIFE INSURANCE COMPANY

RECEIPT FOR PAYMENT AND CONDITIONAL LIFE INSURANCE AGREEMENT

THOMAS A. BENSON $10,000   LIFE POLICY - PARTICIPATING
Name of Proposed Insured   Face Amount   Plan

Received of _THOMAS A. BENSON_
the sum of $ _241.60_ for the policy applied for in the application to THE COUNCIL INSURANCE COMPANY (CL) with the same date and number as this receipt. Checks, drafts, and money orders are accepted subject to collection.

NEW YORK, N.Y., Nov 1 19 80 . G.R. Washington _____ Agent.
Place and Date

CONDITIONAL LIFE INSURANCE AGREEMENT

When premium is paid at the time of application, complete this Agreement and give to the Applicant. No other Agreement will be recognized by the Company. If premium is not paid—do not detach.

I. No Insurance Ever in Force. No insurance shall be in force at any time if the proposed insured is not an acceptable risk on the Underwriting Date for the policy applied for according to CL's rules and standards. No insurance shall be in force under an Additional Benefit for which the proposed insured is not an acceptable risk.

II. Conditional Life Insurance. If the proposed insured is an acceptable risk on the Underwriting Date, the insurance shall be in force subject to the following maximum amounts if the proposed insured dies before the policy is issued:

Life Insurance			Accidental Death Benefit	
Age at Issue	Policies Issued at Standard Premiums	Policies Issued at Higher Premiums	Age at Issue	Maximum Amount
0-24	$ 500,000	$250,000	0-14	$ 25,000
25-45	1,000,000	500,000	15-19	50,000
46-55	800,000	400,000	20-24	75,000
56-65	400,000	200,000	25-60	150,000
66-70	200,000	100,000	Over 60	-0-
Over 70	-0-	-0-		

Reduction in Maximum Amounts. The maximum amounts set forth in the preceding table shall be reduced by any existing CL insurance on the life of the proposed insured with an Issue Date within 90 days of the date of this Agreement or by any pending prepaid applications for CL insurance on the life of the proposed insured with an Underwriting Date within 90 days of the date of this Agreement.

Termination of Conditional Life Insurance. If the proposed insured is an acceptable risk for the policy applied for according to CL's rules and standards only at a premium higher than the premium paid, any insurance under this Agreement shall terminate on the date stated in a notice mailed by CL to the applicant unless by such date the applicant accepts delivery of the policy and pays the additional premium required.

Underwriting Date. The Underwriting Date is the date of page 2 (90-2) of the application or the date of the medical examination [if required, otherwise the date of the nonmedical, page 4 (90-4)], whichever is the later.

III. Premium Adjustment. If the proposed insured is an acceptable risk for the policy applied for only at a premium higher than the premium paid and dies before paying the additional premium required, that additional premium shall be subtracted from the insurance benefit payable to the beneficiary.

IV. Premium Refund. Any premium paid for any insurance or Additional Benefit not issued or issued at a higher premium but not accepted by the applicant shall be returned to the applicant.

NOT A "BINDER"—NO INSURANCE WHERE SECTION I APPLIES—NO AGENT MAY MODIFY.

12

PART I — Life Insurance Application To *The COUNCIL Life Insurance Company*

IMPORTANT NOTICE—This application is subject to approval by the Company's Home Office. Be sure all questions in all parts of the application are answered completely and accurately, since the application is the basis of the insurance contract and will become part of any policy issued.

1. Insured's Full Name (Please Print-Give title as Mr., Dr., Rev., etc.)

MR. THOMAS A. BENSON

Single ☐ Married ☑ Widowed ☐ Divorced ☐ Separated ☐

Mo., Day, Yr. of Birth: APRIL 6, 1943
Ins. Age: 37
Sex: M
Place of Birth: BOSTON, MASS.
Social Security No.: 000-00-0000

2. Addresses last 5 yrs.

Mail to ☐ Home: Present — 217 E. 62 STREET, NEW YORK, N.Y. — 10017 — NEW YORK — 6 yrs
☑ Business: Present — PEPPER, GRINSTEAD, & CROUCH 55 E. 49TH ST — 10017 — NEW YORK — 7 yrs

3. Occupation

Present: Title — ATTORNEY — Describe Exact Duties — REPRESENTS CLIENTS IN LEGAL MATTERS — 7 yrs

4. a) Employer
b) Any change contemplated? Yes ☐ (Explain in Remarks) No ☑

5. Have you ever — Yes / No
a) been rejected, deferred or discharged by the Armed Forces for medical reasons or applied for a government disability rating? ☐ ☑
b) applied for insurance or for reinstatement which was declined, postponed, modified or rated? ☐ ☑
c) used LSD, heroin, cocaine or methadone? ☐ ☑

6. a) In the past 3 years have you
(i) had your driver's license suspended or revoked or been convicted of more than one speeding violation? ☐ ☑
(ii) operated, been a crew member of, or had any duties aboard any kind of aircraft? ☐ ☑
(iii) engaged in underwater diving below 40 feet, parachuting, or motor vehicle racing? ☐ ☑
b) In the future, do you intend to engage in any activities mentioned in (ii) and (iii) of a) above? ☐ ☑
(If "Yes" to 5a or any of 6, complete Supplemental Form 3375)

7. Have you smoked one or more cigarettes within the past 12 months? ☑ ☐

8. Are other insurance applications pending or contemplated? ☐ ☑

9. Do you intend to go to any foreign country? ☑ ☐

10. Will coverage applied for replace or change any life insurance or annuities? (If "Yes", submit Replacement Form) ☐ ☑

11. Total Life Insurance in force $ 35,000 None ☐

12. Face Amount $ 10,000 Plan WL
Accidental Death ☑ Waiver of Premium ☐
Purchase Option—Regular ☐ Preferred ☐ PEP ☐ GOR ☐
____ units of Wife's Term—name: ____
$____ initial amount Decreasing Term, ____ Years
(Joint ☐) (Mot. Pro. ☐) (Straight Line ☐)
Children's Term ☐ Other: ____

13. Auto. Prem. Loan provision operative if available? Yes ☐ No ☑

14. Dividend Option
Additions (for other than Term policies) ☐ Deposits ☐
Reduce premium, if applicable, otherwise cash ☑
Supplemental Protection (Keyman only) ☐
1 Year Term—any balance to
Deposits ☐ Additions ☐ Reduce prem. (cash if mo.) ☐

15. Beneficiary—for children's, wife's or joint insurance as provided in contract; for other insurance as follows, subject to policy's beneficiary provisions:
(Name) (Relationship to Insured)
1st HELEN M. BENSON — WIFE — if living, if not
2nd DAVID A. BENSON — SON — if living, if not
3rd — if living, if not
the executors or administrators of: Insured ☑ Other (use Remarks) ☐
(Joint beneficiaries will receive equally or survivor, unless otherwise specified.)

16. Flexible Plan settlement (personal beneficiary only) ☐

17. Rights—During Insured's lifetime all rights belong to
Insured ☑ Other: ____
Trustee ☐ (attach Trust)
(After Insured's death as provided in contract on wife's insurance.)

18. Premium—Frequency ANNUAL Amt. Paid $ 241.60 None ☐
Have you received a Conditional Receipt? Yes ☑ No ☐

REMARKS [Include details (company, date, amt., etc.) for all "Yes" answers to questions 4b, 5b, 5c, 8, 9 and 10]

Q9: PLANS VACATION IN SWITZERLAND

I agree that: (1) No one but the Company's President, a Vice-President or Secretary has authority to accept information not contained in the application, to modify or enlarge any contract, or to waive any requirement. (2) Except as otherwise provided in any conditional receipt issued, any policy issued shall take effect upon its delivery and payment of the first premium during the lifetime of each person to be insured. Due dates of later premiums shall be as specified in the policy.

Dated at NEW YORK, N.Y. on NOVEMBER 1 19 80 Signature of Insured: Thomas A. Benson

Signature of Applicant (if other than Insured) who agrees to be bound by the representations and agreements in this and any other part of this application ____
(Name) (Relationship) (Complete address of Applicant)

Countersigned by Ed Haley
Field Underwriter (Licensed Resident Agent)

13

PART IA	Statements Forming Part Of Application To *The COUNCIL Life Insurance Company* [Complete this Part if any Non-Medical or Family Insurance is Applied For]

1. Name of Insured **THOMAS A. BENSON**   Ins. Age **37**   Height **6** ft. **1** in.   Weight **185** lbs.

2. If Family, Children's, Wife's or Joint Insurance desired, other family members proposed for insurance:

Wife (include maiden name)	Ins. Age	Mo., Day, Yr. of Birth	Height ft. in.	Weight lbs.	Life in Force $	Place of Birth

Children	Sex	Ins. Age	Mo., Day, Yr. of Birth	Children	Sex	Ins. Age	Mo., Day, Yr. of Birth

3. Has any eligible dependent (a) been omitted from 2? Yes ☐ No ☐ (b) applied for insurance or for reinstatement which was declined, postponed, modified or rated or had a policy cancelled or renewal refused? Yes ☐ No ☐ (Give name, date, company in 8)

4. Have you or anyone else proposed for insurance, so far as you know, ever been treated for or had indication of (underline applicable item)   Yes No

a) high blood pressure? (If "Yes", list drugs prescribed and dates taken.)   ☐ ☑

b) chest pain, heart attack, rheumatic fever, heart murmur, irregular pulse or other disorder of the heart or blood vessels?   ☐ ☑

c) cancer, tumor, cyst, or any disorder of the thyroid, skin, or lymph glands?   ☐ ☑

d) diabetes or anemia or other blood disorder?   ☐ ☑

e) sugar, albumin, blood or pus in the urine, or venereal disease?   ☐ ☑

f) any disorder of the kidney, bladder, prostate, breast or reproductive organs?   ☐ ☑

g) ulcer, intestinal bleeding, hepatitis, colitis, or other disorder of the stomach, intestine, spleen, pancreas, liver or gall bladder?   ☐ ☑

h) asthma, tuberculosis, bronchitis, emphysema or other disorder of the lungs?   ☐ ☑

i) fainting, convulsions, migraine headache, paralysis, epilepsy or any mental or nervous disorder?   ☐ ☑

j) arthritis, gout, amputation, sciatica, back pain or other disorder of the muscles, bones or joints?   ☐ ☑

k) disorder of the eyes, ears, nose, throat or sinuses?   ☐ ☑

l) varicose veins, hemorrhoids, hernia or rectal disorder?   ☐ ☑

m) alcoholism or drug habit?   ☐ ☑

5. Have you or anyone else proposed for insurance, so far as you know, (underline applicable item)   Yes No

a) consulted or been underlined examined or treated by any physician or practitioner in the past 5 years?   ☑ ☐

b) had, or been advised to have, an x-ray, cardiogram, blood or other diagnostic test in the past 5 years?   ☑ ☐

c) been a patient in a hospital, clinic, or other medical facility in the past 5 years?   ☐ ☑

d) ever had a surgical operation performed or advised?   ☑ ☐

e) ever made claim for disability or applied for compensation or retirement based on accident or sickness?   ☐ ☑

6. Are you or any other person proposed for insurance, so far as you know, in impaired physical or mental health, or under any kind of medication?   ☐ ☑

7. Weight change in last 6 months of adults proposed for insurance: **N.A.**

Name	Gain	Loss	Cause

8. Details of all "Yes" answers. For any checkup or routine examination, indicate what symptoms, if any, prompted it and include results of the examination and any special tests. Include clinic number if applicable.

Question No.	Name of Person	Illness & Treatment	No. of Attacks	Dates: Onset- Recovery	Doctor, Clinic or Hospital and Complete Address
5a	THOMAS A. BENSON	ANNUAL CHECKUP	—	—	LIFE EXTENSION INSTITUTE
5b	THOMAS A. BENSON	ROUTINE OF ANNUAL CHECKUP	—	—	"
5d	THOMAS A. BENSON	TONSILLECTOMY-AGE 5	1	JUNE 1949	BOSTON HOSPITAL 2 PITTS STREET, BOSTON, MASS.

So far as may be lawful, I waive for myself and all persons claiming an interest in any insurance issued on this application, all provisions of law forbidding any physician or other person who has attended or examined, or who may attend or examine, me or any other person covered by such insurance, from disclosing any knowledge or information which he thereby acquired.

I represent the statements and answers in this and in any other part of this application to be true and complete to the best of my knowledge and belief, and offer them to the Company for the purpose of inducing it to issue the policy or policies and to accept the payment of premiums thereunder. I also agree that payment of the first premium (if after this date) shall be a representation by me that such statements and answers would be the same if made at the time of such payment.

Dated at **NEW YORK, N.Y.** on **NOV. 1** 19 **80**   Signature of Insured **Thomas A. Benson**

Witnessed by **Ed Hadley**   Signature of Wife (if insured) _____
Field Underwriter (Licensed Resident Agent)

AUTHORIZATION

For purposes of determining my eligibility for insurance, I hereby authorize any physician, practitioner, hospital, clinic, institution, insurance company, Medical Information Bureau, or other organization or person that has records or knowledge of me or my health to give any such information to the Council Life Insurance Company.

If application is made to The Council Life Insurance Company for insurance on any member of my family, this authorization also applies to such member. A photostatic copy of this authorization shall be as valid as the original.

Signed on **NOVEMBER 1** , 19 **80**   **Thomas A. Benson**
Signature of Insured

14

3

Disability Insurance

If you absolutely had to, you could do without life insurance. If state law didn't demand it, you could probably also do without auto insurance. If you could replace your home out of your earnings and savings, you could even manage without homeowners insurance. Similarly, if you could handle unanticipated medical bills without too much problem, health insurance would not be a necessity.

But compared to all of the other policies, disability insurance is something you most certainly should not be without, particularly if you are the family breadwinner and the family depends on your income.

Why is disability insurance so important? Because disability insurance is really "income replacement" insurance. It provides you with a good portion of the cash you and your family need to live on during a period of disability. For example, if have a heart attack and are unable to work, or if you are the victim of a car wreck and you spend a long time in the hospital and at home recovering, you would be considered disabled. With no income coming in, your family would suffer greatly. You will be watching it happen without being able to do much about it.

Your spouse's income might not be enough to keep the family going and your kids might have to do without a lot of things that they previously had. It's even possible that your family might not eat as well.

Remember that while you are alive, your income is your most valuable asset. Your income generates all your accumulated assets, such as your house and car. If you don't have your income for a lengthy period of time, you could get into deep financial trouble.

If you have very limited money to spend on insurance, spend it on disability before you spend it on life. Why? Because the chances are much greater that you will be totally disabled for some period of time before you turn 65, than you will die before that age.

Calculating Disability Needs

Just how much income will you have to replace? Although a precise amount cannot probably be ascertained, by using the accompanying worksheet and other income information, you can determine your need fairly closely.

Basically, you need to figure your annual living expenses. From that subtract all sources of income, including investments and Social Security, which you *may* get if you are disabled. The worksheets used here are based on those from the Health Insurance Association of America.

Group Disability Coverage

Employers certainly recognize the importance of disability insurance. Many of them provide it as a fringe benefit for their employees in the form of group disability insurance. *No worker who is offered disability coverage, especially if it is totally paid for by the employer, should turn it down.*

If your employer doesn't provide it, you might be a member of an organization such as the Kiwanis or a professional group like the National Education Association or a trade union that provides group disability coverage. And, as with all types of group insurance, the group disability insurance is probably your best buy.

Group disability benefits offered by employers can either be in the form of short-term or long-term disability benefits. Short-term disability usually is keyed to salary and provides income replacement for as long as two years.

Long term disability, on the other hand, provides benefits

Monthly Expenses

	Today	If Disabled
Mortgage or Rent (Include property taxes)	$ _____	$ _____
Utilities (Oil, gas, electric, water, phone)	$ _____	$ _____
Home Maintenance/Repairs	$ _____	$ _____
Food	$ _____	$ _____
Clothing	$ _____	$ _____
Insurance		
Auto	$ _____	$ _____
Home	$ _____	$ _____
Life	$ _____	$ _____
Health	$ _____	$ _____
Total	$ _____	$ _____
Installment Payments	$ _____	$ _____
Transportation (Gas, oil, maintenance, parking, etc.)	$ _____	$ _____
Medical and Dental Care	$ _____	$ _____
Education	$ _____	$ _____
Family Spending Money	$ _____	$ _____
Recreation, Entertainment, Hobbies, Vacation, Dues	$ _____	$ _____
Total Monthly Expenses	$ _____	$ _____

Substitute Income to Pay Expenses When Disabled

	Monthly Benefit	Waiting Period	Benefit Period
Group Disability Insurance (From your employer or union)	$ _____	_____	_____
Social Security	$ _____	_____	_____
State Plans	$ _____	_____	_____
Worker's Compensation	$ _____	_____	_____
Credit Disability (In some auto loans or home mortgages)	$ _____	_____	_____
Other income sources (Stocks, bonds, spouse's income)	$ _____	_____	_____
Personally Owned Disability Insurance	$ _____	_____	_____
Total Monthly Substitute Income	$ _____		

Note: Benefits are often coordinated, so that one program's payments are reduced in recognition of benefits from another program, such as Social Security or Worker's Compensation. Ask your agent about "coordination of benefits."

for the employee's lifetime. Again, the benefits are paid on the basis of the worker's salary at the time the disability occurred.

Most employer sponsored disability plans stipulate that any benefits the disabled individual receives from Social

Security or Workers' Compensation (state administered plans that payoff if you are injured at work) will be deducted from any amount payable under the disability plan.

Self-inflicted or intentional injuries as well as disability caused by a war injury are generally excluded from these group policies.

Group vs. Individual Coverage

It is always a good idea to get group coverage on any type of insurance that you can. Even if the insurance is not provided free by an employer, it will be cheaper than individual coverage. However, with group disability insurance, there is one disadvantage you should be aware of:

Group disability benefits, if paid for by an employer, are taxable, while individual coverage benefits are not. If you pay the premiums, the benefits you receive are non-taxable. If somebody else pays the premiums, the benefits are taxable.

Another disadvantage to group disability coverage is that it's not *portable,* or *convertible.* That means you can't take it with you when you leave one employer and go to another, or if you leave one employer and become self-employed. With an individually purchased policy you are always covered as long as you continue to pay premiums, no matter how or where you work.

Because group disability insurance benefits may be taxable, you might do what many savvy insurance buyers do— also buy an individual policy. Those benefits that you collect from the individually purchased policy will remain untaxed.

What Do You Get?

Disability insurance differs in one major way from health insurance. Health insurance pays for hospital and doctors costs incurred as the result of an injury or accident. Disability provides the insured with *money.* You use this money to replace a hefty portion of income lost as the result of disability from an injury or accident. It does not pay hospital or doctor bills.

You might be able to get disability insurance that replaces 100% of your lost income for as long as you are disabled. But coverage like that would be very expensive. And it is certainly not necessary that *all* of your former income be replaced.

Here's why: While you are disabled you will no longer be going to your office, so you won't have to pay the costs of commuting to and from work. Also, you needn't replace your clothes as often because you will undoubtedly be spending most of your time in bedclothes or very casual clothes. In addition, you won't have other business-related expenses.

But the big thing you need not worry about are taxes. Because you aren't drawing a salary, no income is coming in. You'll be paying a good deal less in taxes, or no taxes at all. The money you get from your disability insurance comes to you, if you paid the premiums yourself, tax-free.

Since your expenses are considerably less, you can—say insurance experts—probably maintain your present lifestyle with about 60% of your income at the time you became disabled. Disability policies replace an agreed upon portion of your income, usually 60%, during a period of disability.

If you are disabled for five months or more, you may, if you meet all the qualifications, be eligible to receive disability benefits from Social Security. But even so, you can only replace about 15% of your average monthly income from Social Security. Also, you must be disabled for a full five months before you can collect from Social Security. A disability policy that starts paying benefits earlier would supplement that well. There is no guarantee by, the way, that you will be eligible for or receive Social Security benefits. You can find out more about Social Security eligibility from your local Social Security Administration office.

Types of Disability Policies

When buying an individual disability policy, you must look for three things:

1) Make sure the policy is *guaranteed* to be *renewable* up to age 65 or 70. This means that the company must renew the policy if you continue to pay the premiums until you reach age 65 or 70, no matter what your health is or what job you have.

2) Look for a policy where the *premium cannot be increased* over the term of the policy. The premium should be the same in the first year as in the last year. The word used in the policy to describe this level premium is *non-cancellable*. The term simply means the premium cannot be increased.

3) Make sure the policy pays benefits if the disability arises from *either an injury OR illness*. Some policies limit coverage to injury, but the best cover both. Don't settle for anything less.

Most disability policies will pay benefits only until the policyholder reaches age 65 for an illness—but for life for an injury.

The non-cancellable, guaranteed renewable policy provides the most protection. As a consequence, it is the most expensive type of disability policy. There are policies available that guarantee renewal but increase the premiums over the life of the policy. These policies are less expensive initially. Because the premium can rise over time, the policyholder may be tempted to drop the coverage if his or her financial situation worsens. Dropping the policy would be undesirable.

Definition of Disability

How disability is defined in the policy is vital. Normally you cannot collect unless you are "totally or permanently disabled." That is interpreted to mean that you are unable to perform the normal duties of your chosen profession.

For example, suppose you are a salesman who calls on customers at their place of business, and because of a disability you are bedridden. You would be considered totally disabled.

Or, if you are a fireman and you can no longer perform the rigorous, physical acts required of a fireman, you are undoubtedly disabled. If you are only partially disabled, that means that you can devote at least part-time to your regular occupation. In this case you won't collect under most disability policies. The disability has to be total.

If you should recover to the point where you can resume your work, then your disability insurance would stop paying. You are once again capable of earning an income, and you no longer need income replacement insurance.

There are some jobs that require little physical exertion to perform. For example, a writer might have a disability that would prevent typing, but he or she could still dictate, even from a bed. A teacher might not be able to stand in front of a classroom, but could lecture from a wheelchair, if necessary. For these people, total disability is not the same. Obtaining disability coverage, although not impossible, is quite expensive.

When you are totally disabled, you cannot work at your occupation, whatever that may be. As you might imagine, defining what your occupation really is can be a problem. The best policies will say you will collect if you can't perform the duties of your "own occupation," the occupation you were pursuing when you became disabled. That occupation is easy to define. Therefore, this kind of policy is the most favorable to the disabled individual. It is also the most expensive policy. If you can afford it, get it.

Other, cheaper policies use the wording "any occupation." That means what it says. You will only collect if you can't perform *any* occupation at all. For example, a former truck driver might be able to find a job as a security guard. A nurse might be able to work as a typist. Obviously, this coverage is not as favorable to the policyholder. It is rare that a person will be so disabled as to be unable to do *any* job. And, with this coverage, if you can perform *any* job, you get no disability, or you get considerably reduced benefits. Avoid this type of policy if you can.

Finally, there are a few policies that have a split definition, something like "unable to perform your own occupation for two years, then any occupation." This is a mid-priced policy, not as useful as the "own occupation" type. It's a compromise choice.

If you can afford it, get a policy that provides you with benefits if you become disabled and can't perform the normal, regular duties of your "own occupation." Remember, under that definition if you get another job outside of your regular occupation, you can still collect some or all of the disability benefits.

How Your Occupation
May Prevent Coverage

Obviously, some occupations are more dangerous than others. If you are in a particularly dangerous trade, such as coal mining or race car driving, your chances of becoming disabled are much higher than average. People in dangerous occupations are usually denied normal disability insurance coverage. For a very hefty premium, it might be possible to find an insurer. The chances are that the search will be long and hard.

If you already have a disability policy that is noncancellable and guaranteed renewable, and you change to a hazardous occupation, the insurance company cannot terminate your coverage. The only circumstance under which a non-cancellable and guaranteed renewable policy can be cancelled is if you don't pay the premiums.

Each company has its own definition of hazardous occupation. The following list is from a well-known insurance company that offers disability insurance. The notation *NE* indicates a hazardous occupation. Those people are

Not Eligible to buy disability insurance from this company. However, there might be another company willing to cover Not Eligible occupations listed here. That's another example of why it pays to shop around for all your insurance needs.

Notice that under the special rules section that people who work at home, no matter what their occupation, can't get disability coverage. This was true for most insurance carriers up until 10 years ago. Now it is available.

Occupation Classifications

This rating contains an alphabetical listing of some common occupations. The underwriter must assess not only the proposed insured's occupational title, but also the nature of the duties performed in that occupation. If the person wishing insurance is required to perform several different tasks, the occupational classification is based upon the most hazardous duty performed.

This company's disability income coverage is designed for the professional/executive/proprietor work force. It has, therefore, limited the availability of policies to the top occupational classes, dividing the most desirable occupations into five groups. Classes are defined as follows:

Class 4AS. Certain professionals and corporate executives. The corporate executives *must* meet the following criteria:

1) Primarily office duties with little or no travel.

2) Compensated by salary.

3) Employed by a well-established, stable firm for at least two years and earns more than $35,000 annually.

Class 4A. A number of select professions.

Class 3A. People engaged mostly in mental work, primarily those with clerical duties or "office only" duties.*

Class 2A. People who are supervisors, technicians, merchants with no delivery or repairing, those with special skills, and others not performing what is generally described as manual labor, although duties may require some physical activity.

Class 2B. People in occupational classifications 2A and 3A* who do not meet minimum income requirements, but who are employed by a professional organization to which disability coverage is provided.

*Special Rules

Government Employees. Federal civil services employees are not eligible for disability insurance because of the accumulating sick leave and disability benefits automatically available with their jobs.

Many state, county, and municipal employees, including public school teachers, are ineligible for disability income coverage because of potential substantial benefits available in their pension retirement plans. Individual underwriting consideration may be given for limited coverage amounts, provided full information including the retirement plan booklet is submitted preliminarily to determine eligibility.

Business at Residence. Disability coverage will not generally be available to individuals who work at their residences. Exceptions may be made in cases where some duties are performed at the residence, but a significant amount of outside activity is required. Normally, exceptions of this type will be granted only with a 60- or 90-day waiting period. This rule will not apply to doctors, dentists, and attorneys who have established offices at their residences, nor to manufacturers' representatives who use their residences as business addresses but whose duties require them to spend almost all of their time calling on clients.

Frequently Encountered Occupations. The accompanying list includes a sample of the types of occupations for which the policy was designed. Disability insurance is not available for those occupations designated NE (Not Eligible).

Some Disability Classifications

Occupation	Class
Accountants	
CPA's	4AS
working for an accounting firm	4A
others	3A
Account Executives	4A
Actors, Entertainers, Singers	NE
Actuaries	4A
Acupuncturists	NE
Adjusters, Insurance	
not fire & marine	3A
fire & marine	2A
Advertising	
agency staff, not freelance	3A
Airline Pilots, Flight Attendants, Crew Members	NE
Air Traffic Controllers	NE
Anesthesiologists	4AS
Anesthetists	3A
Antique Dealers	
sales only	3A
others	NE
Apartment House	
managers only	2A
Appliance Repair & Service	NE
Appraisers, Real Estate	3A
Architects (except Landscape Architects)	4AS
Artists	
commercial only, working away from home	3A
others	NE
Attorneys	4AS
Authors	NE
Automobile Sales & Service	
New Car Franchise	
owners & dealers	3A
salesmen	2A
service & parts manager	2A
Used Car Dealers and Salesmen	NE
Service Station Owners & Operators	NE

Occupation	Class
Bailiffs	
in court only	3A
Bakeries	
office & counter	2A
others	NE
Banks	
officers, tellers, bookkeepers	3A
armored car drivers, guards	NE
Barbers	NE
Bartenders	NE
Beauty Parlors	
owners, operators, beauticians	NE
Bill Collectors	2A
Biochemists	3A
Biologists	3A
Bond Brokers	3A
Bookkeepers	3A
Building & Construction	
Engineers, on site visits	3A
Engineers, on site supervision	2A
Contractors	
office not at residence	3A
others, not supervising at job site	2A
supervisory	NE
Building Services	
superintendents, managers	2A
Bus Drivers	NE
Business Machines	
dealer, sales, operators	3A
service & repair	2A
Butchers	NE
Cabinet Makers/Assemblers	NE
Cashiers	
store, theater, restaurant	NE
Caterers	
office only	3A
Supervisory and others	NE
Chemists	
consulting or office only	4A
in lab (no special hazard)	3A

Occupation	Class
Chiropractors	2A
Civil Engineers	
office only	4A
others	3A
Clergymen	3A
Clerks	
office	3A
counter	2A
Collectors	
accounts only	2A
others	NE
Comptrollers (not CPA's)	3A
Computing Machines	
operators	3A
service	2A
Cooks & Chefs	NE
Copyists	
office only	3A
Court Reporters	3A
Decorators, Interior	
consulting only (not at residence)	3A
Dentistry	
dentists	4AS
hygeinists, office work	3A
lab owners (supervisory only)	3A
lab work	2A
Dermatologists	4AS
Designers	3A
Dieticians	
not in food preparation	3A
In food preparation	2A
Draftsmen	
office only	3A
Druggists (not Pharmacists)	3A
Dry Cleaning	
office & counter only	2A
others	NE
Editors	
offices only	3A

Occupation	Class
Engineers, Graduate	
office & consulting only	4A
others (on site inspection only)	3A
Executives	
corporate, office managers	3A
Exterminators	
officer, proprietors only	2A
supervisory and all others	NE
Farmers	
supervisory only	2A
supervisory working	NE
Flight Attendants	NE
Florists	
store duties only	3A
others	NE
Forepersons	
supervising NE workers	NE
others	2A
Furniture Store	
owners or salesmen, no delivery duties	
10 or more full-time employees	3A
other, no delivery	2A
Geologists	
office	3A
field, non-hazardous	2A
Golf Courses	
proprietor, managers	2A
club professional (not touring)	2A
others	NE
Government Employees	
federal	NE
county, state, municipal	*
Grocery Sales	
office and administration	3A
managers (not stocking shelves)	2A
others	NE
Guards, Detectives, Policemen	NE
Gunsmiths	2A
Gynecologists	4AS

Occupation	Class
Hairdressers	NE
Hardware Store	
proprietor & managers only	2A
Health Officials	
office only	3A
field, no hazards	2A
Hospitals, Sanitariums	
managers, administration, nursing	
directors and dieticians	3A
nurses, supervisory or office only	3A
other nurses, full-time	2A
nurses of the insane	NE
Hotels, Motels, Inns	
proprietors, managers	3A
clerks	2A
Household Appliances	
dealers & salesmen	2A
installers, servicemen	NE
Inspectors	
building, insurance, safety	2A
Insurance	
adjusters (not fire or marine), agents	
brokers, office	3A
Interpreters	
full-time	3A
Janitors	NE
Lab or Medical Technicians	
no use of radium atomic energy,	
cobalt, explosive, or acids	2A
radium technicians giving treatment	NE
Landscape Architects (no manual duties)	2A
others	NE
Laundries	
office & counter only	2A
Librarians	3A
Locksmiths	2A
Lumber Industry	
office only	2A
others	NE

Occupation	Class
Manicurists	NE
Meteorologists	3A
Meter Readers	2A
Ministers	3A
Music Teachers, School or College	3A
Musicians	NE
Newspapers	
editors, office work	3A
reporters	2A
photographers	2A
Nurse Practitioner	3A
Nurses	
office or hospital supervisory (RN's)	3A
other RN's and hospital LPN's	2A
private duty	NE
Obstetricians	4AS
Occupational Therapists	2A
Office Workers	
general	3A
Ophthalmologists	4AS
Opticians	
selling & fitting only	3A
shopwork	2A
Optometrists	
selling & fitting only	4A
shopwork	2A
Orthodontists	4AS
Orthopedists	4AS
Osteopaths	4AS
Paramedics	3A
Pediatricians	4AS
Pharmacists	4A
Photographers & Cameramen	
commercial, studio only	3A
newspaper, newsreel, or TV, not free-lance	2A
aerial	NE

Occupation	Class
Physical Therapists	2A
Physicians & Surgeons	4AS
Physician's Office Attendants	3A
Physicists	
no lab work	4A
lab work (no special hazard)	3A
Physiotherapists	2A
Piano Tuner	2A
Podiatrists	4AS
Priests	3A
Printing & Publication	
printers	2A
type founders, etchers	NE
Psychiatrists	4AS
Psychologists	4AS
Rabbis	3A
Real Estate Agents/Brokers	3A
Receptionists	3A
Reducing Salon & Health Spa	NE
Reporters	
court	3A
newspaper	2A
Restaurants (Secondary Liquor Sales Only)	
proprietors & managers, supervisory only	2A
head waiters, maitre d'hotels	2A
waiters, cooks, others	NE
Salesmen—Not Classified Elsewhere	
calling on accounts only, not door to door	3A
manufacturer reps	3A
door to door	NE
delivery	NE
Sanitation Services	
owners & operators (office only)	2A
Speech Therapist	3A
Statisticians	3A
Stenographers	3A
Stockbrokers	3A
Surveyors	2A

Occupation	Class
Taxidermists	2A
Taxicab Companies	
owners & proprietors, office only	2A
all others	NE
Teachers	
administration	3A
academic & commercial in classroom	3A
music-school	3A
others in schools	2A
private in home	NE
Telephone Switchboard Operators	2A
Therapists	
occupational	2A
physical, physiotherapist	2A
Timekeepers	2A
Travel Agents	3A
Typists	3A
Veterinarians	
treating household pets only	4AS
others	3A
Welfare Workers (not Federal Employees)	
office only	3A
others	NE

Besides your occupation, there may be three other circumstances under which a company may deny you disability coverage.

☐ You may have too much "passive" income. Passive income is money you receive from rents, royalties or investments. The exact cutoff for "too much" passive income varies with the carrier. If more than 50% of your regular income is passive, it is doubtful that any disability insurer will insure you. The reason is that disability insurance is an income-based coverage, and an applicant for disability insurance must be able to *prove* his or her income. That's easy when you make a steady salary, but much harder when you get income from sources that could change or vanish tomorrow.

☐ Similarly, if your net worth is too high, you may be denied disability coverage. Again, what's too high varies with the company.

☐ Finally, if you are self-employed, you may be denied coverage. Why? Because to be given coverage in the first instance, you have to be able to prove with certainty what your income is. Self-employed people have difficulty proving their income to the satisfaction of insurance companies. In fact, most companies will not sell disability to self-employed individuals. Again, shopping around and working with a competent insurance broker may produce a good disability policy to fit your needs.

Waiting Periods

It is quite possible to buy a disability insurance policy that will cover you from the first day of your disability, but such a policy would be enormously expensive. *The longer you can wait before you begin receiving benefits the cheaper the policy will be.*

Because most people are up and around about three months after an illness or minor injury, 90 days has been used as the traditional waiting period for most disability policies to start paying. If you are bedridden for three months or more, the chances are that the incapacity will be a long one.

However, just because three months is the standard waiting period doesn't mean that you have to buy a policy adhering to that. If you can afford to be without income for six months because you have six months worth of salary in savings, then you should lengthen the waiting period to six months. If you can wait a year, do so. By doing that you will substantially cut down on your premium. That's the best way to get a "discount" on disability insurance premiums.

The idea of disability insurance is to protect you against catastrophic loss—a disability that rendered you unable to make a living for a long period of time. If you lengthen out the waiting period as much as possible, you can buy much more coverage for the same premium. That coverage should protect you well against a long term disability.

Common Riders

Disability policies as a rule don't have a great number of riders available. There are only three that are worth your consideration. Whether you want to get any should be determined by your financial situation and your family circumstances at the time you buy or review your disability coverage:

Purchase Option

It allows you to buy more coverage as you get older, or at the onset of some event, such as the birth of a child, or your marriage. At these points, it is especially important that your income be protected. Your income must have increased significantly in order to be eligible for these purchase options. Again, income is the determining factor in deciding how much disability insurance you need.

This rider is more and more valuable as you grow older

because statistically your chances of being disabled grow. It's worth considering, but expensive.

Social Security Rider

Since you now know that a disabled person isn't paid by Social Security until he has been disabled for five months, many disability insurance companies offer a rider that pays you a certain amount (above your regular benefit) each and every month for each month you don't collect Social Security benefits. If you have the Social Security rider, and you also have a 90-day waiting period, you can still collect additional benefits for months four and five (assuming a six-month waiting period) of a disability because you will not be collecting Social Security during those months. Since, by the way, there is no guarantee that you will ever receive Social Security, it may be a good rider to have.

These riders will cost you more, but by judiciously shopping around, it may be possible to find a disability insurer who will give you one or both at a fair price.

Although 90 days is the average elimination or waiting period, if you really want to cut down on the costs of disability insurance you can find policies with 180- or even 360-day waiting periods. Remember that the waiting period is the time you must wait before benefits are paid to you, so be careful when you choose.

COLA Rider

The letters of this rider stand for *cost-of-living-adjustment*. COLA provides for an annual upward increase in your benefit based on a certain percentage, such as 6% or 7%. Suppose that your benefit is $1000 a month, and you have purchased the COLA rider with a 6% increase per year. The increase is figured on an annual, compounded basis. After the first year, you would receive $1060 per month, the next year $1122.63 per month and so on. This rider may be quite expensive, but if you were to be disabled for a period exceeding say 10 years, the inflation adjustment would be a godsend.

Not all companies selling disability insurance, of course, offer all of these riders, so be sure to ask about them if you want one or more.

Premium Costs

Life insurance and disability insurance have one thing in common. The later in life you buy it, the more it will cost you. That's because, the older you get, the more chances of your being disabled for a lengthy period of time. For example, more people have heart attacks in their 50's than in their 30's. Age is a criterion used by all insurance companies.

The best time to buy disability coverage is when you are young. The following chart shows some typical premiums for disability insurers based on the age of the individual purchasing the policy.

How much coverage should you buy? As an example, an executive or professional can generally get a monthly benefit under the following guidelines:

Income vs. Recommended Monthly Benefit

Income	Monthly Benefit
$ 25,000	$ 1,250
30,000	1,500
50,000	2,500
75,000	3,750
100,000	5,000
125,000	6,250
150,000	7,500
200,000	10,000

If you are willing to settle for a smaller monthly benefit, you can cut the cost of your premium considerably. For example, if you make $50,000 a year and are willing to pay for a monthly coverage of $1250 instead of $2500, you could save half your premium payment. What does it cost? Annual premiums for quality disability coverage might run as follows per $1000 of monthly benefit to age 65.

Annual Premium Cost vs. Waiting Period

Age	30-Day Wait	60-Day Wait	90-Day Wait
30	$ 398	$ 319	$ 213
35	460	373	328
40	563	466	415
45	698	587	520
50	857	733	623
55	1034	893	730
60	1219	1049	840

To understand this table, remember that the dollar figures used represent a *yearly* premium for each $1000 a *month* in benefits.

Length of Benefits

Policies are designed for nearly every conceivable need. You can buy a policy, for example, that will limit the length of time you can collect benefits to two years or five years, rather than until you are 65. The shorter the length of time benefits must be paid, the cheaper the policy. However, you should think long and hard about limiting your benefit period. If that's all you can afford, then go ahead. Some coverage is better than none. But if you can stretch out the benefit period for as long as possible, you will receive benefits for that period. If possible try to get "lifetime" coverage or coverage to age 65.

To sum up then, discounts on disability insurance are available by:

☐ Lengthening out the waiting period before benefits are paid.

☐ Shortening the period when benefits are paid.

☐ By cutting the amount of the benefit that is paid to you.

Women's Rates

Unfortunately, women have to pay more than men for the same disability coverage. Why? The insurance companies believe women make more disability claims than men.

Here is a comparison showing disability premium rates for men and women of the same age for the identical policy. There is no such thing as a family disability policy, nor can a husband cover a non-working wife out of his employer's group policy. A woman must fend for herself in the disability marketplace.

Annual Premium Cost Comparison of Males & Females

Age	$1000 Benefit		$1500 Benefit		$2500 Benefit	
	Male	Female	Male	Female	Male	Female
30	$ 398	$ 465	$ 597	$ 698	$ 995	$1163
35	460	542	690	813	1150	1355
40	563	652	845	978	1408	1630
45	698	779	1047	1169	1745	1948
50	857	896	1286	1344	2143	2240
55	1034	1034	1551	1551	2585	2585
60	1219	1219	1829	1829	3048	3048

Note: Premiums from three companies offering disability insurance were averaged for this table. Figures based on a 30-day waiting period.

Employed women must make sure that they are covered by their employer's disability coverage, especially if it is free or relatively inexpensive. Individual policies will cost more under all conditions.

Notice, however, in this table, that older women (55 years of age and older) pay the identical amount for disability as do men. It is primarily younger women who pay more for disability insurance than men of a comparable age.

How Much Income Should Be Replaced?

For the average individual, a disability policy should cover approximately 60% of his or her present income. You may need more or less than the average, depending on your particular circumstances.

If you can do with less than 60%, any disability insurance you do buy will be cheaper. Here's who can probably afford to buy coverage of less than 60% of replacement income:

□ If your employer fully covers you for 60% of your income loss under a group disability policy, you may need little or no additional coverage.

□ If a good deal of your income comes from investments, you may have enough income to keep you going through a period of disability.

□ If you get most of your income from commissions or regular bonuses, you might want to arrange with your employer to pay earned commissions and bonuses out to you on a deferred basis, should you become disabled.

□ Self-employed workers can make similar arrangements with their steady clients and customers.

□ You can, if you so desire, self-insure yourself by funding a separate savings or money market fund equal to at least six months salary that you can draw on in the event of disability. The average period of disability, according to industry figures is three to four months.

□ Under the present tax laws, you are permitted to withdraw funds from your individual retirement account (IRA) or Keogh Plan account if disability should occur. Note that no adverse tax liability results from such a withdrawal.

You may need more than 60% coverage when:

□ You own your own business, especially if it is an individual proprietorship. A large amount of disability income may be needed to keep the business going while your laid up.

□ If you have the extra expense of supporting an ill or aging family member or you pay child support or you have a child attending or are planning to send a child to college, more than 60% might be in order.

□ If you have an adjustable-rate mortgage that is not protected by mortgage disability insurance. A one or two point increase in the interest rate could be devastating and may require more than 60% replacement of your income.

Since these factors keep changing, you need to periodically review your disability insurance needs.

Disability Credits on Other Policies

Figuring how much substitute income you will need during a period of disability is difficult. If you have disability riders on your life, auto or homeowners policies that pay the premiums on those policies during a period of disability, your job is a little bit easier.

These riders are expensive but should be considered when figuring your disability income needs. Knowing that these policies will be taken care of is not only a financial but also an emotional relief for many individuals.

Similarly, if you have taken out disability insurance when you got an auto loan or your home mortgage, those loans can also be paid while you are disabled. Some lenders require such coverage for a loan. Check with your auto and home mortgage lenders to find out if you do have it. If you do, any additional disability policies you buy need not cover those payments. You will need to know how many months of disability are required before these benefits kick in.

If you can get benefits from other sources when you become disabled, then you probably don't need disability insurance. Disability insurance is for those who are not fully taken care of by other programs.

Social Security and Disability Benefits

When people think of Social Security, they almost always think about old-age pensions. That, however, is just one part of the Social Security program. The other part is one that provides benefits for disabled individuals. And it is no small amount either. According to the Social Security Administration, more than $18 billion in disability benefits was paid out in 1985.

The exact amount of benefits available to you is determined by your present salary and how many years you have been paying into Social Security. A middle-aged individual who has been paying into Social Security will be eligible for more benefits than a young person who has only been paying into the system for a few years.

Not everyone is eligible to receive Social Security disability payments. If you do qualify, benefits for a permanent or an indefinite disability are not paid until you have been disabled for a five full months.

If you have been disabled and collecting Social Security for two years, you automatically qualify for Medicare, which will help you pay for many of your medical bills. See the discussion *What You Must Know About Medicare,* page 146.

To find out if you qualify and what your benefits would be if you become permanently disabled, contact your local Social Security office.

You may qualify for other benefits as well. For instance:

□ If you are a government employee you may be eligible for Civil Service disability benefits.

□ The Veterans Administration gives pension disability benefits to former service people with service related disabilities.

□ If you are injured at work, you are most likely eligible to receive state Workers Compensation benefits. Your employee benefit office should be able to give you all the relevant information concerning this program.

□ If you are a member of a labor union, you have access to group disability benefits. Again, your union business representatives should be able to fill you in.

□ Some fraternal, professional and charitable organizations cover their members with free disability insurance.

□ Former coal miners are covered under federal and (some) state Black Lung programs.

□ Depending on the nature of your disability and your need for rehabilitation you may qualify for state vocational rehabilitation benefits.

□ Some states provide for a Cash Sickness Program.

□ SSI or Supplemental Security Income is available to qualified low income or welfare recipients.

When you add up all these benefits, you may find that you don't need private disability insurance. Your employer, for example, may provide you with group benefits that include disability insurance. If you are not covered by an employer, or some other program, provides you with only limited benefits, then you should consider getting your own private disability insurance.

Managing Your Disability Coverage

Another often overlooked aspect of disability coverage is the proper management of available benefits. Social Security benefits are not available until five months of total disability have elapsed; your employer-sponsored group disability policy may have a ninety day waiting period before you receive benefits. So, how can you insure your income for the first three months of a disability?

You could purchase (or your employer could provide) a short-term (1-90 days) disability policy.

Many employers provide both long-and short-term disability policies for their employees, so their employees are covered no matter how long or short a period they are disabled. Most short-term policies don't last longer than six months.

If you need to buy a disability policy from a private insurer to supplement your employer-sponsored disability policy, you can save money by putting a six-month waiting period on your private policy. By having such a long waiting period, you can cut your premiums significantly. Depending on the length of the coverage of the short-term disability policy, you can integrate it with a long-term policy. Try to make the waiting period of the long-term policy equal to the maximum of the short-term policy.

Most privately issued disability policies won't replace more than 60% of your income and Social Security. If you do receive it, it will probably replace no more than 15% of your income. Therefore, the most you can expect to get is about 75% of your total income from these sources. But since not everybody is eligible for Social Security Disability, you shouldn't count on receiving it.

Disability After 65

Many personal and most corporate disability policies will stop paying benefits when the disabled individual reaches age 65. Social Security disability benefits, however, are still available after 65. Medicare will also pick up some costs after that age, but for the most part those benefits are medical benefits, not income substitution benefits.

However, if you are working past age 65 and your group disability benefits run out, most employers will make sure you are adequately covered for disability under a supplemental or similar type of policy that will be available.

Also, some individual policies will cover you up until the age of 72 if you are working. They may be a bit more expensive at that age then they were earlier, put the coverage is useful to have, especially when you realized that the older you are, the greater are the chances that you will become disabled.

Questions to Ask
When Buying Disability Insurance

1) Do I really need disability insurance or am I sufficiently covered by my employer or through a fraternal organization or labor union?

2) How much income will I need to have replace if I become disabled?

3) How long can I afford to wait before benefits become payable?

4) For what period of time will disability benefits be paid?

5) Will I be eligible for Social Security?

6) If so, how much?

7) How is total disability defined under this policy?

8) Am I totally covered if I can't perform the regular duties of my regular occupation?

9) Have I considered all available riders?

10) Does the cost of disability insurance fit into my overall insurance budget?

4

Health Insurance

You don't have to be told how expensive health care has become. The costs of doctors, hospitals and post-operative care seem to increase daily. It is no exaggeration to say that two or more weeks in the hospital can bankrupt a family without insurance protection.

And because medical costs are so high, medical insurance premiums are, too. They have increased as medical costs have increased. That's why a family protected by an employer's group health policy has a most important fringe benefit.

But even the best employer group policies usually require some out-of-pocket expense from the employee. The expense might be in the form of a high deductible or an employee contribution to the plan.

If you don't have access to a group policy through an employer or a fraternal or professional association, you'll have to buy an individual policy. The deductibles on those are quite high—from $250 to $2,500—for affordable policies.

Even so, whether you have a group policy or an individual policy, you may find yourself reaching deep into your own pocket for some money to pay a portion of your family's medical expenses during the year. That's because no health insurance policy, no matter how comprehensive, will pay for *all* medical expenses incurred. For example, you'll probably have to pay for routine checkups yourself.

For that reason, you'd be very smart to set up a separate bank or investment account to take care of the un-reimbursed portion of medical expenses. By drawing on that account only when you get a medical bill that insurance doesn't pay for, you can lower your medical insurance premium by increasing your deductible.

If you add to the account periodically, you'll probably sleep better at night, too, because you won't have to worry about looking for money to pay unexpected medical bills.

Group Health Insurance

It is vital for every individual with group health coverage to know *exactly* what that coverage is *before* you need to use it. You should know, for example, if all medical visits by all family members are covered? What is the deductible? Are you and your family covered for visits to a psychiatrist or an acupuncturist? Are you totally covered from your first day in the hospital if you or a family member should be hospitalized? How about maternity benefits?

You must also remember that group health coverages, especially those obtained through employment, don't last a lifetime. Most of these benefits cease if you retire or leave your employer prior to retirement. Then you have to get your own coverage.

Another thing you'll want to check on your group health coverage is what the waiting period is before you are eligible for coverage. Three or six months of employment is common.

Some group policies allow all employees whether they have a *pre-existing condition*—a condition you have prior to coverage, such as pregnancy—or not to be covered under the plan. That's an excellent feature to have.

It's only by knowing *exactly* what you already have that you can make an intelligent decision on what you may additionally need. This is the only way to be fully protected against the high cost of medical care. You may even discover that the group policy you have obviates extra, individual coverage. But that decision should be made only after weighing all the necessary factors.

Because most group policies don't cover you for all medical procedures, you might consider supplementing a group policy with an individual policy that fills the "holes."

Also, if you lose your job because of retirement or termination, you could find yourself without any employer-sponsored group coverage. You might have to get individual health insurance.

Even typical group policies can be seriously out of date and need supplementing. A typical group policy, for example, may pay $200 a day for a hospital room when a room actually costs $400 a day. Unless you have supplemental coverage, that extra $200 a day will come out of your pocket.

Be aware that some group policies may strictly define the term *hospital*. Treatment at a clinic, nursing home or alcoholism treatment center, might not be covered.

There are some medical procedures and treatments customarily excluded under most group policies. These include:

- ☐ Cosmetic surgery (unless caused by injury)
- ☐ Examinations for hearing aids and eyeglasses
- ☐ Expenses for a work-related injury where you are eligible for worker's compensation.
- ☐ Immunizations
- ☐ Routine checkups

As mentioned earlier, the biggest problem with group policies is that they terminate either at age 65 or when you leave your employer. The most important feature of any group policy is whether you can *convert it into an individual policy so you have no break in coverage.* The group policy should be convertible without you and your family members having to take a physical examination.

Of course, individual coverage will cost you more than the group policy did. But *continuity of coverage* is the most important factor here, not cost.

If, on the other hand, you are planning on retiring, a good group policy will continue to provide some coverage after you become eligible for Medicare. The best of these are the ones where the employer foots all or part of the premium during your golden years.

Newly Terminated Employees

If you had a job where you had group health benefits, and you have recently been let go, there is some good news. The U.S. Congress has recently come to the rescue with a new law that will help you to keep your former health insurance benefits for 18 months while you search for a new job.

Widows and widowers of people who were covered under a group health plan, and their dependents, can at their option be covered up to 36 months under the provisions of this new statute. Although you have to pay for the coverage yourself, you are assured of continued health insurance coverage.

Many details of the law still have to be clarified. If *you* terminate employment, you should inquire whether you are eligible for this extended group coverage. The law only applies to employers who employ 20 or more people on a regular basis. If you worked for a smaller company, you won't qualify.

Types of Coverage

There are essentially two kinds of health insurance: *basic health insurance* and *major medical insurance*. Usually each is sold separately because many buyers choose just one or the other. There are also *comprehensive plans* combining the two coverages.

Basic Health

Basic health coverage usually encompasses some of the following services performed in a hospital:

- [ ] Room and board in a hospital for a set number of days. 120 is commonly used.
- [ ] Normal nursing services.
- [ ] X-rays.
- [ ] Laboratory tests.
- [ ] Drugs and medications.

□ Simple surgical procedures performed on an in-patient or out-patient bases.

Away from the hospital, the following services are typically covered:

□ Doctors visits.

□ Physician-ordered diagnostic tests and procedures, such as stress tests or CAT scans.

□ Laboratory tests ordered by your physician.

Major Medical

Major medical insurance is designed to pay for those charges resulting from a major illness or accident. It covers a long hospital stay and generally those items not covered or fully covered under the basic plan, such as:

□ Surgical fees.

□ Private duty nurses.

□ Oxygen and blood services.

□ Outpatient care.

□ Drugs and appliances.

Many people buy major medical plans without having basic coverage. They do this because they assume that they can handle the less expensive health care services, but they want to be protected from the huge costs incurred due to a serious or major health problem. The philosophy here is to insure major expenditures and to use "self-insurance" for medical expenses that would be covered under a basic policy.

If your employer gives you health insurance as a fringe benefit, it is most likely basic coverage. If your employer also offers a major medical plan, so much the better.

Essentially, major medical takes over where basic coverage leaves off. Depending on the particular policy, there are usually no limitations on hospital days or total expenses for a covered injury or illness. If there is a limit, it will probably be in the range of $1 million.

Many basic plans also offer dental and eye coverage as

part of the basic package. Psychiatric and acupuncture treatments are also available with some plans. Of course, the broader the coverage, the more expensive the insurance will be.

Features of a Good, Basic Policy

There are a number of features common to all good, basic health policies, whether offered to an individual or group:

- □ They are all renewable.
- □ They provide coverage for your entire family from day one of the birth of your children until they leave home, age 23 in some cases.
- □ All congenital problems and illnesses are covered.
- □ There is no maximum charge per illness.
- □ All hospital room and board charges are covered, regardless of the prevalent rate at the time of your illness or the hospital you choose. Remember, though, to check the definition of the word *hospital*.
- □ Full coverage of home health care expenses are covered, including limited nursing care and such devices as oxygen tanks and masks, as well as wheelchairs, etc.
- □ There are reasonable pre-existing-condition limitations.

Premium Costs

One of the realities of the health insurance business is that only a handful of companies offer comprehensive health insurance for individuals. As a consequence, there are few, if any, discounts available. And most of the policies look pretty much alike.

Even though you might qualify as a "preferred risk" for life insurance because you don't drink or smoke and so on, you probably can't shop around for a discount in health insurance. Few companies and low competition make the cost of premiums similar.

In fact, because of the high costs involved in issuing and underwriting health policies, some companies who offered health insurance in the past have abandoned the business. Unfortunately, group policies may be unavailable.

Even the most popular and widespread group policies, such as Blue Cross/Blue Shield can often be just as expensive as an individual policy from a commercial insurer. This means that the prospects for saving money by shopping around on health insurance premiums are slim. This is one reason why Health Maintenance Organizations (HMOs) and other organizations and programs that emphasize *preventive care* are flourishing.

Pre-existing Conditions

Most health policies *will not* insure you immediately for an illness or injury that you already have when you apply for the insurance. You may, however, be able to get coverage after a waiting period.

For example, if you have diabetes when you apply for health insurance, an insurance company won't pay for all your diabetes-related treatments from then on because the diabetes is a *pre-existing condition.*

Most of the pre-existing clauses exclude you only from treatment for a certain period of time. The wording will read something like this: "We will not cover any costs resulting from a pre-existing condition for three years". That means that after the three years, if you should have a diabetic condition that results in your hospitalization or other treatment the insurance company will pay for it.

A liberal pre-existing clause can be good for you and your family. If, however, you are all in good health when you apply for the insurance, then there is little or nothing to worry about.

The best idea, however, is to buy health insurance when

you are young and in good health. That way, if you buy a non-cancellable or guaranteed renewable policy, you will be covered later in life when your good health might change.

In the case of a child born with a medical problem, unless the child is covered from the moment of birth, the insurance company *will not* cover the child if the policy contains a pre-existing condition clause.

Exactly what constitutes a pre-existing condition has been the subject of many lawsuits. The key is the definition in the policy and the insurance company's reading of that definition. If you have some kind of ongoing medical problem and you buy health insurance, don't expect to get coverage for those problems for the pre-existing condition limitation set out in the policy.

Some group policies waive the pre-existing condition clause for people who join the group. Therefore, if you have a serious medical condition that could keep you from getting coverage for that condition immmediately, try to find a group situation where a waiver exists. It is probably your best bet.

Choosing the Right Policy

There is no standard, individual health insurance policy. As a result premiums can vary from policy to policy. However, it is vital that you don't shop for a health policy solely on the basis of price alone. Of equal importance is what the policy *excludes* from payment.

In fact, certain diseases or certain medical procedures and treatments may be excluded. For instance, one policy might include treatment for cancer, but exclude psychiatric treatment. Or a policy might exclude chiropractic and acupuncture treatment while including eye examinations. *Usually the more comprehensive the policy, the more expensive it will be.*

The right choice is the most comprehensive policy you can buy at a price that you can afford. Obviously, if the policy excludes treatment for heart disease and heart disease runs in your family, you should forego that policy. But if it excludes injuries suffered as a result of a motorcycle accident, and you don't own a motorcycle and never will, then that policy should be considered.

If you are concerned only about exceptionally large hospital bills, there are a few comprehensive major medical policies available with deductibles as high as $15,000. Because these deductibles are so high, the policies are cheap. They could make a good choice for those who have a large amount of money stashed away for any medical emergencies that might arise.

Health Insurance Strategy

Insurance experts agree that as far as health insurance is concerned, you should insure yourself and your family against *the worst imaginable circumstances*. For example, if you were to be the victim of an accident and you would have to stay in the hospital for six months, that would cost you a huge amount of money. Insure against that.

The best strategy is to take the highest deductible you can afford. Self-insure yourself for what you consider small bills. It is the large, enormous medical bills that you want to insure against, not the routine yearly trips to the doctor's office for a check-up or prescription. You will pay less for insurance, yet when you do have to collect on a coverage, you will have received the most for your premium dollar.

Also, the younger and healthier you are when you apply for health insurance the better. Following are some other strategies you should consider when planning your health insurance program:

☐ If your employer provides you with an option of taking group health insurance or an HMO, weigh the benefits and costs on a family basis. There is no one answer for everyone.

☐ If your health insurance funds are limited, buy major medical coverage first. Since major medical covers the financially catastrophic incidents, you will be getting the most coverage for your insurance dollar that way.

◻ If both you and your spouse work and you both have health insurance coverage, go over your respective policies and coverages and eliminate overlapping coverages. This strategy will probably save you money.

Also try to figure out if it would be cheaper if one spouse would do better by being covered under the other spouse's health insurance plan. Not all employers provide for spousal coverage, but if one of your employers does, it may be cheaper to cover both of you under one policy.

◻ Although it may be difficult to contemplate, women should find out if their health insurance will continue and what their options are should they become divorced or widowed.

◻ Find out what your state Medicaid insurance offers if you find that you cannot afford health insurance coverage of any sort.

◻ If you are over 65, carefully choose a "Medigap" policy. It must coordinate properly with Medicare or you will be wasting money on duplicate, overlapping or unneeded coverages.

◻ Remember, a hospital indemnity policy should never be purchased as a primary health insurance product. Rather, it should always be viewed as a supplement to a basic health policy. Its purpose is to help you meet out-of-pocket expenses that your health insurance coverage may not meet.

Hospital Indemnity Policies

Surely you've seen or heard ads for hospital indemnity policies. "$50.00 a day for every day in the hospital. You can spend the money any way you wish."

There is nothing terribly wrong with these policies. They are relatively cheap, and do pay you a set number of dollars per day. However, they are a *supplement* to health insurance, definitely not a substitute for it.

There are two things you must understand about these policies:

1) They pay a fixed dollar amount per day, and it normally does not rise with inflation. So if you bought a policy today and used it 15 years from now, $50 or $100 a day would probably be less than it seems today.

2) These policies usually do not begin paying you from your first day in the hospital. Often, there is a waiting period such as 7 or 10 days. So you aren't paid anything for short stays in the hospital. And short stays are most common.

Of course, the longer you wait before you start collecting the cash payments under a hospital indemnity policy, the lower the premium. Most policies don't carry a guarantee that the premium won't go up during the time you own the policy. Read the the fine print carefully if you decide to buy one.

Most of these policies are available through the mail, directly from the insurer. Some companies specialize in this market. They may not be particularly well known, so you should check them out through your insurance department's consumer division first.

Senior citizens can benefit particularly from these policies since the age cut-off on a number of these policies is 70 or 75 years, or even later. They can act as a Medicare supplement as well.

Dreaded Disease Policies

Some companies will offer insurance coverage in the event you develop a so-called *dreaded disease*. Cancer is the disease most commonly insured against, but it is by no means the only one.

Because the odds are you won't get a particular disease, buying this kind of insurance policy is a waste of money. These policies usually cover only a certain number of days of treatment or a certain course of treatment.

Quite often, those health problems that might be excluded from a health policy under regular circumstances will be sold as a single sickness or dreaded disease policy.

Also, these policies are for the most part overpriced. They are a very poor buy for the average insurance customer and should be avoided. *usdezaīl*

Blue Cross and Blue Shield

Probably the best known of all health insurance plans are the "Blues," Blue Cross and Blue Shield. They offer group and individual coverages to a large variety of people all over the country. Blue Cross is hospital coverage, similar to major medical. Blue Shield coverage pays doctor bills and surgical fees, the way basic medical plans offered by the commercial carriers do.

However, not all premiums charged by Blue Cross or Blue Shield are the same nationwide. The premiums are based on the cost of medical services in a particular area. Within one rating area, all individuals, regardless of age and sex, will pay the same premium for an identical policy.

For example, if you live in New York City, you can expect to pay more for Blue Cross and Blue Shield coverage than a person buying the identical coverage in Omaha, Nebraska. That's because the cost of hospital stay and doctor fees are higher in New York City than in Omaha.

For the most part, Blue Cross and Blue Shield group plans around the country waive any pre-existing condition problems. Another fine feature of Blue Cross coverage is that if you are covered in one state and you are hospitalized in another with higher fees, reciprocal agreements allow Blue Cross to pay the higher fee. Essentially you have nationwide coverage with Blue Cross.

A Blue Cross or Blue Shield policy should be evaluated just as you would any other health insurance product. But in one area—maternity benefits—it seems to be superior to other products. As a result, young couples in their childbearing years often choose the Blues over other coverages.

Blue Cross and Blue Shield plans are established and run by non-profit organizations. Their premiums are therefore said to be lower than commercial policies. Even so, you should evaluate the policies on your own. Analyze the benefits you are getting for the premium you are paying. That's the only sensible way to evaluate health insurance.

In the course of your shopping around for health insurance, don't forget to consider the Blues. They may just turn out to be your best bet.

Women and Health Insurance

Women who buy health insurance on their own will usually find that it costs them about 15% more than their male counterparts for the same policy. The reason is that women, up until age 55, have statistically more health claims than men do.

After age 55, the premiums for men and women become identical. At around age 60, women actually pay 10% less then men. These price differentials are reflected only in individual commercial policies.

There are really only two solutions for women who are looking to pay less. If you qualify as a dependent under a spouse's or family member's group employment policy, then you should be insured under that policy.

Failing that, you might explore purchasing a Blue Cross and Blue Shield policy. These policies are age-and sex-neutral in their pricing—everybody pays the same amount for the same benefits. But, as mentioned, Blue Cross and Blue Shield policies are not necessarily cheaper than commercial policies. Sometimes they are and sometimes they're not. Remember, there is no standard health policy, and the benefits offered vary considerably from company to company. Some shopping may be required to find the policy that suits your needs best.

Cost Containment and HMOs

Since health insurance pays for services rendered, it is in the interest of health insurers to work at keeping the cost of medical services as low as possible. However, as we all know, the costs of all kinds of medical services have skyrocketed in the last decade.

In response to this problem, some health insurance plans, particularly Blue Cross and Blue Shield, have issued what are essentially *rate cards,* informing doctors, hospitals and policyholders of the maximum amount they will pay for any particular medical procedure.

For example, the plan might say that the maximum paid for an appendectomy will be $900. Doctors who accept these medical plans usually agree to abide by these maximums. This motivates the medical community to be as cost effective as possible and thereby make more profit.

Another response has been the formation of *Health Maintenance Organizations,* or *HMOs.* An HMO is a group of physicians who together render comprehensive health care to patients. However, instead of accepting health insurance payments, the physicians are paid out of a flat monthly fee all patients pay. This fee doesn't change, no matter how much medical attention the patient needs from month to month.

HMOs have become a great alternative for many people. As a matter of fact, many companies offer their employees the *option* of choosing an HMO or a group health insurance plan. The fees you pay an HMO *may* be less than health insurance coverage. If you are offered such an option, you should compare costs.

Many Blue Cross and Blue Shield plans around the country also sponsor HMOs. If you have a Blue Cross plan, you should definitely take a look at its HMO offering to see if it might suit your needs. This HMO option may be less expensive then the Blue Cross plan itself.

HMOs do have one feature that has limited their use in some parts of the nation—the patient has no choice of physician or hospital. You must use a doctor or hospital affiliated with your particular HMO. Of course, there is usually not such a limitation with traditional health insurance.

первая Initially, an HMO may look more expensive, but remember that you pay only a fixed monthly fee. With health insurance, every time you visit a physician or have some health treatment, you may have to pay the deductible amount. If your insurance doesn't cover the entire amount of the bill, you will have to pay for the remainder as well. So, overall, HMOs may turn out to be cheaper, depending on your history of doctor visits and overall health and that of your family members.

Typical HMO offerings include:
- Routine medical checkups.
- Continuous care.
- Emergency procedures.
- Prescription coverage. Most HMOs offer this coverage.

What You Must Know About Medicare

Medicare is a federal health insurance program available to people age 65 and older, or to younger individuals who are totally disabled or who suffer from end-stage kidney disease.

Medicare was never designed to be an all-inclusive health insurance program, and it is not. Its function has always been to relieve older Americans of *some* of their health care costs, but not all. You should be aware of the fact that at age 65 you automatically become eligible for Medicare *whether you are working or not.*

Medicare is divided into two parts, known as Part A and Part B. Part A is essentially hospital insurance. Part B covers physician's and surgeon's charges both in and out of the hospital.

Part A coverage is available without charge to everyone eligible for Medicare. People who are not automatically eligible can get Part A coverage, but they must pay for it. The premium is currently $214 a month. Part A coverage has a deductible of $520 in 1987, applicable to everybody.

Part B coverage is optional, so you must pay a monthly premium to obtain it. In 1986 the monthly premium was $15.50. There is also a yearly deductible that must be met under Part B. At the time of this writing, that deductible is $75.

All of these figures are subject to change on an annual basis. It is important that all Medicare recipients know what these changes are from year to year so that they can evaluate their insurance needs in a rational manner.

The following table details the types of facilities Medicare recipients can use and the types of services that are paid. Under Part A it is vital to understand that Medicare does not pay for the costs of custodial care in a nursing home. Medicare, does, however, pay for medical and nursing services rendered in a nursing home subject to certain limitations.

Since Medicare will pay for an unlimited number of home visits by doctors, nurses, therapists and other health professionals, it is much wiser, if possible, for a Medicare patient to be treated in the confines of his or her home rather than a nursing home.

Medicare Services

Part A

Services	Facilities That Can Be Used
Semi-private room, meals, nursing services, special facility, rehabilitation facility or hospice.	Hospital, skilled nursing facility, rehabilitation care units, operating and recovery room, medical supplies and appliances, rehabilitation services and if billed by the hospital, drugs, laboratory and radiology services. Also, unlimited home visits by health care professionals.*

Part B

Emergency Rooms and outpatient clinics.	Physicians and surgeons fees, diagnostic tests, prosthetic devices, medical supplies, independent lab tests, ambulance services, radiology and pathology services, physical and speech therapy, dental surgery, some chiropractic services and limited outpatient psychiatric care. Also, unlimited home visits by health care professionals.

*Doctor services while one is in the hospital are paid only under Part B.

Benefit Period

Since older people often have serious illnesses requiring long stretches in the hospital, Medicare has had to limit the number of days it will pay for hospital services under Part A. Presently, Medicare pays for up to 90 days of hospitalization for each benefit period. For the first 60 days, Medicare pays all the costs. For the 61st through 90th day, the patient must pay $130 a day. However, remember that you must pay a $520 deductible (in 1987) no matter how long or short your stay in the hospital.

A benefit period under Medicare begins when you are hospitalized and ends when you have been out of the medical facility for 60 days in a row. If you should have to enter the hospital again on the 61st day after you left, your 90 day period would begin anew and you would have to pay the deductible as well.

Each Medicare patient under Part A also has 60 "lifetime reserve" days, which come into use only if you must spend more than 90 consecutive days in a hospital in a benefit period. However, these days are not renewable with each new benefit period. They are a lifetime benefit and once they are used, you can never use them again. Even with the lifetime reserve days, the Medicare patient must still pay (in 1987) $260 a day, Medicare will then pick up the rest.

Under Part B, there is a $75 (in 1986) deductible each year. But in Part B Medicare only picks up the cost of 80% of "allowable" medical charges. That means you must pay the other 20%. But, because of the definition of allowable, your out-of-pocket expense could even be higher.

Here's why: Medicare makes a determination as to what an allowable charge should be for a medical service rendered under the program. For example, if a physician charges a Medicare patient $1,000 for a service that Medicare pegs at $800, all you would get would be the $640 from Medicare—80% of the allowable charge of $800. Your out-of-pocket expense then would be $360, the $200 difference between the physician's fee and the Medicare allowable schedule *plus* the 20% co-insurance amount.

Physician's are *not* required to charge fees that conform only to the Medicare allowable fee schedule. They can charge their customary fee. You may have to bargain with the physician or surgeon to keep to the Medicare schedule so that you won't have to pay anything over and above the normal 20% that you are responsible for under Part B.

Filling Gaps

As you can see, Medicare certainly does not pay for all the medical costs of those eligible to receive it. Here is where supplemental insurance comes in.

If you are 65 and older, you are not working, and you had a group health plan either at work or through a professional or fraternal organization, that plan may provide "Medigap" coverage for you upon retirement. Those coverages, even if you have to pay for them yourself, are still cheaper than an individual policy covering the Medicare gap.

If you are currently covered by a group plan, you may be able to convert it to a Medicare supplement when you reach 65. If your policy is convertible, you should certainly consider conversion when you reach 65. This conversion option is a valuable feature, one you might want to consider if you are now shopping for health insurance. Conversion is allowed without taking a medical examination.

If you are 65 years old and are working, you are still eligible for Medicare. Your employer (unless the firm employs 20 people or less) must offer you the opportunity to remain under the current company health plan with Medicare supplementing those benefits. If you take this option, the employer must pay for all benefits covered under the employee health plan before Medicare must pay.

Individual Insurance

If you don't have a group plan, or if your present plan is

недосточи

either inadequate or won't carry over after age 65, you may have to purchase what is known as a "medical expense policy." This policy is intended to cover the Medicare gaps.

You should, of course, determine if the benefits outweigh the costs on any policy of this type before you buy it. Different policies may have different benefits, so be sure you check out all the different policies available. A knowledgeable insurance agent should be able to assist you in this task.

Of course, you can also purchase a hospital indemnity policy which pays you a set amount of cash for each day you are in the hospital after a certain number of days. Remember, though, these policies may need periodic updating because their benefits are paid in fixed dollars and inflation must be considered.

Finally, there are the Medicare Supplement Policies themselves.

Medicare Supplement Policies

The following information on Medicare Supplement Policies comes from the Health Insurance Association of America's pamphlet entitled *How To Use Private Health Insurance With Medicare* and it is used with their permission.

This type of policy is specifically designed to cover the co-payments not covered by Medicare and to pay Medicare eligible expenses after Medicare's limits have been reached. It is available only to people who are age 65 or older.

Some policies may cover the Part A or Part B deductibles or both, and some may cover services which Medicare does not cover at all, such as out-of-hospital prescription drugs.

But there are some expenses that even Medicare supplement policies probably will not pay for, such as dental or foot care, eyeglasses, hearing aids, routine examinations, or cosmetic surgery. Although some nursing home care may be covered, *custodial care usually is not.* Always check policy exclusions carefully. It is just as important to know what is not covered as to know what is.

Most states have adopted minimum standards that Medicare supplement policies issued in that state must meet. These standards include:

1) Coverage of Part A hospital co-payments for the 61st through 90th days and for hospital reserve days.

2) Coverage of 90% of Part A expenses for an additional 365 days of hospitalization over the lifetime of the policy.

3) Coverage of 20% of Part B allowable expenses up to at least $5000 in a calendar year—although the policy may impose a calendar year deductible of up to $200.

4) Pre-existing conditions may not be excluded after the policy has been in force for six months.

5) Coverage of Medicare co-payment amounts must be changed automatically to coincide with changes in the co-payment.

6) Individual policies and group policies sold through the mail must meet a 60% loss ratio; other group policies subject to the minimum standards must meet a 75% loss ratio. (A loss ratio reflects the total amount of benefits compared to the total amount of premiums).

7) The insured is entitled to a "free look." The policy may be returned if the insured is not satisfied for any reason, and the premium will be refunded. The insured has 30 days to return policies purchased through the mail and 10 days to return policies purchased from agents.

8) The insurance company must provide the insured with an outline of coverage and a buyer's guide.

Any questions or doubts you have about your state's laws should be directed to your state insurance department. The department can also help you with questions about policies, insurance companies, or agents.

Money-Saving Tips on Health Insurance

◻ Most health insurance policies allow you a "second look." That is, they permit you to change your mind within 10 days of initially signing the policy. You can cancel the policy within that period and get your money back.

❑ Because so many health risks are associated with smoking, if you are a heavy smoker, you may be unable to get coverage, regardless of your age. But if you have recently quit smoking, you may obtain coverage if the company feels you will not smoke again.

❑ Diabetics may also find it impossible to get coverage because diabetes leads to so many other health problems.

❑ If you like the idea of a hospital indemnity policy, you can have more than one. These policies are relatively cheap. You can buy two or more and collect on all of them if you are hospitalized for a lengthy period of time.

❑ Start a health emergency fund of your own. There will always be some out-of-pocket expenses associated with an illness, even with Medicare and a sound supplementary health insurance plan. If possible, keep your emergency fund in a joint savings account so someone else can get to it if you cannot.

❑ Coverage of skilled nursing services, either in a nursing facility or at home, are available under Medicare and some insurance policies—if you meet the qualifications—to help you avoid the higher costs of long periods of hospitalizaton.

❑ Your choice of physician and surgeon should depend on your confidence in their skills. But don't hesitate to ask them about their fees and how they are to be paid. Remember to ask whether they will accept Medicare "assignment."

❑ Your choice of supplementary health insurance should be made carefully. Investigate, weigh benefits, compare, ask questions and don't be satisfied until you get answers you understand.

❑ Claim forms should be made out carefully and fully. If they're not, delays may cost you money and concern.

❑ Check your bills, and watch for deductibles which you must pay first.

❑ Don't over-insure. There are better things to do with your money than pay premiums that duplicate or overlap other insurance coverage.

◻ Keep your health insurance up to date. Some policies adjust to inflation better than others. But the cost of health care continues to rise, so make sure the benefits of your policies have not been outdated. Review them annually.

◻ Don't drop one policy and buy another with similar benefits merely because the second one looks a little better, or is a little less expensive. You could delay benefits under a brand new policy, because of waiting periods and pre-existing condition limitations.

◻ Keep your health insurance policies in one place that is readily accessible and tell those close to you where they are. Then make a list of the policy numbers and the companies that issued them in case the originals are lost or misplaced.

◻ Check for pre-existing condition limitations that reduce or eliminate coverage of current health problems for certain periods of time.

◻ Check your right to renew. Beware of policies that let the company refuse to renew your policy on an individual basis. These policies provide the least permanent coverage.

◻ Take your time. Do not let a brief enrollment period pressure you into buying a policy.

◻ If you continue to work past age 65, you and your Medicare eligible spouse may choose to remain covered by your employer's group health plan. Check with your employer for the advantages of doing so.

◻ Know with whom you are dealing. A company must meet certain qualifications to do business in your state. This licensing helps protect you, and agents must carry proof of state licensing. If the agent cannot show such proof, do not buy insurance from that person. A business card is not a license.

◻ Check with your state insurance department if you have any questions about the policy, the agent or the company represented. The department cannot make a purchase decision for you, but it can tell you if the company you are dealing with is reputable and the policy meets state standards.

□ Other helpful booklets include *Your Medicare Handbook*, available from any Social Security office and *A Guide to Health Insurance for People with Medicare*, available from the Health Care Financing Administration, state insurance departments and companies selling Medicare supplement policies.

Questions to Ask
When Buying Health Insurance

1) What are the exclusions in the policy I want to buy?

2) Have I thoroughly shopped the health insurance market?

3) Are all my health insurance needs met by my or my spouse's employee family health policy?

4) If I am covered by a group policy, is it fully convertible to an individual policy so I am covered by health insurance at all times?

5) Do I have the proper mix of basic coverage and major medical coverage?

6) Is the policy fully renewable?

7) Is my whole family covered from birth?

8) What are the pre-existing condition limitations?

9) Does my policy pay for today's full cost of hospital room-and-board charges?

10) Have I investigated prepaid health plans, such as HMOs, that might suit my needs best?

5

Auto Insurance

In practically every state in the union, you can't drive unless you have some type of auto insurance. As a matter of fact, driving without insurance is considered a crime in some states. If you are a driver, it's obviously one of your most important insurance decisions.

Essentially, there are no great differences in auto policies from company to company. There are, however, big differences in how much you pay for an auto insurance policy.

The following factors determine the cost of premiums you pay for the policy you want:

□ The type of car you drive. Since a smaller car will have more damage done to it in an accident than a larger car, the smaller car will cost you more in premiums if you have collision insurance.

□ The age of the car. As soon as you drive a car out of the showroom, it has already depreciated in value. *Auto insurers will never pay you more than the "book value" of your car.* The older the car, the less valuable it is, hence the lower the premium.

□ Your driving record. This is probably the most important factor in determining the premium you will pay. If you haven't been in an accident in 20 years, you will pay less for insurance than the average person. A driver who regularly causes accidents or gets a great number of traffic tickets will pay more than average.

□ Where you live. All auto insurers divide cities, states and towns into rate-making territories based on the experience of all the drivers and auto owners in that vicinity. Since, if your area has a higher incidence of car theft than a neighboring area, your premium for theft insurance will be higher.

☐ How much coverage you want. For lots of coverage you will have to pay more. In every state, you must carry a minimum amount of coverage according to law, but many people prefer to increase that coverage to protect themselves from large losses.

☐ The amount of deductible. If you think that you can pay the costs of repairing you car after minor damage, say one that costs $300, then you should take that for your deductible. Every driver must decide what costs he or she is willing to assume. Remember, the higher the deductible, the lower the premium.

Book Value

As mentioned earlier, no matter how much insurance you have or want, an auto insurer will never pay more than the *market,* or *book,* value of your car. This value is the present value according to publicly known standards. These standards are published in books detailing those values. The two books most companies use are the *NADA Official Used Car Guide* and the *Kelley Blue Book.* They are available at most libraries, lending institutions and used-car dealers.

Market value includes a charge for depreciation and general wear and tear. Different cars may depreciate at different rates. Consult the books to determine the value of your car at any time.

Policy Terminations

If you are unable to get auto insurance, or if your policy is terminated even though you have paid the premium and are still willing to do so, the reason is undoubtedly your driving record. Many companies will also automatically terminate a policyholder convicted of driving while intoxicated (DWI). If you have a number of moving violations within a short space of time, you may be terminated as well.

Different companies have different rules as to who is

terminated and who isn't. If one company terminates you or turns you down, another one may take you on. Your agent should be able to help you find coverage somewhere.

As a last resort, there is the uninsured motorist pool coverage most states have for drivers unable to get coverage elsewhere. Sometimes called *assigned risk,* these pools charge their policyholders higher premiums than regular insurance policies because these people are higher risk drivers than average. If your driving record improves, you may be able to get regular coverage again, but you will have to shop around.

Some companies have a reputation for terminating people after one small accident. To check a company's termination record, call your state insurance department. The department can probably give you specific information about a company's performance and service. Check with the state department before you finally settle on any one policy.

Types of Coverage

No matter which company you buy from, the standard auto insurance policy contains seven types of coverage. It is important that you understand what you are covered for *before* you start paying premiums for auto insurance.

In alphabetical order, these coverages are:

Bodily Injury Liability

Under this coverage, you are protected if you negligently cause an accident that injures or kills another person. The insurance company will pay for the legal costs and any legal liability that you may be responsible for. Because of the real possibility of a high jury award against you, this coverage is a necessity.

Collision Coverage

This portion of your auto coverage pays for the cost of repairing damage to your own car. That damage could be caused by your hitting another automobile, a tree, a telephone pole, etc. When a collision occurs that was not your fault, you make a claim to your company. They will normally pay you the full amount of the damages, minus any deductible you carry.

If the accident was not your fault, your company must then try to collect from the other person's insurance company or from the driver if he or she is not insured. If your company is successful in collecting from the other party or the other party's insurance company, you may even get your deductible back.

Since the chances of a collision occurring are significantly higher than your injuring or killing somebody, collision coverage constitutes the major component of your auto insurance premium.

Again, since the insurer will never pay you more than the current market value of your car, there can come a point when what you will recover from the insurance company will be closer to the premiums it costs to insure the car. When this happens, you can drop collision coverage.

That point, in most cases, is five years. This recommendation is based on the fact that a car depreciates to about one third its purchase price in five years. If you buy a car for $15,000, five years later the market value of your car would be around $5,000 or less. If you were to get into a wreck that would cause $11,000 worth of damage to fix, you would only get the $5,000 book value of the car and be out of pocket $6000 if you decide to have the car fixed.

Many drivers, instead of dropping collision coverage altogether on a car five years or older, will cut back on the amount of collision they hold. This is normally done by increasing your deductible. Remember, the higher the deductible, the lower the premium. If dropping collision altogether scares you, at least increase the deductible. That will save you some money.

Comprehensive Coverage

Comprehensive is sometimes called *other than collision coverage*. Since so many non-accident related things can also happen to a car, it is a necessity that you have comprehensive coverage. Comprehensive coverage includes, theft, glass breakage, damage from vandalism or from fire, flood or other Acts of God.

If your car is stolen or damaged, it is the value of your car at the time that determines the amount of your recovery. Some companies will also pay you for costs incurred in getting substitute transportation, such as a rental car, for a specific period of time.

Medical Payments Coverage

This portion of auto insurance pays for all doctor and related hospital bills that come about as the result of an accident, *no matter who is at fault*. Not only are your medical bills covered, but so are those of your passengers, regardless of who they are.

Note that if you are injured while riding in someone else's car, that person's insurance will pay for your medical bills. But, if your bills exceed the amount of that person's coverage, your own auto insurance would pay the excess amount up to the limit of your coverage.

Property Damage Liability

This portion of the typical auto insurance policy pays for your damage if you are at fault in causing damage to another driver's car or other property. For instance, if you were found responsible for an accident that totaled another car, your insurance would pay for the market value of that car. If the driver was carrying valuables in the car that were damaged or destroyed, the insurance would pay for those losses as well.

Underinsured Motorists Coverage

This covers you in situations where even though another negligent driver is insured, the injuries and property damage suffered by you exceed the limits of his or her policy. At that point your coverage would take over.

This is normally considered an optional type of coverage. It is vital, however, that every driver include it in his or her own policy. Most drivers will only comply with the minimum legal requirements of coverage. If you have an accident and don't have Underinsured Coverage, you could find yourself paying out of your own pocket for injuries and damage that were not your fault.

Uninsured Motorists Coverage

Some people drive without coverage, even if doing so is against the law. You could have an accident with an uninsured motorist, so you might need this kind of coverage. This provision also covers you if you are the victim of a hit-and-run accident.

It is not strictly necessary that you carry all seven parts of the typical auto insurance policy. For example, if your car is 10 years old, collision and comprehensive are not necessary. All you will get from the insurance company is the market value of the car.

Similarly, if you have health and disability coverage, you might consider doing away with the underinsured motorists coverage portion of the policy.

All companies allow you to drop and add coverage as needed with a resultant change in the premium. If the coverage is broadened, the premium will go up. Less coverage lowers premiums.

If you are employed and your employer provides you with good health and major medical coverage, you may be able to cut down on medical payments coverage. This is a prime example of an overlapping coverage that, if eliminated, can save you money on your overall insurance outlay.

In addition, if you live in a state with no-fault auto insurance, you don't need medical payments coverage. This is already covered under no-fault provisions. Further discussion follows.

No-Fault Auto Insurance

Many states have a *no-fault* insurance system. Although the details vary from state to state, essentially no-fault provides that the insured's company will pay for all losses incurred in an accident. Each company pays no matter who was at fault in causing the accident.

This system is intended to cut down on the number of lawsuits started to determine who was actually at fault in an accident. Under this system, the insurance carriers ascertain between themselves who was at fault. They settle their financial differences after paying their policyholders.

In states where no-fault laws exist, drivers are restricted from suing another driver. Exactly what those limitations are is spelled out in the laws of each state affected. So far, the system seems to have worked in paring down the number of auto-related lawsuits.

Regardless of whether you live in a no-fault state, the seven basic coverages found in the typical auto insurance policy work the same. No-fault just affects lawsuits.

For the most part, no-fault pertains to physical injuries and medical expenses, normally not to property damage. As a result, you can limit the amount of bodily injury liability you cover. You should carry the maximum amount of property damage liability that you can afford.

Remember, if you carry collision coverage, damage to your own car is covered. Property damage liability covers the cost of repairing damage to another person's automobile.

No-fault claims are paid very quickly, usually within 30 days after the necessary paperwork is completed. If you make a claim and you haven't gotten your money within that period, check with the insurer to find out what the problem is. If you don't get any satisfaction from them, carry your complaint to the state insurance department.

Some Cars May Be Uninsurable

As with companies offering life insurance, auto insurers can also pick and choose the customers they want. If a company doesn't like the car you drive, or if you live in a high-crime area, no insurer has to insure you. If you can find a company that will insure you, you may pay up to three times the average cost for your coverage.

For example, many insurers will not insure Jeep Cherokees because the companies believe these vehicles turn over very easily if not driven properly. The claims rate on Jeep Cherokees has been so high that few insurers will cover them.

Similarly, few companies will insure a Corvette because that car (no matter which year) is a particular favorite of thieves. A number of other high-powered sports cars fall into the same category.

Since auto buyers almost always must have insurance, such "rejects" are put into the assigned risk pool in their state. These assigned risk people pay from two to three times as much for insurance as their non-assigned risk friends and neighbors.

If you are a savvy auto buyer, you will check out the "insurability" of the automobile you are going to purchase before you complete the deal. Although insurability should not be your final criterion as to which car you might buy, it should definitely be part of your thinking.

Auto insurance companies determine part of the premium's cost on where your car is located most of the time. That means where it is "garaged." If you do a good deal of driving in high-crime, primarily urban areas, but your car can be garaged out of town, do that. You will cut down the cost of your premium.

Auto Insurance Discounts

Not all auto policies will give all the discounts mentioned here. But by shopping around and asking the right questions, you may find policies with many of these discounts. Of course you should fit your particular needs to the discount. Here are available discounts:

Good driving record. What constitutes a good driving record varies from insurer to insurer. If you or any member of your family has an unblemished driving history, you are certainly eligible for a discount ranging from 5% to 30%, depending on the company. A small fender-bender 10 years ago may count against you with some companies. With others it won't. It's important then for you to determine the company's definition of a good driving record. One company may be more liberal in this regard than another. As a result, you may qualify for a good driver discount with one insurer and not with another.

Multicar discount. If you have more than one car and insure them with the same company, you can almost always get a 5% to 25% discount.

Mature age discounts. Drivers who are 50 years of age or older probably qualify for a discount with most insurers. With some the age is 55, with others 60 or 65. The discount can be as much as 20%.

Installation of anti-theft devices. Sirens, alarms, and certain types of devices that lock up the steering wheel may get you a discount from 5% to 30% on the comprehensive part of your coverage. Ask your insurer or your agent what kinds of devices qualify for discounts. Be sure the cost of the device is more than offset by the premium savings over the life of the car.

Driver training and defensive driving courses. If you have ever taken driver education, or a course in defensive driving, each course may be worth as much as a 10% discount to you. Don't take these courses just to qualify for the discounts. Take them because you want to become a better driver. Remember, the best discounts are given to the best drivers. If these courses allow you to become a better driver, you will benefit from them in the long run in lowered auto premium costs.

Restricted mileage. If you drive 7500 miles or less each year, most insurance companies will give you a discount because you are on the road less. Consequently there is less chance of your being in an accident.

Car pools. The same reasoning holds true for drivers who use their cars once or twice a week as a car pool vehicle and don't drive to work in that same car the rest of the week.

Passive seat belts and air bags. If your car is equipped with operable passive seat belts (the kind that automatically belt you in when you turn on the ignition or close the door) or airbags, you may get a 10% to 20% discount from a number of insurers.

A "safe" car. Certain car models are better made or are cheaper to fix than others, so they rate a discount. (The latest up-to-date rating of safe cars starts on page 172.) The cost of insurance should be a factor in your ultimate buying decision about a particular model of automobile.

Some states mandate a discount of up to 10% for automobiles equipped with "crash proof" bumpers. These bumpers can withstand low speed collisions, usually up to 10 mph.

Non-smokers. Some insurers give non-smokers a break on auto insurance by including a small discount of up to 5% for those who don't light up. Insurers feel that smokers who reach for the auto lighter or an ash tray could lose their concentration and be more likely to cause an accident.

Rural location. If you live on a farm, rural or low-traffic area, some companies will give a discount because your chances for an accident are considerably reduced.

If your teenager is driving your car and you are covering him or her with your policy, the following discounts should be checked out.

Good student discount. If your youngster has a B average, or better, in school, the chances are a discount can be obtained.

Driver training. If your teen driver has completed an approved state driver's education course, such as one offered at most high schools, another discount will usually be given.

Restricted driving. If your teenager drives your car less than 15% of its total annual mileage, you may get a discount from certain insurers.

College. If your son or daughter is more than 100 miles from home in college and is not driving your car while there, a discount will undoubtedly be given.

Proper Coverage

Virtually every state requires that every driver in that state have auto insurance of a minimum amount. The minimums are usually expressed in terms of "split limits." For example, the state may mandate that for residents of their state, all drivers must have at least *10/20/5*. These figures specify different amounts of coverage, as follows:

□ The first figure represents $10,000. It is the maximum a driver must be insured for the liability of injuring one person in one accident. Or, it indicates the maximum amount that the insurance company will pay for injuries to any one person who might be injured, in this example $10,000.

□ The second number stands for $20,000 and refers to the maximum amount the company will pay if two or more people are injured.

□ The third number represents $5,000 of property damage that is covered for in the event of an accident. This usually involves damage to another car.

Know the minimums you must carry. If you are at fault, and you must pay, your insurer will only pay for those minimums you have. *You* are responsible for paying any amount that exceeds the minimum.

Juries often award huge amounts to the victims of auto accidents these days. So every driver, especially those with substantial assets to protect, should undoubtedly purchase auto insurance with much higher minimums. As with all forms of insurance, the higher the amount of protection, the higher the premium.

It is very common and most desirable these days to buy auto insurance with bodily injury liability limits of $100,000 to $300,000—or even more. And since cars are expensive, you should also have a higher property damage liability limit. $50,000 should cover you fully.

It is also a good idea to add umbrella coverage for liability of to $1,000,000 or more.

Buy as much insurance as you can afford, and supplement it with an umbrella policy. If you take advantage of all the available discounts, and you maintain a good driving record, your auto insurance premiums need not be overwhelming.

Umbrella Coverage

For the benefits you get, *umbrella policies are the best buy in insurance today.* These relatively cheap policies raise your liability coverage to a million dollars or more, and are available as additions to your auto or homeowners policies.

Liability insurance protects you from paying a high legal award that might be assessed against you by a jury. For example, if you have injured someone in an auto accident and you are found negligent in a court of law, the jury could award a judgement against you of hundreds of thousands of dollars. Liability insurance makes that payment the insurance company's responsibility.

(cont.)

Suppose that you have auto insurance of 100/300/50 (for more see Chapter 5), which is quite common today. That means that if you are sued and must pay as the result of an auto accident, the insurance company will only pay up to $300,000 for bodily injuries to two or more people. However, with juries routinely awarding much more than that to accident victims, many people—especially those with a large number of assets or a business to protect—need higher coverages to insulate them from the possibility of a high jury award.

The umbrella policy does just that. For an additional $100 or so annually, you can be protected up to $1,000,000 or more for liability. There are umbrella policies available that offer protection up to $5,000,000 for those who really think they need it.

Before you buy umbrella coverage, most companies require that you have either $100,000 worth of liability coverage on your home or $300,000 worth of liability protection on your car. In most situations, $100 or so will buy you $1,000,000 worth of coverage.

An umbrella policy increases your liability coverage. It is not necessary to buy an umbrella that covers auto liability and another that covers your homeowners. It's all combined in one policy.

Even though you can probably buy an umbrella policy from either your auto or homeowner's insurer at a discount, you may get even a better deal elsewhere on an umbrella. Shop around for the best umbrella coverage you can find.

Umbrella policies then, provide a cushion against large negligence awards that could wipe you out financially. The same company that sells you your homeowners or auto policy will probably also offer umbrella coverage. If you purchase your auto and homeowners policies from the same company, you may be able to buy an umbrella policy that will cover both at a discount.

Model and Type of Car

Collision coverage pays for damage to your car in the event of an accident. A large portion of your premium payment goes towards collision protection. But not everybody pays the same for this collision coverage. It also depends on the make and model of the car being covered.

It's a fact that some cars are better made than others and can withstand the effects of a collision better than others. As a rule, the larger the car, the less the damage that will be done. Hence the less money spent on repairs.

Insurance carriers can only go by the history of a certain event before they can determine a premium. If a certain make and model of automobile is less costly to repair than another, your premium will be less than if you owned the flimsier car.

All auto insurers use the same data gathered by the Highway Loss Data Institute in Washington, D.C. Reproduced here is the August 1985 report based on crash data from 1982 to 1984 model autombiles sold in the U.S.

A high deductible will cut down on your auto premiums substantially. But if you are insuring a relatively "crashworthy" auto, you can also expect to pay less for your auto insurance. You might want to take that fact into consideration before you buy any new or used car.

Highway Loss Data Institute
Injury & Collision Loss Experience

How To Use This Information

The Highway Loss Data Institute (HLDI) is a nonprofit, public service organization. It is closely associated with and funded through the Insurance Institute for Highway Safety. HLDI gathers, processes, and publishes data on the ways insurance losses vary among different kinds of vehicles.

The listings summarize the recent insurance injury and collision loss experience of passenger cars. Results are based on the loss experience of 1982-84 cars. Most popular car models are listed, but some are not because there are relatively few of them on U.S. highways and hence, insufficient insurance coverage, or "exposure," data to obtain reliable results.

Injury losses are presented in terms of frequency of insurance claims filed under Personal Injury Protection (PIP) coverage. Two measures of injury losses are presented—overall and severe:

1) The *overall injury loss* result for a particular car model is the frequency of all medical claims filed under PIP coverage, regardless of the magnitude of the losses.

2) The *severe injury loss* result represents the frequency of claims for paid medical losses exceeding $500. (For some cars, no severe injury loss result is shown because of insufficient data to compute this figure.)

Collision losses are presented in terms of average loss payments per insured vehicle year.

All losses are stated in *relative terms,* with 100 representing the result for all cars in each loss category—overall injury, severe injury, and collision. Thus, an injury or collision result of 122 is 22% higher (worse) than average. A result of 96 is 4% lower (better) than average. Cars are listed within each body style and size group in ascending sequence of their overall injury claim frequency result.

The results are adjusted or standardized to eliminate possible distortions due to two non-vehicle factors: operator age and deductible amount.

The injury and collision loss experience of the cars shown in the table is based on model years 1982-84 but provides a good prediction of the experience of current models of the same cars. This is because the loss experience of particular cars generally is consistent from one model year to another. However, in some cases completely new or redesigned cars models are given the same series name as earlier, discontinued models.

The listings show very wide variations in the injury and collision loss experience of various vehicles on the nation's highways. Many of the cars with the worst injury results have claim frequencies double those of many of the vehicles with the best experience.

Most of the cars with the best overall results (injury and collision) are larger station wagons, passenger vans, and four-door models.

The cars with the worst overall results (injury and collision) are small, two-door models, predominantly Japanese imports. Small sports and specialty models tend to have especially bad collision results, but most do not have particularly bad injury results.

Station Wagons/Passenger Vans

	Overall Injury	Severe Injury	Collision
Small			
Volkswagen Vanagon	73		67
Mercury Lynx	83		68
Toyota Tercel 4WD	91		75
Ford Escort	95	92	72
Subaru DL/GL 4WD	98	101	118
Subaru DL/GL	100	95	97
Nissan Sentra	108	109	87
Midsize			
Volvo 240	56	43	93
American Eagle 30	69	65	54
Ford LTD	76		70
Oldsmobile Firenza	80		61
Chevrolet Celebrity	83		62
Dodge Aries	91	80	69
Plymouth Reliant	93	77	68
Pontiac 2000	94		79
Chevrolet Cavalier	94	88	70
Chrysler Le Baron	95		91
Nissan Maxima	100		106
Large			
Oldsmobile Custom Cruiser	54	47	83
Buick Electra	59		98
Dodge Caravan	63		51
Plymouth Voyager	67		46
Chevrolet Caprice	69	60	68
Mercury Grand Marquis	69		79
Ford Crown Victoria	70		89

Four-Door Cars

	Overall Injury	Severe Injury	Collision
Small			
Saab 900	71		139
Honda Accord	89	85	104
Volkswagen Rabbit	92	75	100
Volkswagen Jetta	97	91	102
Mazda 626	100	85	107
Nissan Stanza	107	93	104
Dodge Omni	114	102	92
Renault Alliance	114	117	101
Ford Escort	117	112	87
Plymouth Horizon	118	104	89
Mercury Lynx	120	116	96
Toyota Corolla	122	131	89
Subaru DL/GL Sedan	125	130	112
Toyota Tercel	127	122	87
Mazda GLC	130	120	121
Pontiac 1000	139	135	95
Isuzu T-Car/I-Mark	140		103
Chevrolet Chevette	143	151	91
Dodge Colt	144		119
Nissan Sentra	145	152	101
Mitsubishi Tredia	155		122
Plymouth Colt	156		114
Midsize			
Chrysler E Class	75		78
Oldsmobile Cutlass	76	68	67
Buick Regal	79	74	71
Pontiac Bonneville	80	76	65
Mercury Topaz	81		82
Pontiac 6000	85	86	80

	Overall Injury	Severe Injury	Collision
Mercury Marquis	86	91	79
Dodge 600	86		81
Oldsmobile Ciera	86	80	81
Chrysler New Yorker	87	98	78
Buick Century	87	86	89
Chrysler Le Baron	88	83	74
Volvo 240	89	93	123
Ford LTD	89	86	80
Peugeot 505	91		139
Toyota Camry	91	89	73
Toyota Cressida	92	111	120
Buick Skylark	92	87	81
Cadillac Cimarron	93	105	97
Chevrolet Celebrity	94	89	74
Chevrolet Citation	94	91	74
Audi 4000	96		154
Oldsmobile Omega	98	92	71
Ford Tempo	100	101	77
Pontiac Phoenix	101		62
Pontiac 2000	109	102	88
Dodge Aries	111	110	80
Plymouth Reliant	112	97	76
Chevrolet Cavalier	112	119	80
Oldsmobile Firenza	113		75
Buick Skyhawk	113	101	85
Nissan Maxima	121	129	115

Large

	Overall Injury	Severe Injury	Collision
Oldsmobile Delta 88	59	53	62
Buick Le Sabre	62	59	64
Oldsmobile Ninety Eight	62	73	66
Mercury Grand Marquis	65	68	61
Buick Electra	66	67	70
Chevrolet Caprice	68	69	66
Ford Crown Victoria	68	78	61
Chry. New Yorker 5th Ave.	69	77	75

	Overall Injury	Severe Injury	Collision
Dodge Diplomat	72		56
Chevrolet Impala	79	79	75
Plymouth Gran Fury	101		77

Two-Door Cars

Small

	Overall Injury	Severe Injury	Collision
Saab 900	70		138
Honda Accord	102	97	116
Nissan Stanza	105		105
Volkswagen Rabbit	106	104	133
Mazda 626	106		149
Volkswagen Scirocco	108		187
Mazda GLC	110	120	107
Honda Prelude	114	119	145
Honda Civic	115		115
Subaru Hardtop	117	123	132
Renault Fuego	118		203
Toyota Celica	120	125	126
Dodge Daytona	122		158
Subaru Hatchback	125		100
Plymouth Horizon	128	123	127
Chrysler Laser	128		128
Toyota Tercel	129	121	95
Ford Escort	130	133	98
Renault Encore	130		103
Dodge Charger	132	124	133
Mercury Lynx	137	134	99
Nissan Sentra	137	136	113
Renault Alliance	138	137	112
Toyota Starlet	148		98
Plymouth Colt	148	154	134
Dodge Colt	149	160	122
Mitsubishi Cordia	151		186
Chevrolet Chevette	154	162	101
Pontiac 1000	155	161	123
Nissan Pulsar	158	162	144

	Overall Injury	Severe Injury	Collision
Midsize			
Oldsmobile Cutlass	88	93	91
Buick Regal	90	93	85
Oldsmobile Ciera	91	82	90
Pontiac Grand Prix	92	98	95
Oldsmobile Omega	92		87
Pontiac 6000	94		110
Buick Skylark	94	89	86
Chevrolet Monte Carlo	98	111	103
Chrysler Le Baron	99	99	85
Ford Thunderbird	100	98	118
Buick Century	100	98	106
Volvo 240	104		145
Dodge 400/600	105		92
Chevrolet Celebrity	107	101	80
Dodge Aries	109	100	89
Mercury Cougar	109	122	126
Chevrolet Citation	111	102	91
Pontiac Phoenix	112		82
Pontiac 2000	118	103	105
Ford Tempo	118		94
Plymouth Reliant	119	115	88
Buick Skyhawk	123	116	99
Oldsmobile Firenza	123		96
Chevrolet Cavalier	126	126	94
Large			
Ford Crown Victoria	65		67
Buick Le Sabre	70	90	66
Oldsmobile Delta 88	70	76	72
Oldsmobile Ninety Eight	71		76
Mercury Grand Marquis	76		63
Chevrolet Caprice	77		50
Buick Electra	81		75

Sports & Specialty Cars

	Overall Injury	Severe Injury	Collision
Small			
Mercedes-Benz 380SL Coupe	57		176
Chevrolet Corvette	63		157
Porsche 944 Coupe	71		226
Nissan 300ZX	100		236
VW Rabbit Convertible	102		112
Mazda RX-7	104	101	164
Pontiac Fiero	119		117
Ford EXP	124	129	122
Midsize			
Lincoln Continental	72		118
BMW 528e/533i	74		162
Audi 5000 4D	79		157
BMW 318i/325e	81		206
Chrysler Le Baron Conv.	87		100
Ford Mustang Convertible	98		103
Toyota Celica Supra	102	106	158
Pontiac Firebird	107	108	167
Mercury Capri	114	109	138
Chevrolet Camaro	116	123	155
Ford Mustang	127	128	149
Large			
Mercedes Benz 300SD/380SE	60		142
Jaguar XJ6	63		189
Mercedes-Benz 300D	64		121
Oldsmobile Toronado	65	62	89
Cadillac De Ville 4D	67	84	94
Cadillac Eldorado	71	78	112
Lincoln Town Car	72	84	103
Buick Riviera	73	83	85
Cadillac Brougham 4D	75	90	91
Cadillac Seville	76	87	122
Cadillac De Ville 2D	81	95	99

Picking an Auto Insurer

Your choice of an auto insurer should not be based just on the cost of the premiums. Service, reliability and termination experience (the number of policyholders the company terminates due to accidents or volume of claims) are just as vital as price.

You will no doubt find that there is not much difference in premiums between companies. Direct writers, such as Allstate or Nationwide, which sell directly to the public through their own salespeople, may be somewhat cheaper.

A policy from a company that sells through independent agents or brokers will probably be a bit higher, because a commission charge is added to the price. Because so many discounts and deductible choices are available, you should not pay the full premium price. However, be sure to ask about and cover fully all the discounts you are eligible for.

Some auto insurers sell very cheap insurance through the mail. You should evaluate those policies the same way you would any other.

Because most auto policies must be renewed on an annual basis, you can always change after one year.

Auto Insurance Riders You Don't Need

Extra coverages are expensive and probably unnecessary. You can probably do without:

Stolen Radio Coverage

An expensive sound system stolen from your car can be costly to replace, but the cost of adding that coverage to your auto policy is not worth the extra premium.

Towing Coverage

Again the cost is not worth the additional outlay. Joining the American Automobile Association (AAA) and getting cheaper towing is more economical than adding a rider to your auto insurance. If you have comprehensive coverage, the costs of towing a car may already be included.

Medical Payments Coverage

As discussed earlier, if you are already covered by health insurance, you probably don't need this optional coverage.

Rental Car Coverage

If you are in an accident and your car cannot be driven for some period of time, some riders pay the cost of renting another car while yours is being repaired. Check the comprehensive portion of your policy. If it is not already included there, you should consider whether you truly need it or not. For example, if you can easily borrow another car while yours is in the shop or if you can use a company car for a short time, this coverage is probably innecessary.

Accidental Death Insurance

This rider is certainly unnecessary if you have life insurance. Your life insurance policy will pay your family whether you die as a result of an accident.

Weekly Disability

This benefit is not needed if you already have a disability insurance policy that covers you if you become disabled as a result of an accident.

About Teenage Drivers

Auto insurance premiums are calculated on the basis of all drivers in your family. If you have a teenager, you know that your auto premium can double or triple once your teen starts driving. Even so, young women have a better history of driving safely, so coverage for female teenage drivers cost less than for male teen drivers.

Besides the discounts available previously mentioned for

teenage drivers, here are some other tips you will find useful if your family includes a teenage driver.

☐ If the teenager uses your car instead of owning one individually, the cost of insurance will be less.

☐ Limit the teenager's access to your car. If the teen drives your car less than 20% of the time it is actually in use, the insurance carrier will probably give you a break. On the other hand, if your teenager is the principal driver of a car registered in his or her own name, that auto insurance will be the most expensive.

☐ Some adults who own their businesses and own company cars allow their children to use the company cars when they are not being driven for business purposes. There will be no rate increase at all under those circumstances, *but the business can be sued* if the teenager has an accident while driving a company car. You will have to decide for yourself if that risk is worth the cost of not having to pay any additional insurance premium on the youngster.

How to Make an Auto Insurance Claim

Instead of waiting until an accident strikes you or your family, save time, money and anxiety by doing three important things *now*:

1) Look through your policies to see what is and isn't covered. The coverages and exclusions in your insurance policies can differ significantly from those of your friends. The best advice is to understand your policies *before* you have a claim. You should know the following:

☐ How much liability insurance you have. This coverage pays for damage you cause to another vehicle or injuries to other people.

☐ Whether your state has no-fault insurance. If so, what coverages does it provide?

☐ Your deductible if you have collision, comprehensive or both.

2) Ask your local insurance agent or company representative to explain anything you don't understand.

3) Read the following information to learn exactly what steps to follow when you have a claim.

At the Scene

Taking the time *now* to review the steps you should follow after an auto accident will help reduce the anxiety surrounding the incident and help you avoid costly and time-consuming mistakes.

1) Stop your car and get help for the injured. Have someone call the police or highway patrol. Tell them how many people were injured and the types of injuries. The police can then notify the nearest medical unit.

Give whatever help you can to the injured but avoid moving anyone so you don't aggravate the injury. Covering an injured person with a blanket and making that person comfortable usually is as much as you can do.

2) Provide the police with whatever information they require. Also ask the investigating officer where you can obtain a copy of the police report, which you may need to support any claim you submit to your insurance company.

3) Try to protect the accident scene. Take reasonable steps to protect your car from further damage, such as setting up flares, getting the car off the road and calling a tow truck. If necessary, have the car towed to a repair shop. *Failure to do this will probably result in your claim being completely refused.* But remember, your insurance company probably will want to have an adjuster inspect it and appraise the damage before you order repair work done.

4) Make notes. Keep a pad and pencil in your glove compartment. Write down the names and addresses of all drivers and passengers involved in the accident. Also note

the license number, make and model of each car involved and record the driver's license number and insurance identification of each driver.

Record the names and addresses of as many witnesses as possible, as well as the names and badge numbers of police officers or other emergency personnel. If you run into an unattended vehicle or object, try to find the owner. If you can't, leave a note containing your name, address and phone number.

Filing Your Claim

If your car is involved in an accident, if it is damaged by fire, flood or vandalism, or if it is stolen, put your insurance to work for you by following these steps in filing your claim:

1) Phone your insurance agent or local company representative. Do it as soon as possible even if you're far from home and even if someone else caused the accident. Ask your agent how to proceed and what forms or documents will be needed to support your claim. Your company may require a "proof of loss" form, as well as documents relating to your claim, such as medical and auto repair bills and a copy of the police report.

2) Supply the information your insurer needs. Cooperate with your insurance company in its investigation, settlement or defense of any claim, and turn over to the company immediately copies of any legal papers you receive in connection with your loss. Your insurer will represent you if a claim is brought against you and defend you if you are sued.

3) Keep records of your expenses. Expenses you incur as a result of an automobile accident may be reimbursed under your policy. Remember, for example, that your no-fault insurer usually will pay your medical and hospital expenses, and possibly such other costs as lost wages and at least part of your costs if you have to hire a temporary housekeeper.

4) Keep copies of your paperwork. Store copies of all paperwork in your own files. You may need to refer to it later.

Little-Known Facts About Auto Insurance

◻ Auto insurance is for a specific automobile. Anybody who is authorized or given permission to drive that car, in or out of your immediate household, is covered by your insurance. If your best friend should borrow your car with your permission and he or she would be involved in an accident with it, your insurance would pay just as if you were the driver.

◻ An insurance agent with the designation *CPCU* next to his or her name is a Certified Property and Casualty Underwriter and as such is an expert on Automobile insurance. This representative should have a good understanding of what policies are available and which discounts you may qualify for.

◻ If you want to sue another driver for being at fault in an auto accident, your auto insurance *will not* pay your legal fees. Your insurance only covers you if *you* are sued.

◻ The insurance law in many states prohibits an insurance carrier from cancelling your auto insurance after the insured makes one claim.

Claim Denial

If your claim for recompense under any insurance policy is denied by an insurance company, you are entitled to be told of the exact nature of the denial. This is where a competent insurance agent can be most helpful. Claim denials can be changed. If your agent is working on the case, a previously denied claim may be turned around.

If you are a policyholder of long standing, you probably stand a better chance of getting the denial reversed than if you are a short-term policyholder who has filed a claim before. Never having filed a claim before may help, too.

If your insurance agent can do nothing for you, you can always complain to your state insurance department. The department may be able to resolve the problem.

Some states have certain procedures that must be followed in making a complaint concerning an insurance claim. Be sure to follow those. In some cases, arbitration may be the answer. Whatever the procedure, it is the duty of the state insurance department to protect the rights of its insurance consumers.

Credit Insurance

When you go to your local car dealer to buy a new car, or when you apply for a loan at a bank, you may be given or offered something called *credit life insurance*. You may also be subjected to a sales pitch for credit accident and health insurance and/or credit disability insurance.

The pitch is the same no matter what type of insurance is being sold. If you should die or become incapacitated, this insurance will pay off your car or loan. You won't be saddled with that debt. You probably don't need this coverage. Besides, it's extremely expensive.

If you have planned your life insurance properly, part of the proceeds of that policy could be used to pay off any existing debts you had. If you already have health and disability insurance, you will have taken all of your debts into consideration when you bought your policy, so no additional coverage, is needed.

Recent press reports have shown that many unwary car buyers and personal loan applicants have had these premium payments factored right into the cost of the loan without being told. So remember, if you have planned your insurance program properly, you do not need an expensive credit or creditor life insurance policy.

Questions to Ask
When Buying Auto Insurance

1) Have I shopped around for the best auto insurance I can find?

2) Have I taken advantage of all discounts that are available?

3) Have I determined properly what kind of deductible I should take?

4) Do I need collision coverage?

5) Have I checked my other coverage to see whether I can cut down on medical payments or liability?

6) Do I have umbrella coverage in case of a very large lawsuit against me?

7) Can I garage my car elsewhere to cut down on my auto premium?

8) Before buying a new car, have I checked what it will cost to insure?

9) Do I know how to make a claim properly under the insurance policy I have?

10) Does my state have "no-fault" insurance? If so, do I know the limitations on it?

Sample Auto Insurance Policy

Immediately following is a sample automobile insurance policy supplied by the Insurance Information Institute. It is written in plain English and is easy to understand. Read through it to get a good idea of what such a policy is like.

PERSONAL AUTO POLICY

SPACE FOR COMPANY NAME, INSIGNIA, AND LOCATION

NOTE:

The Policy Declarations are shown on page 3.

The "Liability" and "Uninsured Motorists" coverages in the Policy provide for a "single" limit of liability. These coverages can be provided with a "split" limit of liability by application of the endorsements on page 17.

THESE POLICY PROVISIONS WITH THE DECLARATIONS PAGE AND ENDORSEMENTS, IF ANY, ISSUED TO FORM A PART THEREOF, COMPLETE THIS POLICY.

BJP8054-3-C (Ed. 8-83)

PP 00 01 (Ed. 6-80)/PP 00 03 (Ed. 8-83)

YOUR PERSONAL AUTO POLICY—QUICK REFERENCE

DECLARATIONS PAGE

Your Name and Address
Your Auto or Trailer
Policy Period
Coverages and Amounts of Insurance

Auto Insurance

```
NAME OF COMPANY

PERSONAL AUTO POLICY
DECLARATIONS
```

Renewal of Number

No. PA
Named Insured and Mailing Address (No., Street, Apt., Town or City, County, State, Zip Code)

Policy Period:
From: To: 12:01 A.M. Standard Time

Description of Auto(s) or Trailer(s)

AUTO	Year	Trade Name — Model	VIN	Symbol	Age
1					
2					
3					
4					

The Auto(s) or Trailer(s) described in this policy is principally garaged at the above address unless otherwise stated:
(No., Street, Apt., Town or City, County, State, Zip Code)

Coverage is provided where a premium and a limit of liability are shown for the coverage.

Coverages	Limit of Liability	Premium Auto 1	Auto 2	Auto 3	Auto 4
A. Liability	$ each accident	$	$	$	$
A. Liability					
Bodily Injury	$ each person / $ each accident	$	$	$	$
Property Damage	$ each accident	$	$	$	$
B. Medical Payments	$ each person	$	$	$	$
C. Uninsured Motorists	$ each accident	$	$	$	$
C. Uninsured Motorists	$ each person / $ each accident	$	$	$	$
D. Damage to your Auto 1. Collision Loss	Actual Cash Value minus $ Deductible	$	$	$	$
2. Other than Collision Loss	$ Deductible	$	$	$	$
Towing and Labor Costs	$ each disablement	$	$	$	$
		$	$	$	$

Endorsements made part of this Policy at time of issue:

Endorsement Premium $

Total Premium Per Auto	$	$	$

Total Premium $

Loss Payee (Name and address)

Countersigned:

By_____
Authorized Representative

THIS DECLARATIONS PAGE WITH PERSONAL AUTO POLICY PROVISIONS OR POLICY JACKET AND PERSONAL AUTO POLICY FORM, TOGETHER WITH ENDORSEMENTS, IF ANY, ISSUED TO FORM A PART THEREOF, COMPLETES THE ABOVE NUMBERED POLICY.

Includes copyrighted material of Insurance Services Office, with its permission.
Copyright, Insurance Services Office, 1979

JDL8054-2-B (Ed. 6-80)

190

PERSONAL AUTO POLICY

AGREEMENT

In return for payment of the premium and subject to all the terms of this policy, we agree with you as follows:

DEFINITIONS

Throughout this policy, "you" and "your" refer to:

1. The "named insured" shown in the Declarations; and
2. The spouse if a resident of the same household.

"We", "us" and "our" refer to the Company providing this insurance.

For purposes of this policy, a private passenger type auto shall be deemed to be owned by a person if leased:

1. Under a written agreement to that person; and
2. For a continuous period of at least 6 months.

Other words and phrases are defined. They are boldfaced when used.

"Family member" means a person related to you by blood, marriage or adoption who is a resident of your household. This includes a ward or foster child.

"Occupying" means in, upon, getting in, on, out or off.

"Trailer" means a vehicle designed to be pulled by a:

1. Private passenger auto; or
2. Pickup, panel truck, or van.

It also means a farm wagon or farm implement while towed by a vehicle listed in 1. or 2. above.

"Your covered auto" means:

1. Any vehicle shown in the Declarations.
2. Any of the following types of vehicles on the date you become the owner:
   a. a private passenger auto; or
   b. a pickup, panel truck or van.

This provision applies only if:

   a. you acquire the vehicle during the policy period;
   b. you ask us to insure it within 30 days after you become the owner; and
   c. with respect to a pickup, panel truck or van, no other insurance policy provides coverage for that vehicle.

If the vehicle you acquire replaces one shown in the Declarations, it will have the same coverage as the vehicle it replaced. You must ask us to insure a replacement vehicle within 30 days only if:

   a. you wish to add or continue Coverage for Damage to Your Auto; or
   b. it is a pickup, panel truck or van used in any business or occupation, other than farming or ranching.

If the vehicle you acquire is in addition to any shown in the Declarations, it will have the broadest coverage we now provide for any vehicle shown in the Declarations.

3. Any **trailer** you own.
4. Any auto or **trailer** you do not own while used as a temporary substitute for any other vehicle described in this definition which is out of normal use because of its:

   a. breakdown;   c. servicing;   e. destruction.
   b. repair;   d. loss; or

Page 1

191

PART A—LIABILITY COVERAGE

INSURING AGREEMENT

We will pay damages for bodily injury or property damage for which any **covered person** becomes legally responsible because of an auto accident. We will settle or defend, as we consider appropriate, any claim or suit asking for these damages. In addition to our limit of liability, we will pay all defense costs we incur. Our duty to settle or defend ends when our limit of liability for this coverage has been exhausted.

"Covered person" as used in this Part means:

1. You or any **family member** for the ownership, maintenance or use of any auto or **trailer.**

2. Any person using **your covered auto.**

3. For **your covered auto,** any person or organization but only with respect to legal responsibility for acts or omissions of a person for whom coverage is afforded under this Part.

4. For any auto or **trailer,** other than **your covered auto,** any person or organization but only with respect to legal responsibility for acts or omissions of you or any **family member** for whom coverage is afforded under this Part. This provision applies only if the person or organization does not own or hire the auto or **trailer.**

SUPPLEMENTARY PAYMENTS

In addition to our limit of liability, we will pay on behalf of a **covered person:**

1. Up to $250 for the cost of bail bonds required because of an accident, including related traffic law violations. The accident must result in bodily injury or property damage covered under this policy.

2. Premiums on appeal bonds and bonds to release attachments in any suit we defend.

3. Interest accruing after a judgment is entered in any suit we defend. Our duty to pay interest ends when we offer to pay that part of the judgment which does not exceed our limit of liability for this coverage.

4. Up to $50 a day for loss of earnings, but not other income, because of attendance at hearings or trials at our request.

5. Other reasonable expenses incurred at our request.

EXCLUSIONS

A. We do not provide Liability Coverage for any person:

1. Who intentionally causes bodily injury or property damage.

2. For damage to property owned or being transported by that person.

3. For damage to property:

a. rented to;

b. used by; or

c. in the care of;

that person.

This exclusion does not apply to damage to:

a. a residence or private garage; or

b. any of the following type vehicles not owned by or furnished or available for the regular use of you or any **family member:**

(1) private passenger autos;

(2) **trailers;** or

(3) pickups, panel trucks, or vans.

4. For bodily injury to an employee of that person during the course of employment. This exclusion does not apply to bodily injury to a domestic employee unless workers' compensation benefits are required or available for that domestic employee.

5. For that person's liability arising out of the ownership or operation of a vehicle while it is being used to carry persons or property for a fee. This exclusion does not apply to a share-the-expense car pool.

6. While employed or otherwise engaged in the business or occupation of:

   a. selling;   c. servicing;   e. parking;

   b. repairing;   d. storing; or

   vehicles designed for use mainly on public highways. This includes road testing and delivery. This exclusion does not apply to the ownership, maintenance or use of **your covered auto** by:

   a. you;

   b. any **family member;** or

   c. any partner, agent or employee of you or any **family member.**

7. Maintaining or using any vehicle while that person is employed or otherwise engaged in any business or occupation (other than farming or ranching) not described in Exclusion 6. This exclusion does not apply to the maintenance or use of a:

   a. private passenger auto;

   b. pickup, panel truck or van that you own; or

   c. **trailer** used with a vehicle described in a. or b. above.

8. Using a vehicle without a reasonable belief that that person is entitled to do so.

9. For bodily injury or property damage for which that person:

   a. is an insured under a nuclear energy liability policy; or

   b. would be an insured under a nuclear energy liability policy but for its termination upon exhaustion of its limit of liability.

   A nuclear energy liability policy is a policy issued by any of the following or their successors:

   a. Nuclear Energy Liability Insurance Association;

   b. Mutual Atomic Energy Liability Underwriters; or

   c. Nuclear Insurance Association of Canada.

10. For liability assumed under any contract or agreement for loss or damage in excess of $1,000 to any vehicle:

    a. rented to;   o. in the care of;

    b. used by; or

    that person. This exclusion does not apply to damages for which a person is legally responsible, other than by contract or agreement.

B. We do not provide Liability Coverage for the ownership, maintenance or use of:

   1. Any motorized vehicle having less than four wheels.

   2. Any vehicle, other than **your covered auto,** which is:

      a. owned by you; or

      b. furnished or available for your regular use.

   3. Any vehicle, other than **your covered auto,** which is:

      a. owned by any **family member;** or

      b. furnished or available for the regular use of any **family member.**

   However, this exclusion does not apply to your maintenance or use of any vehicle which is:

      a. owned by a **family member;** or

      b. furnished or available for the regular use of a **family member.**

LIMIT OF LIABILITY The limit of liability shown in the Declarations for this coverage is our maximum limit of liability for all damages resulting from any one auto accident. This is the

Page 3

most we will pay regardless of the number of:

1. **Covered persons;**
2. Claims made;
3. Vehicles or premiums shown in the Declarations; or
4. Vehicles involved in the auto accident.

We will apply the limit of liability to provide any separate limits required by law for bodily injury and property damage liability. However, this provision will not change our total limit of liability.

OUT OF STATE COVERAGE

If an auto accident to which this policy applies occurs in any state or province other than the one in which **your covered auto** is principally garaged, we will interpret your policy for that accident as follows:

If the state or province has:

1. A financial responsibility or similar law specifying limits of liability for bodily injury or property damage higher than the limit shown in the Declarations, your policy will provide the higher specified limit.

2. A compulsory insurance or similar law requiring a nonresident to maintain insurance whenever the nonresident uses a vehicle in that state or province, your policy will provide at least the required minimum amounts and types of coverage.

No one will be entitled to duplicate payments for the same elements of loss.

FINANCIAL RESPONSIBILITY REQUIRED

When this policy is certified as future proof of financial responsibility, this policy shall comply with the law to the extent required.

OTHER INSURANCE

If there is other applicable liability insurance we will pay only our share of the loss. Our share is the proportion that our limit of liability bears to the total of all applicable limits. However, any insurance we provide for a vehicle you do not own shall be excess over any other collectible insurance.

PART B—MEDICAL PAYMENTS COVERAGE

INSURING AGREEMENT

We will pay reasonable expenses incurred for necessary medical and funeral services because of bodily injury:

1. Caused by accident; and
2. Sustained by a **covered person.**

We will pay only those expenses incurred within 3 years from the date of the accident.

"Covered person" as used in this Part means:

1. You or any **family member:**
   a. while **occupying;** or
   b. as a pedestrian when struck by;
   a motor vehicle designed for use mainly on public roads or a trailer of any type.
2. Any other person while **occupying your covered auto.**

EXCLUSIONS

We do not provide Medical Payments Coverage for any person for bodily injury:

1. Sustained while **occupying** any motorized vehicle having less than four wheels.

2. Sustained while **occupying your covered auto** when it is being used to carry persons or property for a fee. This exclusion does not apply to a share-the-expense car pool.

3. Sustained while **occupying** any vehicle located for use as a residence or premises.

4. Occurring during the course of employment if workers' compensation benefits are required or available for the bodily injury.

Page 4

194

5. Sustained while **occupying** or, when struck by, any vehicle (other than **your covered auto**) which is:

   a. owned by you; or

   b. furnished or available for your regular use.

6. Sustained while **occupying** or, when struck by, any vehicle (other than **your covered auto**) which is:

   a. owned by any **family member**; or

   b. furnished or available for the regular use of any **family member.**
   However, this exclusion does not apply to you.

7. Sustained while **occupying** a vehicle without a reasonable belief that that person is entitled to do so.

8. Sustained while **occupying** a vehicle when it is being used in the business or occupation of a **covered person.** This exclusion does not apply to bodily injury sustained while **occupying** a:

   a. private passenger auto;

   b. pickup, panel truck, or van that you own; or

   c. **trailer** used with a vehicle described in a. or b. above.

9. Caused by or as a consequence of:

   a. discharge of a nuclear weapon   c. civil war;
      (even if accidental);   d. insurrection; or

   b. war (declared or undeclared);   e. rebellion or revolution.

10. From or as a consequence of the following, whether controlled or uncontrolled or however caused:

    a. nuclear reaction;   c. radioactive contamination.

    b. radiation; or

LIMIT OF LIABILITY

The limit of liability shown in the Declarations for this coverage is our maximum limit of liability for each person injured in any one accident. This is the most we will pay regardless of the number of:

1. **Covered persons;**   3. Vehicles or premiums shown in the Declarations; or

2. Claims made;   4. Vehicles involved in the accident.

Any amounts otherwise payable for expenses under this coverage shall be reduced by any amounts paid or payable for the same expenses under Part A or Part C.

No payment will be made unless the injured person or that person's legal representative agrees in writing that any payment shall be applied toward any settlement or judgment that person receives under Part A or Part C.

OTHER INSURANCE

If there is other applicable auto medical payments insurance we will pay only our share of the loss. Our share is the proportion that our limit of liability bears to the total of all applicable limits. However, any insurance we provide with respect to a vehicle you do not own shall be excess over any other collectible auto insurance providing payments for medical or funeral expenses.

PART C—UNINSURED MOTORISTS COVERAGE

INSURING AGREEMENT

We will pay damages which a **covered person** is legally entitled to recover from the owner or operator of an **uninsured motor vehicle** because of bodily injury:

1. Sustained by a **covered person;** and

2. Caused by an accident.

The owner's or operator's liability for these damages must arise out of the ownership, maintenance or use of the **uninsured motor vehicle.**

Any judgment for damages arising out of a suit brought without our written consent is not binding on us.

Page 5

195

"Covered person" as used in this Part means:

1. You or any **family member.**

2. Any other person **occupying your covered auto.**

3. Any person for damages that person is entitled to recover because of bodily injury to which this coverage applies sustained by a person described in 1. or 2. above.

"Uninsured motor vehicle" means a land motor vehicle or trailer of any type:

1. To which no bodily injury liability bond or policy applies at the time of the accident.

2. To which a bodily injury liability bond or policy applies at the time of the accident. In this case its limit for bodily injury liability must be less than the minimum limit for bodily injury liability specified by the financial responsibility law of the state in which **your covered auto** is principally garaged.

3. Which is a hit and run vehicle whose operator or owner cannot be identified and which hits:

    a. you or any **family member;**

    b. a vehicle which you or any **family member** are **occupying;** or

    c. **your covered auto.**

4. To which a bodily injury liability bond or policy applies at the time of the accident but the bonding or insuring company:

    a. denies coverage; or

    b. is or becomes insolvent.

However, **"uninsured motor vehicle"** does not include any vehicle or equipment:

1. Owned by or furnished or available for the regular use of you or any **family member.**

2. Owned or operated by a self-insurer under any applicable motor vehicle law.

3. Owned by any governmental unit or agency.

4. Operated on rails or crawler treads.

5. Designed mainly for use off public roads while not on public roads.

6. While located for use as a residence or premises.

EXCLUSIONS

A. We do not provide Uninsured Motorists Coverage for bodily injury sustained by any person:

1. While **occupying,** or when struck by, any motor vehicle owned by you or any **family member** which is not insured for this coverage under this policy. This includes a trailer of any type used with that vehicle.

2. If that person or the legal representative settles the bodily injury claim without our consent.

3. While **occupying your covered auto** when it is being used to carry persons or property for a fee. This exclusion does not apply to a share-the-expense car pool.

4. Using a vehicle without a reasonable belief that that person is entitled to do so.

B. This coverage shall not apply directly or indirectly to benefit any insurer or self-insurer under any of the following or similar law:

1. workers' compensation law; or

2. disability benefits law.

LIMIT OF LIABILITY

The limit of liability shown in the Declarations for this coverage is our maximum limit of liability for all damages resulting from any one accident. This is the most we will pay regardless of the number of:

1. **Covered persons;**

2. Claims made;
3. Vehicles or premiums shown in the Declarations; or
4. Vehicles involved in the accident.

Any amounts otherwise payable for damages under this coverage shall be reduced by all sums:

1. Paid because of the bodily injury by or on behalf of persons or organizations who may be legally responsible. This includes all sums paid under Part A; and

2. Paid or payable because of the bodily injury under any of the following or similar law:

   a. workers' compensation law; or
   b. disability benefits law.

Any payment under this coverage will reduce any amount that person is entitled to recover for the same damages under Part A.

OTHER INSURANCE

If there is other applicable similar insurance we will pay only our share of the loss. Our share is the proportion that our limit of liability bears to the total of all applicable limits. However, any insurance we provide with respect to a vehicle you do not own shall be excess over any other collectible insurance.

ARBITRATION

If we and a **covered person** do not agree:

1. Whether that person is legally entitled to recover damages under this Part; or
2. As to the amount of damages;

either party may make a written demand for arbitration. In this event, each party will select an arbitrator. The two arbitrators will select a third. If they cannot agree within 30 days, either may request that selection be made by a judge of a court having jurisdiction. Each party will:

1. Pay the expenses it incurs; and
2. Bear the expenses of the third arbitrator equally.

Unless both parties agree otherwise, arbitration will take place in the county in which the **covered person** lives. Local rules of law as to procedure and evidence will apply. A decision agreed to by two of the arbitrators will be binding as to:

1. Whether the **covered person** is legally entitled to recover damages; and

2. The amount of damages. This applies only if the amount does not exceed the minimum limit for bodily injury liability specified by the financial responsibility law of the state in which **your covered auto** is principally garaged. If the amount exceeds that limit, either party may demand the right to a trial. This demand must be made within 60 days of the arbitrators' decision. If this demand is not made, the amount of damages agreed to by the arbitrators will be binding.

PART D—COVERAGE FOR DAMAGE TO YOUR AUTO

INSURING AGREEMENT

We will pay for direct and accidental loss to **your covered auto**, including its equipment, minus any applicable deductible shown in the Declarations. However, we will pay for loss caused by **collision** only if the Declarations indicate that Collision Coverage is provided.

"**Collision**" means the upset, or collision with another object of **your covered auto**. However, loss caused by the following are not considered "collision":

1. Missiles or falling objects;
2. Fire;
3. Theft or larceny;
4. Explosion or earthquake;
5. Windstorm;
6. Hail, water or flood;
7. Malicious mischief or vandalism;
8. Riot or civil commotion;
9. Contact with bird or animal; or
10. Breakage of glass.

If breakage of glass is caused by a **collision,** you may elect to have it considered a loss caused by **collision.**

Page 7

197

TRANSPORTATION EXPENSES

In addition, we will pay up to $10 per day, to a maximum of $300, for transportation expenses incurred by you. This applies only in the event of the total theft of **your covered auto**. We will pay only transportation expenses incurred during the period:

1. Beginning 48 hours after the theft; and
2. Ending when **your covered auto** is returned to use or we pay for its loss.

EXCLUSIONS

We will not pay for:

1. Loss to **your covered auto** which occurs while it is used to carry persons or property for a fee. This exclusion does not apply to a share-the-expense car pool.
2. Damage due and confined to:
   a. wear and tear;
   b. freezing;
   c. mechanical or electrical breakdown or failure; or
   d. road damage to tires.

This exclusion does not apply if the damage results from the total theft of **your covered auto.**

3. Loss due to or as a consequence of:
   a. radioactive contamination;
   b. discharge of any nuclear weapon (even if accidental);
   c. war (declared or undeclared)·
   d. civil war;
   e. insurrection; or
   f. rebellion or revolution.
4. Loss to equipment designed for the reproduction of sound. This exclusion does not apply if the equipment is permanently installed in **your covered auto.**
5. Loss to tapes, records or other devices for use with equipment designed for the reproduction of sound.
6. Loss to a camper body or **trailer** not shown in the Declarations. This exclusion does not apply to a camper body or **trailer** you:
   a. acquire during the policy period; and
   b. ask us to insure within 30 days after you become the owner.
7. Loss to any vehicle while used as a temporary substitute for a vehicle you own which is out of normal use because of its:
   a. breakdown;
   b. repair;
   c. servicing;
   d. loss; or
   e. destruction.
8. Loss to:
   a. TV antennas;
   b. awnings or cabanas; or
   c. equipment designed to create additional living facilities.
9. Loss to any of the following or their accessories:
   a. citizens band radio;
   b. two-way mobile radio;
   c. telephone; or
   d. scanning monitor receiver.

This exclusion does not apply if the equipment is permanently installed in the opening of the dash or console of the auto. This opening must be normally used by the auto manufacturer for the installation of a radio.

Page 8

198

10. Loss to any custom furnishings or equipment in or upon any pickup, panel truck or van. Custom furnishings or equipment include but are not limited to:

    a. special carpeting and insulation, furniture, bars or television receivers;

    b. facilities for cooking and sleeping;

    c. height-extending roofs; or

    d. custom murals, paintings or other decals or graphics.

LIMIT OF LIABILITY

Our limit of liability for loss will be the lesser of the:

1. Actual cash value of the stolen or damaged property; or

2. Amount necessary to repair or replace the property.

PAYMENT OF LOSS

We may pay for loss in money or repair or replace the damaged or stolen property. We may, at our expense, return any stolen property to:

1. You; or

2. The address shown in this policy.

If we return stolen property we will pay for any damage resulting from the theft. We may keep all or part of the property at an agreed or appraised value.

NO BENEFIT TO BAILEE

This insurance shall not directly or indirectly benefit any carrier or other bailee for hire.

OTHER INSURANCE

If other insurance also covers the loss we will pay only our share of the loss. Our share is the proportion that our limit of liability bears to the total of all applicable limits.

APPRAISAL

If we and you do not agree on the amount of loss, either may demand an appraisal of the loss. In this event, each party will select a competent appraiser. The two appraisers will select an umpire. The appraisers will state separately the actual cash value and the amount of loss. If they fail to agree, they will submit their differences to the umpire. A decision agreed to by any two will be binding. Each party will:

1. Pay its chosen appraiser; and

2. Bear the expenses of the appraisal and umpire equally.

We do not waive any of our rights under this policy by agreeing to an appraisal.

PART E—DUTIES AFTER AN ACCIDENT OR LOSS

GENERAL DUTIES

We must be notified promptly of how, when and where the accident or loss happened. Notice should also include the names and addresses of any injured persons and of any witnesses.

A person seeking any coverage must:

1. Cooperate with us in the investigation, settlement or defense of any claim or suit.

2. Promptly send us copies of any notices or legal papers received in connection with the accident or loss.

3. Submit, as often as we reasonably require, to physical exams by physicians we select. We will pay for these exams.

4. Authorize us to obtain:

    a. medical reports; and

    b. other pertinent records.

5. Submit a proof of loss when required by us.

ADDITIONAL DUTIES FOR UNINSURED MOTORISTS COVERAGE

A person seeking Uninsured Motorists Coverage must also:

1. Promptly notify the police if a hit and run driver is involved.

2. Promptly send us copies of the legal papers if a suit is brought.

Page 9

ADDITIONAL DUTIES FOR COVERAGE FOR DAMAGE TO YOUR AUTO

A person seeking Coverage for Damage to Your Auto must also:

1. Take reasonable steps after loss to protect **your covered auto** and its equipment from further loss. We will pay reasonable expenses incurred to do this.
2. Promptly notify the police if **your covered auto** is stolen.
3. Permit us to inspect and appraise the damaged property before its repair or disposal.

PART F—GENERAL PROVISIONS

BANKRUPTCY

Bankruptcy or insolvency of the **covered person** shall not relieve us of any obligations under this policy.

CHANGES

This policy contains all the agreements between you and us. Its terms may not be changed or waived except by endorsement issued by us. If a change requires a premium adjustment, we will adjust the premium as of the effective date of change.

We may revise this policy form to provide more coverage without additional premium charge. If we do this your policy will automatically provide the additional coverage as of the date the revision is effective in your state.

LEGAL ACTION AGAINST US

No legal action may be brought against us until there has been full compliance with all the terms of this policy. In addition, under Part A, no legal action may be brought against us until:

1. We agree in writing that the **covered person** has an obligation to pay; or
2. The amount of that obligation has been finally determined by judgment after trial.

No person or organization has any right under this policy to bring us into any action to determine the liability of a **covered person**.

OUR RIGHT TO RECOVER PAYMENT

A. If we make a payment under this policy and the person to or for whom payment was made has a right to recover damages from another we shall be subrogated to that right. That person shall do:

1. Whatever is necessary to enable us to exercise our rights; and
2. Nothing after loss to prejudice them.

However, our rights in this paragraph do not apply under Part D, against any person using **your covered auto** with a reasonable belief that that person is entitled to do so.

B. If we make a payment under this policy and the person to or for whom payment is made recovers damages from another, that person shall:

1. Hold in trust for us the proceeds of the recovery; and
2. Reimburse us to the extent of our payment.

POLICY PERIOD AND TERRITORY

This policy applies only to accidents and losses which occur:

1. During the policy period as shown in the Declarations; and
2. Within the policy territory.

The policy territory is:

1. The United States of America, its territories or possessions;
2. Puerto Rico; or
3. Canada.

This policy also applies to loss to, or accidents involving, **your covered auto** while being transported between their ports.

TERMINATION

Cancellation. This policy may be cancelled during the policy period as follows:

1 The named insured shown in the Declarations may cancel by:
   a. returning this policy to us; or
   b. giving us advance written notice of the date cancellation is to take effect.

Page 10

200

2. We may cancel by mailing to the named insured shown in the Declarations at the address shown in this policy:

   a. at least 10 days notice:

   (1) if cancellation is for nonpayment of premium; or

   (2) if notice is mailed during the first 60 days this policy is in effect and this is not a renewal or continuation policy; or

   b. at least 20 days notice in all other cases.

3. After this policy is in effect for 60 days, or if this is a renewal or continuation policy, we will cancel only:

   a. for nonpayment of premium; or

   b. if your driver's license or that of:

   (1) any driver who lives with you; or

   (2) any driver who customarily uses **your covered auto;**

   has been suspended or revoked. This must have occurred:

   (1) during the policy period; or

   (2) since the last anniversary of the original effective date if the policy period is other than 1 year.

Nonrenewal. If we decide not to renew or continue this policy, we will mail notice to the named insured shown in the Declarations at the address shown in this policy. Notice will be mailed at least 20 days before the end of the policy period. If the policy period is other than 1 year, we will have the right not to renew or continue it only at each anniversary of its original effective date.

Automatic Termination. If we offer to renew or continue and you or your representative do not accept, this policy will automatically terminate at the end of the current policy period. Failure to pay the required renewal or continuation premium when due shall mean that you have not accepted our offer.

If you obtain other insurance on **your covered auto,** any similar insurance provided by this policy will terminate as to that auto on the effective date of the other insurance.

Other Termination Provisions.

1. If the law in effect in your state at the time this policy is issued, renewed or continued:

   a. requires a longer notice period;

   b. requires a special form of or procedure for giving notice; or

   c. modifies any of the stated termination reasons;

   we will comply with those requirements.

2. We may deliver any notice instead of mailing it. Proof of mailing of any notice shall be sufficient proof of notice.

3. If this policy is cancelled, you may be entitled to a premium refund. If so, we will send you the refund. The premium refund, if any, will be computed according to our manuals. However, making or offering to make the refund is not a condition of cancellation.

4. The effective date of cancellation stated in the notice shall become the end of the policy period.

TRANSFER OF YOUR INTEREST IN THIS POLICY
Your rights and duties under this policy may not be assigned without our written consent. However, if a named insured shown in the Declarations dies, coverage will be provided for:

1. The surviving spouse if resident in the same household at the time of death. Coverage applies to the spouse as if a named insured shown in the Declarations; or

2. The legal representative of the deceased person as if a named insured shown

Page 11

In the Declarations. This applies only with respect to the representative's legal responsibility to maintain or use **your covered auto.**

Coverage will only be provided until the end of the policy period.

TWO OR MORE AUTO POLICIES	If this policy and any other auto insurance policy issued to you by us apply to the same accident, the maximum limit of our liability under all the policies shall not exceed the highest applicable limit of liability under any one policy.

In Witness Whereof, we have caused this policy to be executed and attested, and, if required by state law, this policy shall not be valid unless countersigned by our authorized representative.

INSERT SIGNATURES AND
TITLES OF PROPER OFFICERS

PP 03 05 (Ed. 8-83)
LOSS PAYABLE CLAUSE

A 1373
(Ed. 8-83)

Loss Payee:

Loss or damage under this policy shall be paid, as interest may appear, to you and the loss payee shown in the Declarations or in this endorsement. This insurance with respect to the interest of the loss payee, shall not become invalid because of your fraudulent acts or omissions unless the loss results from your conversion, secretion or embezzlement of **your covered auto.** However, we reserve the right to cancel the policy as permitted by policy terms and the cancellation shall terminate this agreement as to the loss payee's interest. We will give the same advance notice of cancellation to the loss payee as we give to the named insured shown in the Declarations.

When we pay the loss payee we shall, to the extent of payment, be subrogated to the loss payee's rights of recovery.

This endorsement must be attached to the Change Endorsement when issued after the policy is written.

Copyright, Insurance Services Office, 1983

A 1373
(Ed. 8-83)

PP 03 03 (Ed. 8-83)
TOWING AND LABOR COSTS COVERAGE

A 1372
(Ed. 8-83)

SCHEDULE

DESCRIPTION OF YOUR COVERED AUTO	LIMIT OF TOWING AND LABOR COSTS COVERAGE	PREMIUM
	$	$
	$	$
	$	$

We will pay towing and labor costs incurred each time **your covered auto** is disabled, up to the amount shown in the Schedule or in the Declarations as applicable to that vehicle. We will only pay for labor performed at the place of disablement.

This endorsement must be attached to the Change Endorsement when issued after the policy is written.

Copyright, Insurance Services Office, 1983

A 1372
(Ed. 8-83)

A 1065
(Ed. 6-80)

PP 03 04 (Ed. 6-80)
COVERAGE FOR TAPES, RECORDS OR OTHER DEVICES

Additional Premium: $

The provisions and exclusions that apply to Part D also apply to this endorsement except Exclusion 5 and any deductible.

We will pay for direct and accidental loss to tapes, records or other devices used with sound reproduction equipment. This coverage applies only if the tapes, records, or other devices:

  1. Are your property or that of a **family member;** and
  2. At the time of loss are in **your covered auto.**

The limit of our liability for all losses as a result of any one occurrence shall not exceed $200.

This endorsement must be attached to the Change Endorsement when issued after the policy is written.

Copyright, Insurance Services Office, 1979

A 1065
(Ed. 6-80)

PP 03 09 (Ed. 6-80)
A 1069
(Ed. 6-80)

SPLIT LIABILITY LIMITS

SCHEDULE

Bodily Injury Liability	$_____ each person
	$_____ each accident
Property Damage Liability	$_____ each accident

The first paragraph of the Limit of Liability provision in Part A is replaced by the following:

LIMIT OF LIABILITY

The limit of liability shown in the Schedule or in the Declarations for "each person" for Bodily Injury Liability is our maximum limit of liability for all damages for bodily injury sustained by any one person in any one auto accident. Subject to this limit for "each person", the limit of liability shown in the Schedule or in the Declarations for "each accident" for Bodily Injury Liability is our maximum limit of liability for all damages for bodily injury resulting from any one auto accident. The limit of liability shown in the Schedule or in the Declarations for "each accident" for Property Damage Liability is our maximum limit of liability for all damages to all property resulting from any one auto accident. This is the most we will pay regardless of the number of:

1. **Covered persons;**
2. Claims made;
3. Vehicles or premiums shown in the Declarations; or
4. Vehicles involved in the auto accident.

This endorsement must be attached to the Change Endorsement when issued after the policy is written.

Copyright, Insurance Services Office, 1979

A 1069
(Ed. 6-80)

A 1085
(Ed. 6-80)

PP 04 01 (Ed. 6-80)

SPLIT UNINSURED MOTORISTS LIMITS

SCHEDULE

Uninsured Motorists Coverage	$_____ each person
	$_____ each accident

The first paragraph of the Limit of Liability provision in Part C is replaced by the following:

LIMIT OF LIABILITY

The limit of liability shown in the Schedule or in the Declarations for "each person" for Uninsured Motorists Coverage is our maximum limit of liability for all damages for bodily injury sustained by any one person in any one accident. Subject to this limit for "each person", the limit of liability shown in the Schedule or in the Declarations for "each accident" for Uninsured Motorists Coverage is our maximum limit of liability for all damages for bodily injury resulting from any one accident. This is the most we will pay regardless of the number of:

1. **Covered persons;**
2. Claims made;
3. Vehicles or premiums shown in the Declarations; or
4. Vehicles involved in the accident.

This endorsement must be attached to the Change Endorsement when issued after the policy is written.

Copyright, Insurance Services Office, 1979

A 1085
(Ed. 6-80)

6

Homeowners Insurance

When most people think of homeowners insurance they automatically think of fire insurance to protect their homes. Yet homeowners insurance covers much more than fires. Homeowners, like auto insurance, is really a package of coverages. It covers you for the loss of your personal possessions and belongings anywhere in the world. If you were to go on a vacation, for example, and your camera was stolen, your homeowners insurance would cover its loss.

This insurance also covers your legal liability in case someone should sue you for something that occurred on your property. If the postal worker should fall over your child's wagon on your porch and sustain extensive injuries, your homeowners coverage would protect you in a lawsuit up to the designated limits of the policy. Standard liability coverage is $25,000, hardly enough to meet today's normal liability needs.

Because juries are awarding huge sums in liability cases, you'd be wise to carry at least $100,000 in liability under the liability portion. You can get more liability coverage if you wish, but it will cost you more. And, in case of a gigantic award, a $1 million umbrella is a necessity.

Since your home is probably your biggest asset, no doubt you will want to insure it against a catastrophic loss. Fire is the most common calamity that homeowners insurance covers. If you have full coverage for all your personal possessions in the home, and a burglar robs your home, you will be covered for those losses.

You can see that homeowners insurance is a broad based package of coverages. You pay for the package with one premium. Besides offering a package of coverages, homeowners policies cover the liability of all members of your family, as well as your pets. If one of your children should hit another child and cause injury, your child would be covered under the homeowners policy, provided your child is under 21 and living at home.

Similarly, if your dog should bite your neighbor, your policy would pay any medical bills incurred by the neighbor. Property damage is also covered. If, for example, you were to borrow your neighbor's expensive, new riding lawn mower and ruin it, your policy would pay for the cost of replacing it.

Two perils that are not covered under any homeowners policy are earthquake and flood damage. Special policies are available from the federal government for individuals who want to protect their homes and possessions from loss in the event of those calamities. Any competent insurance agent will be able to tell you about and obtain earthquake or flood insurance if you need it.

Types of Coverage

Homeowners policies cover four main areas of exposure:

1) Damage to your home and any other structures on your property such as a garage and/or a tool shed.

2) Liability for which you are found responsible in most situations in all parts of the world. If a claim is filed against you for causing a person injury or damage to property, your homeowners liability will pay for all expenses and legal awards up to the limit of the policy.

3) Damage to all of your personal property, with some exceptions, such as your car.

4) Living expenses if your home is rendered uninhabitable due to fire or other covered peril. This coverage includes the payment of hotel bills and restaurant tabs for you and your family until you can move back into your home. This is sometimes called *loss of use coverage*.

One coverage that many people don't realize they have under a homeowners policy is coverage for the loss of credit cards. If your credit cards are lost or stolen, most policies cover that loss.

With all credit cards, if someone else charges on your card without your authorization, you are only liable for $50 worth of charges, even if you have no credit card insurance. If you have a homeowners policy, you are protected for even that $50. Therefore, if you have homeowners insurance, you don't need separate coverage for credit cards. You can then ignore the solicitation of credit card protection bureaus.

How Much Coverage?

Since your home is the largest asset covered by homeowners insurance, it is the focal point for determining how much coverage you need. You need to insure your home for not its market value, but for its *replacement value*.

The market value of your home is what you could get for it if you sold it today. That figure includes the land the house is on, sidewalks and driveways and any other things that cannot burn up in a fire.

Replacement cost, on the other hand, is the amount that it would cost you to fully replace that same house today. Replacement cost is a much more difficult dollar amount to estimate. It is particularly difficult if your home is an older home with special fixtures, such as chandeliers or specialized built-ins.

By definition, replacement value is a figure that is less than the market value. If you were to hire an appraiser, that individual should ask if the appraisal is for real estate or for insurance purposes. A real estate appraisal includes all the grounds, together with other factors concerning recent sales of comparable homes. For an insurance appraisal just your home is appraised.

You need not, however, insure your home for 100% of its replacement value. To collect the full replacement cost, you need to insure the home for no more than 80% of its replacement cost. For example, if the replacement cost of your home is $100,000 today, you only have to insure it for $80,000 to gain a full recovery from the insurance company.

Why only 80%? Few fires or other casualties cause 100% damage. Usually, a much smaller amount of damage is done and that's what you are protecting against. For that reason, most insurance companies recommend and most people obtain 80% coverage.

This doesn't mean that you can't get coverage for 100% of the replacement value. But the extra cost of the premium probably isn't worth the risk of total destruction. Coverage at 80% satisfies the needs of the great majority of homeowners. But you must have 80% coverage. If you have less than 80% coverage, you will not recover the full cost of even a partial loss.

Here's why: Suppose the replacement value of your home is $100,000 and you have it covered for up to $50,000, or 50% of your home's replacement value. If a fire does $25,000 worth of damage to your house, your insurance would only pay 50% of the amount or $12,500. If you had the 80% coverage, you would get back the entire $25,000.

It is especially important to insure up to the replacement cost if you are a new homeowner. When people buy a house, they often make the very big mistake of insuring the house for only the amount of the mortgage. They forget that they may already have a good deal of equity in the house in the form of the down payment they put in to buy it.

Buying a $100,000 house, for example, may require a 15% down payment. That's $15,000. If you insure the house for only the $80,000 and a fire totally destroys the home, you have essentially lost your down payment.

Also, If you remodel your home, you should also take a new look at your homeowner's insurance. In most cases, remodeling will increase the replacement value of your home.

Therefore, if you insured your $100,000 house for $100,000, you would get $100,000 for a total loss of the house. You would also be paid $50,000 for the lose of its contents, $10,000 if an unattached structure was totally destroyed, and $20,000 in additional living expenses. Your total recovery would be $180,000.

If you carried 50% of full replacement value, all your other coverages are cut in half. You would receive

$25,000 for the contents,

$5,000 for an unattached garage,

$10,000 in additional living expenses.

Your total recovery would be $90,000.

Remember, when you buy homeowners insurance, you are purchasing a package of coverages. That means you can choose the amounts of coverage you want for each item. If the contents of your home are only worth $20,000, you can insure them for that amount and no more.

Your premium is, of course, pegged to the amount of coverage that you want. If you have lower coverages than the standard, you will pay less in premiums.

On the other hand, if you have contents worth more than standard coverage, you'll pay higher premiums. You should essentially design your own homeowners insurance package to suit your needs. A competent insurance agent can help you assess your real needs and get what you want.

Many insurers offer *inflation guard* policies. These policies increase your coverage automatically as inflation increases. The increases are based on rises in the Consumer Price Index or some other common measure of inflation. When your coverage increases, your premiums will be raised.

Because the inflation guard operates automatically, it is not necessary for the policyholder to contact the insurer each and every year to increase the value of his or her coverage. The necessary adjustments are made annually by the insurer.

A Vital Preparatory Step

Homeowners insurance is based on the value of your home and your personal possessions. The most important thing you can do is to get an accurate assessment of the true value of these items. That way you can insure them properly.

Determining exactly what you have is just as important as how much it is worth. Surprisingly, many people don't know what they own after a disaster strikes. They aren't paid for items forgotten, so they lose money.

This potential problem is easily solved. Before you buy your first, or your next, homeowners insurance policy, *prepare a household inventory complete with pictures and detailed information about all of your valuables, including your furniture and furnishings, along with antiques and important collectibles.* Still photos are fine, but a videotape is better.

This information and the pictures or tape should, of course, be stored in a fireproof safe deposit box away from your home. That way if there should be a fire or other serious calamity, you will have an accurate and up-to-date list of all your household items. Make one or two copies of the pictures or tape as well as the written information. Leave one copy of each with your insurance agent and the other with a relative or attorney.

Similarly, your house itself should be appraised each time you renew your policy. The worst mistake you can make is to underinsure your home. If you don't have a good idea of its value at all times, you could lose a lot in the event of fire.

Besides having your home appraised, you might want to have its contents appraised as well. If you have antiques, works of art or other valuables you want to insure, have them appraised as well.

Appraisals cost money, but that shouldn't stop you from making sure you have the proper coverage. And when you have appraisals performed for insurance purposes, those fees are fully deductible under present tax laws.

Once you know what your house and its contents are worth, then you will be able to accurately determine how much homeowners insurance you need.

To aid you in making appraisal determinations, you should keep copies of receipts and other sales information whenever you buy an item of some value that will be placed in the home.

Documentary proof of value is always the best. No insurance company will dispute the worth of an item when you have written proof of what you paid for it. There might be some dispute as to the wholesale and retail price of an item, but since insurance recoveries are mainly based on replacement value, retail value is usually an acceptable measure.

Keep the written and visual records of your possessions away from your home, and do the same thing with receipts and other price documentation. A bank or credit union safe deposit box is a logical choice.

Getting Coverage

Homeowners and auto insurance are similar in the way the product is priced. First, companies establish rating territories. The same policy will cost more in some territories; less in others. A company's loss experience is a major factor in premium determination from year to year. And for homeowners insurance a number of factors are considered by the insurance company before determines how much you'll have to pay for coverage. For example:

□ If your house is built of brick or stone rather than wood, your premium will be lower.

□ If you live in a rural area, where the fire department is far away, you may have to pay more than the individual whose home is closer to fire protection.

□ Also, if your home is far from a usable source of water, your premium cost will probably be higher. It may take longer to put out a fire on your property.

▢ If you live in an urban area with a high crime rate, you may have to pay an enormous sum for homeowners insurance—if you can get it at all. Because the insurance company feels it assuming a higher-than-normal risk, your premiums are higher than normal.

If You Are Denied Coverage

Because of a property's location some individuals are denied coverage. Because no insurance company can be forced to take you, some states have provided for an assigned risk pool for homeowners insurance. Just about every state has an assigned risk or FAIR plan for automobile insurance, but fewer offer coverage for homeowners.

These plans are run by the state. Inquire about your eligibility if you have been denied coverage by the standard commercial carriers. You should also check with your state insurance department. The department may be able to help you get the coverage you need.

Being denied coverage because of where you live could be a form of *redlining* (a practice of denying coverage to people just because they live in a declining or poor neighborhood) and is probably illegal. In that case the state insurance department is the first place you should go.

Federal Crime Insurance

If you happen to live in an area where you can't get theft insurance from a commercial carrier, the federal government offers federal crime insurance. Typically, the cost is $120 for $10,000 worth of coverage. The deductible is $250, or 5% of the loss, whichever is greater. You must comply with certain minimum safety standards, such as the installation of locks, for your residence.

For more information: Write to Federal Crime Insurance, P.O. Box 41033, Washington, D.C. 20014. You can also call the toll-free number (800) 638-8780.

Federal Flood Insurance

This is available to residents of areas that have complied with federal land use and control regulations regarding flooding. The community must also qualify under the Federal Flood Emergency Program.

Quite extensive coverage of $35,000 per home and $185,000 for multi-family structures is available. There is a $500 deductible.

To see whether you qualify, and for more information, write to: Computer Sciences Corporation, P.O. Box 459, Lanham, Maryland 20706. Or phone (800) 638-6620.

Types of Homeowners Policies

Available policies are classified according to the risks that are covered.

HO 1

This basic policy is also known as *Homeowners 1*. It is the cheapest and covers the following perils:
- Fire, lightning and smoke damage.
- Windstorm and hail.
- Burglary and theft.
- Explosion.
- Glass breakage.
- Vehicle or aircraft damage.
- Riot and civil commotion.
- Vandalism and malicious mischief.
- Bodily injury liability.
- Damage to property of others.
- Cost of legal defense in liability cases.
- Medical payments.
- Personal property located at home.
- Personal property away from home, while traveling.
- Additional living expenses.

HO 2

Also called the *broad form policy*, it adds six additional coverages not available under HO 1. It also costs approximately 10% more. The additional risks covered are:

□ Falling objects.

□ Damage from weight of ice or snow.

□ Water damage from your home's plumbing system.

□ Freezing of the plumbing system.

□ Electrical damage to appliances.

□ Rupture of water heaters and heating systems.

HO 3

This is the most popular form of homeowners insurance, the *Special Form* policy. Here, your home is covered for *all risks of physical loss except those specifically excluded*. Examples of exclusions include:

□ Normal wear and tear.

□ Mechanical breakdown.

□ Vandalism if the home has been unoccupied for more than 30 days.

□ Continuous water seepage over a specified time period.

The biggest difference between HO 2 and HO 3 is that the coverage for your personal possessions is not as extensive as the coverage for the house. Under HO 3, contents coverage is only for those perils named in HO 2.

HO 4

This is a special policy available to renters or owners of cooperative apartments. It is discussed separately.

HO 5

The most expensive homeowners policy (it could be as much as twice the cost of HO 1) is the *Comprehensive Form* policy, better known as HO 5. It is also called an *all risks* policy. It covers both the dwelling and your personal possessions from anything and everything *unless the risk is specifically excluded*. Those exclusions are typically flood, earthquake, war and nuclear accident.

HO 6

This is a policy for owners of condominium apartments.

HO 8

There is no HO 7. HO 8 is a special policy available to owners of older structures that cannot be replaced today. Therefore the structure is insured not for its replacement value but for its actual cash value.

Choosing Among These Policies

Most people buy HO 3 because they feel they can do with slightly less coverage on their contents. Many items of furniture, for example, can be replaced fairly inexpensively. The big ticket items such as the house itself are insured up to the limit.

If you don't want to take any chances, then HO 5 is for you. It is the most expensive homeowners policy you can buy. Yet, most people feel most comfortable with HO 3. It gives the most protection for the insurance dollar. Remember, when you start adding coverages, the cost of any policy goes up. For homeowners, HO 3 is probably the best bet.

Valuable Personal Possessions

Not all your possessions are fully covered under standard homeowners policies. Coverage for jewelry, furs, watches and currency is severely restricted. For example, if you lose an expensive mink cost to a thief, a homeowners policy would pay no more than $1,000 for the loss.

The same holds true for the loss of jewelry and important papers such as deeds and wills, manuscripts, passports and stamps. Silverware, cameras, and firearms are other items that have limits on recovery.

Obviously, a $1000 return on a $5000 mink cost is insufficient. To get the additional coverage you need you can purchase a *personal articles floater*. With this floater you agree with the insurance company on a value, and the premium is then pegged to that value.

The name *floater* is very descriptive of what that insurance does. It actually floats with the property wherever it goes. If your jewelry is stolen while you are in Europe on vacation, you are covered under the floater. The coverage follows the item insured wherever it may be.

You must prove the value of the item covered either by submitting an appraisal from a recognized expert in the field or by forwarding a copy of the sales slip from the purchase of the item. Of course, if you bought the item some time ago, or you inherited it you may not have a sales slip. In that case the insurance company may demand an appraisal. Normally, you'll have to pay for that appraisal yourself.

You may have to purchase a separate floater for each item that you want insured over and above the policy's regular limits. Discounts are normally available for floaters.

For example, you can probably get a discount on the floater for jewelry, if the items covered under the floater are routinely kept in a bank safe deposit vault and are taken out only when they will be worn. Similarly, if an expensive fur is stored for the summer months in a licensed and insured fur vault, you could get a discount on the floater.

Just as you should shop around for the basic homeowners policy, you can also shop for a personal articles floater. You can buy the floater from one company and your homeowners policy from another.

Homeowners Insurance Discounts

Most homeowners insurance companies give discounts to homeowners who:

☐ Don't smoke. Obviously, non-smokers have less chance

217

of causing a fire than people who do. Depending on the company, the discount could amount to 5% or more.

☐ Install burglar alarms. If you put in the kind of alarm that is hooked up to the local police station, your discount may be even higher.

☐ Hook up a sprinkler system. An operating sprinkler system is one of the best defenses against a serious house fire.

☐ Put in smoke detectors or smoke alarms. Smoke detectors are another protection against house fires. A detector will warn you once the smoke rises to a dangerous level. Most insurers give approximately a 3% break for them. Install smoke detectors on each level of the house.

☐ Install dead bolt locks. These will help in keeping out burglars. They aren't foolproof, but they may slow burglars down or deter them altogether.

☐ If you keep jewelry, currency and valuable papers in a bank safe deposit vault, the majority of insurers will give you a discount of approximately 5%.

☐ Participate in the personal property identification system sponsored by the local police department. This practice usually involves etching your social security or state driver's license number permanently on to valuable personal belongings such as computers, television sets and stereo equipment. If properly etched, such personal items can be returned to you if stolen. Check with your local police authorities. This can save you another 5% or more on your homeowners premium.

☐ Some companies give discounts to senior citizens on the theory that they are more likely to be home and to keep an unwanted burglar from entering the house.

☐ New houses may qualify for a discount because they are, on the whole, better fireproofed than older ones.

☐ An all wood house is more fire prone than one made of all brick or stone. Some insurers will therefore give a discount for a house primarily constructed of brick or stone.

Overall, the best way to save on homeowners coverage is

to combine the highest deductible you can afford with any or all of the discounts mentioned here. Not every company will offer all the discounts cited, but some may offer many.

Endorsements

An *endorsement* is an additional coverage that is added on to the standard policy. Since the extra coverage doesn't apply to everyone, you must add it if you want to be covered.

A common endorsement is the second home endorsement. If you own a second home, you can cover it simply by adding it on to your existing homeowners policy. It isn't necessary to buy a new policy.

Naturally, because an endorsement is an additional coverage, you will have to pay more for it. Different companies may price their endorsements differently. When you look for homeowners coverage, be sure to consider, any endorsements you need so you get the coverage you really need.

Another endorsement you might consider, especially if you own an older house, is the "increased cost of construction" endorsement. If, for example, your town requires all new construction to be built with fireproof materials, that means that if your present house was totally destroyed and a new one was built, it would probably cost you more to build a new fireproof house than the replacement value of your former home.

Many insurers are offering personal computer endorsements on homeowners policies. If you own a computer, look into adding this endorsement to your homeowners policy. It may be cheaper than insuring the computer under a separate policy. Be sure you get replacement cost coverage.

Homeowners for Tenants

Also known as HO 4, there is a "homeowners" policy

specifically designed for renters and owners of cooperative apartments. Since renters and co-op owners don't own the building they reside in, all they can cover are the contents of the housing unit and the tenant's liability.

The landlord (or the owner's association in the case of a cooperative) must insure the building the unit is in against fire and all the other perils or risks that may occur.

The contents coverage is based on the actual cash value of the items insured. Normally, a tenant's policy can be purchased for as little as $100, depending on the size of the unit and the number and worth of the items to be insured.

If you are a renter and you lose your belongings in a fire or other normally insured calamity, your landlord is not responsible for your loss. A tenant should insure his or her own belongings to the limit of affordability.

If You Work at Home

Many professionals, including doctors, dentists, lawyers and accountants work out of their homes. They have an office in their homes where they meet patients or clients and actually practice their professions.

Those areas devoted to a business are routinely not covered by standard homeowners policies. To protect those areas of your home, you must obtain the appropriate business insurance coverage. This coverage, typically, is rather expensive.

Termination of Your Policy

Insurance carriers are in business to sell policies, not to terminate them. Therefore, a company must, from its own point of view, have a good reason to terminate a policy. Companies can terminate a homeowners policy under the following circumstances:

□ Failure to pay the premium on time. Unlike life insurance companies, property and casualty companies usually provide no grace period for policyholders to pay their premium. *Pay on time or you could be cancelled.*

Policyholders should be aware of the fact that their homeowners policy expires on a certain date. If you don't renew your policy before the expiration date, you could be left without any insurance on your home. If your home should burn during that period, you would not be covered.

Therefore, it is vital that you know exactly when your homeowners policy expires most policies are in force for one year at a time. Be sure to renew your policy before it expires.

☐ A 'material" misrepresentation made on your insurance application. What constitutes "material" may be a company-by-company definition. If you claimed that you had never been convicted of arson, for example, when in fact you had, that would undoubtedly be a material misrepresentation.

☐ Leaving your house vacant or your insured property unattended for a specified length of time, as stated in the policy, could also cause you to lose your coverage.

☐ Knowingly increasing the risk of a hazard occurring. If you store a flammable liquid in your basement or allow your children to play with fireworks, your company may not cover you.

☐ A physical change in the property that renders it uninsurable.

☐ A number of claims being filed that evidence a pattern of failure to follow commonsense safety rules and procedures. When you get your policy, read it. Pay particular attention to the wording regarding termination. Since most companies interpret this very strictly, you must know the exact circumstances under which your policy can be terminated.

Other Factors

Also, once the policy period is up, a company does not have to renew you. There is no such thing as guaranteed-renewable homeowners insurance. The reason for non-renewability may have nothing to do with you as a policyholder. It may be a change in direction by the insurance carrier or something else over which you have no control.

From time to time, insurers have been known to cancel out a policy because of the decline of a particular neighborhood. If there is an increased risk of crime or fire, the company may refuse to renew a policy. If that occurs, you might want to contact your state's superintendent of insurance to see whether or not the problem can be resolved. It is possible that a form of redlining is going on. Redlining is illegal almost everywhere.

Filing a Claim

The proper filing of a claim involves a series of consecutive steps that should be followed to the letter. Your policy specifies these, but here are the general steps:

1) Immediately contact the local law enforcement authorities if a theft or break-in has occurred.

2) Get a copy of any police report that has been prepared.

3) As soon as possible, contact your insurance agent or the company that has your homeowners insurance policy. See the questions on page 224.

4) Find your copy of your personal inventory of your possessions. Determine which items are missing or have been destroyed. Be sure you have the pictures or videotape as well.

5) If physical damage has occurred, make temporary repairs to protect the property from further damage. Keep all receipts connected with the repairs.

6) Take a series of after-the-fact photos. These should be before-and-after pictures—before and after repairs are made. That way the insurance company can be shown the true extent of the damage. You should get your own independent estimate or appraisal of the damage so that it can

be compared to the insurance company's estimate.

7) Be sure you have a copy of your policy. Check to make sure you have followed the claims procedure detailed in your policy.

8) If a dispute should develop concerning the claim, you should try to work it out with your insurance carrier first, if you can't you have the right, in many states, to have an arbitrator hear the claim.

Other Tips on Buying a Homeowners Policy

☐ As with all insurance policies, pay your homeowners premium once a year. Although the amount will be high for a one shot payment, it will be lower than if you pay the bill off in installments.

☐ Try to get your auto insurance and your homeowners policy from the same company. Almost all of them offer a discount for people who do that.

☐ Try not to make a number of small claims. Insurers are more likely to cancel out a policyholder who makes "nickel and dime" claims than one who makes a legitimate large claim. The best way to handle this problem is by raising your deductible. Remember, the purpose of insurance should be to pay for large losses, not to compensate you for small ones.

☐ Although most homeowner policies are sold for only one year at a time, some companies offer policies of three or five years duration. Those longer term policies will probably be cheaper, but be sure that you have an inflation guard rider that automatically increases your coverage (and your premium) as inflation grows.

☐ If you own a swimming pool, make sure you have at least $500,000 worth of liability coverage in the event of an accident.

Questions to Ask Before Filing a Claim

You will probably want to ask these questions of your

agent or insurance company if an accident has occurred that you think you might have a claim for.

1) Is this incident covered?

2) Does the amount of the claim exceed my deductible? Your insurance company will pay any amount that is higher than the deductible.

3) What documents or information do you need from me to process my claim as thoroughly and speedily as possible?

4) Should I get damage estimates? If so, how many are required?

Questions to Ask
When Buying Homeowners Insurance

1) Have I prepared a household inventory complete with pictures and other vital information?

2) Do I know the exact replacement value of my home and its contents?

3) If so, is my home covered for at least 80% of its replacement cost?

4) Are the contents of my home insured for their full replacement value?

5) Have I shopped around for the policy that most suits my needs?

6) Have I taken advantage of all discounts and have I placed the deductible at a level that I can comfortably afford the policy?

7) Do I have an umbrella policy?

8) Do I review my coverage regularly?

9) Do I know exactly when my policy expires so I can renew it without being uncovered by insurance?

10) Do I know how to file a claim under this policy?

Sample Homeowners Insurance Policy

Immediately following is a sample homeowners insurance policy supplied by the Insurance Information Institute. It is written in plain English and is easy to understand. Read through it to get a good idea of what such a policy is like.

Homeowners Policy

TYPE OF COMPANY

THIS POLICY JACKET WITH THE HOMEOWNERS POLICY FORM, DECLARATIONS PAGE AND ENDORSEMENTS, IF ANY, ISSUED TO FORM A PART THEREOF, COMPLETES THE ABOVE NUMBERED POLICY.

YOUR HOMEOWNERS POLICY—QUICK REFERENCE

DECLARATIONS PAGE
Your Name
Location of Your Residence
Policy Period
Coverages
Amounts of Insurance
Deductible

NOTE: This Policy is completed by attachment of the Declarations on page 20 and Form HO-3 on page 21.

In Witness Whereof, we have caused this policy to be executed and attested, but this policy shall not be valid unless countersigned by our authorized representative.

```
INSERT SIGNATURES AND
TITLES OF PROPER OFFICERS
```

NAME OF COMPANY

HOMEOWNERS POLICY
DECLARATIONS

RENEWAL OF NUMBER

No. H

Named Insured and Mailing Address (No., Street, Apt., Town or City, County, State, Zip Code)

Policy Period: Years   From: To: ☐ 12:01 A.M.   ☐ 12:00 Noon, Standard Time
                                                                    at the **residence premises**.

The **residence premises** covered by this policy is located at the above address unless otherwise stated: (No., Street, Apt., Town or City, County, State, Zip Code)

Coverage is provided where a premium or limit of liability is shown for the coverage.

Coverages and Limit of Liability	Section I Coverages				Section II Coverages	
	A. Dwelling	B. Other Structures	C. Personal Property	D. Loss of Use	E. Personal Liability Each occurrence	F. Medical Payments to Others Each person
	$	$	$	$	$	$

Premium	Basic Policy Premium	Additional Premiums			Total Prepaid Premium	Premium if paid in installments	Payable: At each Inception (and) anniversary / At subsequent
	$	$	$	$	$	$	$	$

Premium for Scheduled Personal Property	$		$	$	$

Form and Endorsements made part of this Policy at time of issue:
Insert Number(s) and Edition Date(s):
Form   Endorsement(s)

Combined Premium	$	$	$	$

DEDUCT-IBLE	SECTION I $	OTHER $	In case of a loss under Section I, we cover only that part of the loss over the deductible stated.

Section II   Other insured locations: (No., Street, Apt., Town or City, County, State, Zip Code)

Mortgagee (Name and address)		Special State Provisions S. Car. Valuation Clause (Cov. A) $

Countersigned:

By_____
Authorized Representative

RATING INFORMATION   FORM: ☐ HO-1 (1) ☐ HO-2 (2) ☐ HO-3 (3) ☐ HO-4 (4) ☐ HO-5 (5) ☐ HO-6 (6) ☐ HO-8 (8)   YEAR OF CONST.   Code

NUMBER OF FAMILIES   HO-1, 2, 3, 5 and 8- house Code   Not Town/Row- (1) 1 (3) 2 (6) 3 4 (6)   Town/ Row- house (1) 1 (3) 2 (2) 3 4 (2)   5 or more (4)   HO-4 or HO-6 Not Rented to Others (1) 1 (1) 2 (1) 3 (1) 4 5 or more (8)   HO-6 Rented to Others (1) 1 (1) 2 (1) 3 (1) 4 5 or more (8)

CONSTRUC-TION   Frame (1) ☐ | Brick, Stone or Masonry Veneer (2) ☐ | Brick, Stone or Masonry (3) ☐ | Frame with Aluminum or Plastic Siding (5) ☐ | Superior or Fire Resistive (4) ☐ | Specially Rated— Not Fire Resistive (8) ☐ | Mobile Homes (6) ☐ | All Other (1) ☐

PROTECTION CLASS: Code   Not more than   feet from hydrant,   miles from Fire Dept.   FIRE DISTRICT OR TOWN:

TERRITORY: Code   PREM. GRP. NO.   DEDUCTIBLES: Type Code   Size Code   Section I $ Other $

STATISTICAL REPORTING INFORMATION (Separate Coding Record Required)   Premium: Prepaid;   If paid in Installments;   Payable at: Inception   Each Anniversary

	Codes	Subline	Number	Classif.	Cov. E Limit	Premium: Prepaid;	If paid in Installments;	Payable at: Inception	Each Anniversary
Earthquake	(	) (—	) (—	) (—	)	$	$	$	$
F.P.L.	(	) (—	) (	) (	)	$	$	$	$
Snowmobiles	(	) (	) (	) (	)	$	$	$	$
Watercraft	(	) (	) (	) (	)	$	$	$	$
End. HO-61	(	) (—	) (	) (—	)	$	$	$	$
ALL OTHER PREMIUMS						$			

(a) The **residence premises** is not seasonal; (b) no **business** pursuits are conducted on the **residence premises**; (c) the **residence premises** is the only premises where you maintain a residence other than **business** or farm properties; (d) the **insured** has no full time **residence employee**(s); (e) the **insured** has no outboard motor(s) or watercraft otherwise excluded under this policy for which coverage is desired. Exception, if any, to (a), (b), (c), (d) or (e)*.

*Absence of an entry means "no exceptions".

THIS DECLARATIONS PAGE, WITH POLICY JACKET, HOMEOWNERS POLICY FORM, AND ENDORSEMENTS IF ANY, ISSUED TO FORM A PART THEREOF, COMPLETES THE ABOVE NUMBERED HOMEOWNERS POLICY.

JDL1776-2 (Ed. 7-82)

**Homeowners 3
Special Form
Ed. 7-77**

AGREEMENT

We will provide the insurance described in this policy in return for the premium and compliance with all applicable provisions of this policy.

DEFINITIONS

Throughout this policy, "you" and "your" refer to the "named insured" shown in the Declarations and the spouse if a resident of the same household, and "we", "us" and "our" refer to the Company providing this insurance. In addition, certain words and phrases are defined as follows:

1. **"bodily injury"** means bodily harm, sickness or disease, including required care, loss of services and death resulting therefrom.

2. **"business"** includes trade, profession or occupation.

3. **"insured"** means you and the following residents of your household:

   a. your relatives;

   b. any other person under the age of 21 who is in the care of any person named above.

   Under Section II, **"insured"** also means:

   c. with respect to animals or watercraft to which this policy applies, any person or organization legally responsible for these animals or watercraft which are owned by you or any person included in 3a or 3b. A person or organization using or having custody of these animals or watercraft in the course of any **business,** or without permission of the owner is not an **insured;**

   d. with respect to any vehicle to which this policy applies, any person while engaged in your employment or the employment of any person included in 3a or 3b.

4. **"insured location"** means:

   a. the **residence premises;**

   b. the part of any other premises, other structures, and grounds, used by you as a residence and which is shown in the Declarations or which is acquired by you during the policy period for your use as a residence;

   c. any premises used by you in connection with the premises included in 4a or 4b;

   d. any part of a premises not owned by any **insured** but where any **insured** is temporarily residing;

   e. vacant land owned by or rented to any **insured** other than farm land;

   f. land owned by or rented to any **insured** on which a one or two family dwelling is being constructed as a residence for any **insured;**

   g. individual or family cemetery plots or burial vaults of any **insured;**

   h. any part of a premises occasionally rented to any **insured** for other tha.~ **business** purposes.

5. **"motor vehicle"** means:

   a. a motorized land vehicle designed for travel on public roads or subject to motor vehicle registration. A motorized land vehicle in dead storage on an **insured location** is not a **motor vehicle.**

   b. a trailer or semi-trailer designed for travel on public roads and subject to motor vehicle registration. A boat, camp, home or utility trailer not being towed by or carried on a vehicle included in 5a is not a **motor vehicle;**

   c. a motorized golf cart, snowmobile, or other motorized land vehicle owned by any **insured** and designed for recreational use off public roads, while off an **insured location.** A motorized golf cart while used for golfing purposes is not a **motor vehicle;**

   d. any vehicle while being towed by or carried on a vehicle included in 5a, 5b or 5c.

6. **"property damage"** means physical injury to or destruction of tangible property, including loss of use of this property.

HO-3 Ed. 7-77   Copyright, Insurance Services Office, 1975, 1977   **Page 1 of 12**

7. "residence employee" means an employee of any **insured** who performs duties in connection with the maintenance or use of the **residence premises,** including household or domestic services, or who performs duties elsewhere of a similar nature not in connection with the **business** of any **insured.**

8. "residence premises" means the one or two family dwelling, other structures, and grounds or that part of any other building where you reside and which is shown as the "residence premises" in the Declarations.

SECTION I—COVERAGES

**COVERAGE A
DWELLING**

We cover:

a. the dwelling on the **residence premises** shown in the Declarations used principally as a private residence, including structures attached to the dwelling; and

b. materials and supplies located on or adjacent to the **residence premises** for use in the construction, alteration or repair of the dwelling or other structures on the **residence premises.**

**COVERAGE B
OTHER
STRUCTURES**

We cover other structures on the **residence premises,** separated from the dwelling by clear space. Structures connected to the dwelling by only a fence, utility line, or similar connection are considered to be other structures.

We do not cover other structures:

a. used in whole or in part for **business** purposes; or

b. rented or held for rental to any person not a tenant of the dwelling, unless used solely as a private garage.

**COVERAGE C
PERSONAL
PROPERTY**

We cover personal property owned or used by any **insured** while it is anywhere in the world. At your request, we will cover personal property owned by others while the property is on the part of the **residence premises** occupied by any **insured.** In addition, we will cover at your request, personal property owned by a guest or a **residence employee,** while the property is in any residence occupied by any **insured.**

Our limit of liability for personal property usually situated at any **insured's** residence, other than the **residence premises,** is 10% of the limit of liability for Coverage C, or $1000, whichever is greater. Personal property in a newly acquired principal residence is not subject to this limitation for the 30 days immediately after you begin to move the property there.

Special Limits of Liability. These limits do not increase the Coverage C limit of liability. The special limit for each following numbered category is the total limit for each occurrence for all property in that numbered category.

1. $100 on money, bank notes, bullion, gold other than goldware, silver other than silverware, platinum, coins and medals.

2. $500 on securities, accounts, deeds, evidences of debt, letters of credit, notes other than bank notes, manuscripts, passports, tickets and stamps.

3. $500 on watercraft, including their trailers, furnishings, equipment and outboard motors.

4. $500 on trailers not used with watercraft.

5. $500 on grave markers.

6. $500 for loss by theft of jewelry, watches, furs, precious and semi-precious stones.

7. $1000 for loss by theft of silverware, silver-plated ware, goldware, gold-plated ware and pewterware.

8. $1000 for loss by theft of guns.

Property Not Covered. We do not cover:

1. articles separately described and specifically insured in this or any other insurance;

2. animals, birds or fish;

3. motorized land vehicles except those used to service an **insured's** residence which are not licensed for road use;

4. any device or instrument, including any accessories or antennas, for the transmitting, recording, receiving or reproduction of sound which is operated by power from the electrical system of a **motor vehicle,** or any tape, wire, record, disc or other medium for use with any such device or instrument while any of this property is in or upon a **motor vehicle;**

5. aircraft and parts;

6. property of roomers, boarders and other tenants, except property of roomers and boarders related to any **insured;**

7. property contained in an apartment regularly rented or held for rental to others by any **insured;**

8. property rented or held for rental to others away from the **residence premises;**

9. **business** property in storage or held as a sample or for sale or delivery after sale;

10. **business** property pertaining to a **business** actually conducted on the **residence premises;**

11. **business** property away from the **residence premises.**

COVERAGE D
LOSS OF USE

The limit of liability for Coverage D is the total limit for all the following coverages.

1. Additional Living Expense. If a loss covered under this Section makes the **residence premises** uninhabitable, we cover any necessary increase in living expenses incurred by you so that your household can maintain its normal standard of living. Payment shall be for the shortest time required to repair or replace the premises or, if you permanently relocate, the shortest time required for your household to settle elsewhere. This period of time is not limited by expiration of this policy.

2. Fair Rental Value. If a loss covered under this Section makes that part of the **residence premises** rented to others or held for rental by you uninhabitable, we cover its fair rental value. Payment shall be for the shortest time required to repair or replace the part of the premises rented or held for rental. This period of time is not limited by expiration of this policy. Fair rental value shall not include any expense that does not continue while that part of the **residence premises** rented or held for rental is uninhabitable.

3. Prohibited Use. If a civil authority prohibits you from use of the **residence premises** as a result of direct damage to neighboring premises by a Peril Insured Against in this policy, we cover any resulting Additional Living Expense and Fair Rental Value loss for a period not exceeding two weeks during which use is prohibited.

We do not cover loss or expense due to cancellation of a lease or agreement.

ADDITIONAL
COVERAGES

1. Debris Removal. We will pay the reasonable expense incurred by you in the removal of debris of covered property provided coverage is afforded for the peril causing the loss. Debris removal expense is included in the limit of liability applying to the damaged property. When the amount payable for the actual damage to the property plus the expense for debris removal exceeds the limit of liability for the damaged property, an additional 5% of that limit of liability will be available to cover debris removal expense.

2. Reasonable Repairs. We will pay the reasonable cost incurred by you for necessary repairs made solely to protect covered property from further damage provided coverage is afforded for the peril causing the loss. This coverage does not increase the limit of liability applying to the property being repaired.

3. Trees, Shrubs and Other Plants. We cover trees, shrubs, plants or lawns, on the **residence premises,** for loss caused by the following Perils Insured Against: Fire or lightning, Explosion, Riot or civil commotion, Aircraft, Vehicles not owned or operated by a resident of the **residence premises,** Vandalism or malicious mischief or Theft. The limit of liability for this coverage shall not exceed 5% of the limit of liability that applies to the dwelling for all trees, shrubs, plants and lawns nor more than $500 for any one tree, shrub or plant. We do not cover property grown for **business** purposes.

4. Fire Department Service Charge. We will pay up to $250 for your liability assumed by contract or agreement for fire department charges incurred when the fire department is called to save or protect covered property from a Peril Insured Against. No deductible applies to this coverage.

5. Property Removed. Covered property while being removed from a premises endangered by a Peril Insured Against and for not more than 30 days while removed is covered for direct loss from any cause. This coverage does not change the limit of liability applying to the property being removed.

6. Credit Card, Forgery and Counterfeit Money. We will pay up to $500 for:

a. the legal obligation of any **insured** to pay because of the theft or unauthorized use of credit cards issued to or registered in any **insured's** name.

We do not cover use by a resident of your household, a person who has been entrusted with the credit card, or any person if any **insured** has not complied with all terms and conditions under which the credit card is issued.

b. loss to any **insured** caused by forgery or alteration of any check or negotiable instrument; and

c. loss to any **insured** through acceptance in good faith of counterfeit United States or Canadian paper currency.

We do not cover loss arising out of **business** pursuits or dishonesty of any **insured**. No deductible applies to this coverage.

Defense:

a. We may make any investigation and settle any claim or suit that we decide is appropriate. Our obligation to defend any claim or suit ends when the amount we pay for the loss equals our limit of liability.

b. If a claim is made or a suit is brought against any **insured** for liability under the Credit Card coverage, we will provide a defense at our expense by counsel of our choice.

c. We have the option to defend at our expense any **insured** or any **insured's** bank against any suit for the enforcement of payment under the Forgery coverage.

SECTION I—PERILS INSURED AGAINST

Coverage A Dwelling and Coverage B Other Structures

We insure for all risks of physical loss to the property described in Coverages A and B except:

1. losses excluded under Section I—Exclusions;

2. freezing of a plumbing, heating or air conditioning system or of a household appliance, or by discharge, leakage or overflow from within the system or appliance caused by freezing, while the dwelling is vacant, unoccupied or being constructed unless you have used reasonable care to:

a. maintain heat in the building; or

b. shut off the water supply and drain the system and appliances of water;

3. freezing, thawing, pressure or weight of water or ice, whether driven by wind or not, to a fence, pavement, patio, swimming pool, foundation, retaining wall, bulkhead, pier, wharf or dock;

4. theft in or to a dwelling under construction, or of materials and supplies for use in the construction until the dwelling is completed and occupied;

5. vandalism and malicious mischief or breakage of glass and safety glazing materials if the dwelling has been vacant for more than 30 consecutive days immediately before the loss. A dwelling being constructed is not considered vacant;

6. continuous or repeated seepage or leakage of water or steam over a period of time from within a plumbing, heating or air conditioning system or from within a household appliance;

7. wear and tear; marring; deterioration; inherent vice; latent defect; mechanical breakdown; rust; mold; wet or dry rot; contamination; smog; smoke from agricultural smudging or industrial operations; settling, cracking, shrinking, bulging, or expansion of pavements, patios, foundations, walls, floors, roofs or ceilings; birds, vermin, rodents, insects or domestic animals. If any of these cause water to escape from a plumbing, heating or air conditioning system or household appliance, we cover loss caused by the water. We also cover the cost of tearing out and replacing any part of a building necessary to repair the system or appliance. We do not cover loss to the system or appliance from which this water escaped.

Under items 2 thru 7, any ensuing loss not excluded is covered.

Coverage C Personal Property

We insure for direct loss to property described in Coverage C caused by:

1. Fire or lightning.

2. Windstorm or hail.

This peril does not include loss to the property contained in a building caused by rain, snow, sleet, sand or dust unless the direct force of wind or hail damages the building causing an opening in a roof or wall and the rain, snow, sleet, sand or dust enters through this opening.

HO-3 Ed. 7-77

This peril includes loss to watercraft and their trailers, furnishings, equipment, and outboard motors, only while inside a fully enclosed building.

3. Explosion.

4. Riot or civil commotion.

5. Aircraft, including self-propelled missiles and spacecraft.

6. Vehicles.

7. Smoke, meaning sudden and accidental damage from smoke.

This peril does not include loss caused by smoke from agricultural smudging or industrial operations.

8. Vandalism or malicious mischief.

9. Theft, including attempted theft and loss of property from a known location when it is likely that the property has been stolen.

This peril does not include loss caused by theft:

    a. committed by any **insured;**

    b. in or to a dwelling under construction, or of materials and supplies for use in the construction until the dwelling is completed and occupied; or

    c. from any part of a **residence premises** rented by an **insured** to other than an **insured.**

This peril does not include loss caused by theft that occurs away from the **residence premises** of:

    a. property while at any other residence owned, rented to, or occupied by any **insured,** except while any **insured** is temporarily residing there. Property of a student who is an **insured** is covered while at a residence away from home if the student has been there at any time during the 45 days immediately before the loss;

    b. unattended property in or on any **motor vehicle** or trailer, other than a public conveyance, unless there is forcible entry into the vehicle while all its doors, windows and other openings are closed and locked and there are visible marks of the forcible entry; or the vehicle is stolen and not recovered within 30 days.

Property is not unattended when any **insured** has entrusted the keys of the vehicle to a custodian.

    c. watercraft, including its furnishings, equipment and outboard motors. Other property in or on any private watercraft is covered if the loss results from forcible entry into a securely locked compartment and there are visible marks of the forcible entry; or

    d. trailers and campers.

10. Falling objects.

This peril does not include loss to property contained in a building unless the roof or an exterior wall of the building is first damaged by a falling object. Damage to the falling object itself is not included.

11. Weight of ice, snow or sleet which causes damage to property contained in a building.

12. Collapse of a building or any part of a building.

This peril does not include settling, cracking, shrinking, bulging or expansion.

13. Accidental discharge or overflow of water or steam from within a plumbing, heating or air conditioning system or from within a household appliance.

This peril does not include loss:

    a. to the appliance from which the water or steam escaped;

    b. caused by or resulting from freezing;

    c. on the **residence premises** caused by accidental discharge or overflow which occurs off the **residence premises.**

14. Sudden and accidental tearing asunder, cracking, burning or bulging of a steam or hot water heating system, an air conditioning system, or an appliance for heating water.

We do not cover loss caused by or resulting from freezing under this peril.

15. Freezing of a plumbing, heating or air conditioning system or of a household appliance.

This peril does not include loss on the **residence premises** while the dwelling is unoccupied, unless you have used reasonable care to:

    a. maintain heat in the building; or

    b. shut off the water supply and drain the system and appliances of water.

16. Sudden and accidental damage from artificially generated electrical current.

This peril does not include loss to a tube, transistor or similar electronic component.

SECTION I—EXCLUSIONS

We do not cover loss resulting directly or indirectly from:

1. Ordinance or Law, meaning enforcement of any ordinance or law regulating the construction, repair, or demolition of a building or other structure, unless specifically provided under this policy.

2. Earth Movement. Direct loss by fire, explosion, theft, or breakage of glass or safety glazing materials resulting from earth movement is covered.

3. Water Damage, meaning:

a. flood, surface water, waves, tidal water, overflow of a body of water, or spray from any of these, whether or not driven by wind;

b. water which backs up through sewers or drains; or

c. water below the surface of the ground, including water which exerts pressure on, or seeps or leaks through a building, sidewalk, driveway, foundation, swimming pool or other structure.

Direct loss by fire, explosion or theft resulting from water damage is covered.

4. Power Interruption, meaning the interruption of power or other utility service if the interruption takes place away from the **residence premises.** If a Peril Insured Against ensues on the **residence premises,** we will pay only for loss caused by the ensuing peril.

5. Neglect, meaning neglect of the **insured** to use all reasonable means to save and preserve property at and after the time of a loss, or when property is endangered by a Peril Insured Against.

6. War, including undeclared war, civil war, insurrection, rebellion, revolution, warlike act by a military force or military personnel, destruction or seizure or use for a military purpose, and including any consequence of any of these. Discharge of a nuclear weapon shall be deemed a warlike act even if accidental.

7. Nuclear Hazard, to the extent set forth in the Nuclear Hazard Clause of Section I—Conditions.

SECTION I—CONDITIONS

1. Insurable Interest and Limit of Liability. Even if more than one person has an insurable interest in the property covered, we shall not be liable:

a. to the **insured** for an amount greater than the **insured's** interest; nor

b. for more than the applicable limit of liability.

2. Your Duties After Loss. In case of a loss to which this insurance may apply, you shall see that the following duties are performed:

a. give immediate notice to us or our agent, and in case of theft also to the police. In case of loss under the Credit Card coverage also notify the credit card company;

b. protect the property from further damage, make reasonable and necessary repairs required to protect the property, and keep an accurate record of repair expenditures;

c. prepare an inventory of damaged personal property showing in detail, the quantity, description, actual cash value and amount of loss. Attach to the inventory all bills, receipts and related documents that substantiate the figures in the inventory;

d. exhibit the damaged property as often as we reasonably require and submit to examination under oath;

e. submit to us, within 60 days after we request, your signed, sworn statement of loss which sets forth, to the best of your knowledge and belief:

(1) the time and cause of loss;

(2) interest of the **insured** and all others in the property involved and all encumbrances on the property;

(3) other insurance which may cover the loss;

(4) changes in title or occupancy of the property during the term of the policy;

(5) specifications of any damaged building and detailed estimates for repair of the damage;

(6) an inventory of damaged personal property described in 2c;

(7) receipts for additional living expenses incurred and records supporting the fair rental value loss;

(8) evidence or affidavit supporting a claim under the Credit Card, Forgery and Counterfeit Money coverage, stating the amount and cause of loss.

3. Loss Settlement. Covered property losses are settled as follows:

a. Personal property and structures that are not buildings at actual cash value at the time of loss but not exceeding the amount necessary to repair or replace;

b. Carpeting, domestic appliances, awnings, outdoor antennas and outdoor equipment, whether or not attached to buildings, at actual cash value at the time of loss but not exceeding the amount necessary to repair or replace;

c. Buildings under Coverage A or B at replacement cost without deduction for depreciation, subject to the following:

(1) If at the time of loss the amount of insurance in this policy on the damaged building is 80% or more of the full replacement cost of the building immediately prior to the loss, we will pay the cost of repair or replacement, without deduction for depreciation, but not exceeding the smallest of the following amounts:

(a) the limit of liability under this policy applying to the building;

(b) the replacement cost of that part of the building damaged for equivalent construction and use on the same premises; or

(c) the amount actually and necessarily spent to repair or replace the damaged building.

(2) If at the time of loss the amount of insurance in this policy on the damaged building is less than 80% of the full replacement cost of the building immediately prior to the loss, we will pay the larger of the following amounts, but not exceeding the limit of liability under this policy applying to the building:

(a) the actual cash value of that part of the building damaged; or

(b) that proportion of the cost to repair or replace, without deduction for depreciation, of that part of the building damaged, which the total amount of insurance in this policy on the damaged building bears to 80% of the replacement cost of the building.

(3) In determining the amount of insurance required to equal 80% of the full replacement cost of the building immediately prior to the loss, you shall disregard the value of excavations, foundations, piers and other supports which are below the undersurface of the lowest basement floor or, where there is no basement, which are below the surface of the ground inside the foundation walls, and underground flues, pipes, wiring and drains.

(4) When the cost to repair or replace the damage is more than $1000 or more than 5% of the amount of insurance in this policy on the building, whichever is less, we will pay no more than the actual cash value of the damage until actual repair or replacement is completed.

(5) You may disregard the replacement cost loss settlement provisions and make claim under this policy for loss or damage to buildings on an actual cash value basis and then make claim within 180 days after loss for any additional liability on a replacement cost basis.

4. Loss to a Pair or Set. In case of loss to a pair or set we may elect to:

a. repair or replace any part to restore the pair or set to its value before the loss; or

b. pay the difference between actual cash value of the property before and after the loss.

5. Glass Replacement. Loss for damage to glass caused by a Peril Insured Against shall be settled on the basis of replacement with safety glazing materials when required by ordinance or law.

6. Appraisal. If you and we fail to agree on the amount of loss, either one can demand that the amount of the loss be set by appraisal. If either makes a written demand for appraisal, each shall select a competent, independent appraiser and notify the other of the appraiser's identity within 20 days of receipt of the written demand. The two appraisers shall then select a competent, impartial umpire. If the two appraisers are unable to agree upon an umpire within 15 days, you or we can ask a judge of a court of record in the state where the **residence premises** is located to select an umpire. The appraisers shall then set the amount of the loss. If the appraisers submit a written report of an agreement to us, the amount agreed upon shall be the amount of the loss. If the appraisers fail to agree within a reasonable time, they shall submit their differences to the umpire. Written agreement signed by any two of these three shall set the amount of the loss. Each appraiser shall be paid by the party selecting that appraiser. Other expenses of the appraisal and the compensation of the umpire shall be paid equally by you and us.

7. Other Insurance. If a loss covered by this policy is also covered by other insurance, we will pay only the proportion of the loss that the limit of liability that applies under this policy bears to the total amount of insurance covering the loss.

8. Suit Against Us. No action shall be brought unless there has been compliance with the policy provisions and the action is started within one year after the occurrence causing loss or damage.

9. Our Option. If we give you written notice within 30 days after we receive your signed, sworn statement of loss, we may repair or replace any part of the property damaged with equivalent property.

10. Loss Payment. We will adjust all losses with you. We will pay you unless some other person is named in the policy to receive payment. Payment for loss will be made within 30 days after we reach agreement with you, entry of a final judgment, or the filing of an appraisal award with us.

11. Abandonment of Property. We need not accept any property abandoned by any **insured.**

12. Mortgage Clause.
The word "mortgagee" includes trustee.
If a mortgagee is named in this policy, any loss payable under Coverage A or B shall be paid to the mortgagee and you, as interests appear. If more than one mortgagee is named, the order of payment shall be the same as the order or precedence of the mortgages.
If we deny your claim, that denial shall not apply to a valid claim of the mortgagee, if the mortgagee:
a. notifies us of any change in ownership, occupancy or substantial change in risk of which the mortgagee is aware;
b. pays any premium due under this policy on demand if you have neglected to pay the premium;
c. submits a signed, sworn statement of loss within 60 days after receiving notice from us of your failure to do so. Policy conditions relating to Appraisal, Suit Against Us and Loss Payment apply to the mortgagee.
If the policy is cancelled by us, the mortgagee shall be notified at least 10 days before the date cancellation takes effect.
If we pay the mortgagee for any loss and deny payment to you:
a. we are subrogated to all the rights of the mortgagee granted under the mortgage on the property; or
b. at our option, we may pay to the mortgagee the whole principal on the mortgage plus any accrued interest. In this event, we shall receive a full assignment and transfer of the mortgage and all securities held as collateral to the mortgage debt.
Subrogation shall not impair the right of the mortgagee to recover the full amount of the mortgagee's claim.

13. No Benefit to Bailee. We will not recognize any assignment or grant any coverage for the benefit of any person or organization holding, storing or transporting property for a fee regardless of any other provision of this policy.

14. Nuclear Hazard Clause.
a. "Nuclear Hazard" means any nuclear reaction, radiation, or radioactive contamination, all whether controlled or uncontrolled or however caused, or any consequence of any of these.
b. Loss caused by the nuclear hazard shall not be considered loss caused by fire, explosion, or smoke, whether these perils are specifically named in or otherwise included within the Perils Insured Against in Section I.
c. This policy does not apply under Section I to loss caused directly or indirectly by nuclear hazard, except that direct loss by fire resulting from the nuclear hazard is covered.

SECTION II—LIABILITY COVERAGES

COVERAGE E PERSONAL LIABILITY

If a claim is made or a suit is brought against any **insured** for damages because of **bodily injury** or **property damage** to which this coverage applies. we will:

a. pay up to our limit of liability for the damages for which the **insured** is legally liable; and

b. provide a defense at our expense by counsel of our choice. We may make any investigation and settle any claim or suit that we decide is appropriate. Our obligation to defend any claim or suit ends when the amount we pay for damages resulting from the occurrence equals our limit of liability.

COVERAGE F MEDICAL PAYMENTS TO OTHERS

We will pay the necessary medical expenses incurred or medically ascertained within three years from the date of an accident causing **bodily injury**. Medical expenses means reasonable charges for medical, surgical, x-ray, dental, ambulance, hospital, professional nursing, prosthetic devices and funeral services. This coverage does not apply to you or regular residents of your household other than **residence employees.** As to others, this coverage applies only:

a. to a person on the **insured location** with the permission of any **insured**; or

b. to a person off the **insured location,** if the **bodily injury:**
   (1) arises out of a condition in the **insured location** or the ways immediately adjoining;
   (2) is caused by the activities of any **insured;**
   (3) is caused by a **residence employee** in the course of the **residence employee's** employment by any **insured;** or
   (4) is caused by an animal owned by or in the care of any **insured.**

SECTION II—EXCLUSIONS

1. **Coverage E—Personal Liability and Coverage F—Medical Payments to Others** do not apply to **bodily injury** or **property damage:**

a. which is expected or intended by the **insured;**

b. arising out of **business** pursuits of any **insured** or the rental or holding for rental of any part of any premises by any **insured.**

This exclusion does not apply to:

   (1) activities which are ordinarily incident to non-**business** pursuits: or

   (2) the rental or holding for rental of a residence of yours:
      (a) on an occasional basis for the exclusive use as a residence;
      (b) in part. unless intended for use as a residence by more than two roomers or boarders: or
      (c) in part, as an office, school, studio or private garage;

c. arising out of the rendering or failing to render professional services;

d. arising out of any premises owned or rented to any **insured** which is not an **insured location;**

e. arising out of the ownership. maintenance. use. loading or unloading of:

   (1) an aircraft;

   (2) a **motor vehicle** owned or operated by. or rented or loaned to any **insured;** or

   (3) a watercraft:

      (a) owned by or rented to any **insured** if the watercraft has inboard or inboard-outdrive motor power of more than 50 horsepower or is a sailing vessel. with or without auxiliary power. 26 feet or more in overall length: or

      (b) powered by one or more outboard motors with more than 25 total horsepower. owned by any **insured** at the inception of this policy. If you report in writing to us within 45 days after acquisition. an intention to insure any outboard motors acquired prior to the policy period. coverage will apply.

f. caused directly or indirectly by war. including undeclared war. civil war. insurrection. rebellion. revolution. warlike act by a military force or military personnel. destruction or seizure or use for a military purpose. and including any consequence of any of these. Discharge of a nuclear weapon shall be deemed a warlike act even if accidental.

Exclusion e(3) does not apply while the watercraft is stored and exclusions d and e do not apply to **bodily injury** to any **residence employee** arising out of and in the course of the **residence employee's** employment by any **insured.**

2. **Coverage E—Personal Liability,** does not apply to:

a. liability assumed under any unwritten contract or agreement, or by contract or agreement in connection with any **business** of the **insured;**

b. **property damage** to property owned by the **insured;**

c. **property damage** to property rented to, occupied or used by or in the care of the **insured.** This exclusion does not apply to **property damage** caused by fire, smoke or explosion;

d. **bodily injury** to any person eligible to receive any benefits required to be provided or voluntarily provided by the **insured** under any worker's or workmen's compensation, non-occupational disability, or occupational disease law; or

e. **bodily injury** or **property damage** for which any **insured** under this policy is also an insured under a nuclear energy liability policy or would be an insured but for its termination upon exhaustion of its limit of liability. A nuclear energy liability policy is a policy issued by Nuclear Energy Liability Insurance Association, Mutual Atomic Energy Liability Underwriters, Nuclear Insurance Association of Canada, or any of their successors.

3. **Coverage F—Medical Payments to Others,** does not apply to **bodily injury:**

a. to a **residence employee** if it occurs off the **insured location** and does not arise out of or in the course of the **residence employee's** employment by any **insured;**

b. to any person, eligible to receive any benefits required to be provided or voluntarily provided under any worker's or workmen's compensation, non-occupational disability or occupational disease law;

c. from any nuclear reaction, radiation or radioactive contamination, all whether controlled or uncontrolled or however caused, or any consequence of any of these.

SECTION II—ADDITIONAL COVERAGES

We cover the following in addition to the limits of liability:

1. **Claim Expenses.** We pay:

a. expenses incurred by us and costs taxed against any **insured** in any suit we defend;

b. premiums on bonds required in a suit defended by us, but not for bond amounts greater than the limit of liability for Coverage E. We are not obligated to apply for or furnish any bond;

c. reasonable expenses incurred by any **insured** at our request, including actual loss of earnings (but not loss of other income) up to $50 per day for assisting us in the investigation or defense of any claim or suit;

d. interest on the entire judgment which accrues after entry of the judgment and before we pay or tender, or deposit in court that part of the judgment which does not exceed the limit of liability that applies.

2. **First Aid Expenses.** We will pay expenses for first aid to others incurred by any **insured** for **bodily injury** covered under this policy. We will not pay for first aid to you or any other **insured.**

3. **Damage to Property of Others.** We will pay up to $250 per occurrence for **property damage** to property of others caused by any **insured.**

We will not pay for **property damage:**

a. to property covered under Section I of this policy;

b. caused intentionally by any **insured** who is 13 years of age or older;

c. to property owned by or rented to any **insured,** a tenant of any **insured,** or a resident in your household; or

d. arising out of:

(1) **business** pursuits;

(2) any act or omission in connection with a premises owned, rented or controlled by any **insured,** other than the **insured location;** or

(3) the ownership, maintenance, or use of a **motor vehicle,** aircraft or watercraft.

HO-3 Ed. 7-77

SECTION II—CONDITIONS

1. Limit of Liability. Regardless of the number of **insureds,** claims made or persons injured, our total liability under Coverage E stated in this policy for all damages resulting from any one occurrence shall not exceed the limit of liability for Coverage E stated in the Declarations. All **bodily injury** and **property damage** resulting from any one accident or from continuous or repeated exposure to substantially the same general conditions shall be considered to be the result of one occurrence.

Our total liability under Coverage F for all medical expense payable for **bodily injury** to one person as the result of one accident shall not exceed the limit of liability for Coverage F stated in the Declarations.

2. Severability of Insurance. This insurance applies separately to each **insured.** This condition shall not increase our limit of liability for any one occurrence.

3. Duties After Loss. In case of an accident or occurrence, the **insured** shall perform the following duties that apply. You shall cooperate with us in seeing that these duties are performed:

a. give written notice to us or our agent as soon as practicable, which sets forth:
(1) the identity of the policy and **insured;**
(2) reasonably available information on the time, place and circumstances of the accident or occurrence; and
(3) names and addresses of any claimants and available witnesses;
b. forward to us every notice, demand, summons or other process relating to the accident or occurrence;
c. at our request, assist in:
(1) making settlement;
(2) the enforcement of any right of contribution or indemnity against any person or organization who may be liable to any **insured;**
(3) the conduct of suits and attend hearings and trials;
(4) securing and giving evidence and obtaining the attendance of witnesses;
d. under the coverage—Damage to the Property of Others—submit to us within 60 days after the loss, a sworn statement of loss and exhibit the damaged property, if within the **insured's** control;
e. the **insured** shall not, except at the **insured's** own cost, voluntarily make any payment, assume any obligation or incur any expense other than for first aid to others at the time of the **bodily injury.**

4. Duties of an Injured Person—Coverage F—Medical Payments to Others.
The injured person or someone acting on behalf of the injured person shall:
a. give us written proof of claim, under oath if required, as soon as practicable;
b. execute authorization to allow us to obtain copies of medical reports and records; and
c. the injured person shall submit to physical examination by a physician selected by us when and as often as we reasonably require.

5. Payment of Claim—Coverage F—Medical Payments to Others. Payment under this coverage is not an admission of liability by any **insured** or us.

6. Suit Against Us. No action shall be brought against us unless there has been compliance with the policy provisions.

No one shall have any right to join us as a party to any action against any **insured.** Further, no action with respect to Coverage E shall be brought against us until the obligation of the **insured** has been determined by final judgment or agreement signed by us.

7. Bankruptcy of any Insured. Bankruptcy or insolvency of any **insured** shall not relieve us of any of our obligations under this policy.

8. Other Insurance—Coverage E—Personal Liability. This insurance is excess over any other valid and collectible insurance except insurance written specifically to cover as excess over the limits of liability that apply in this policy.

SECTION I AND SECTION II—CONDITIONS

1. Policy Period. This policy applies only to loss under Section I or **bodily injury** or **property damage** under Section II. which occurs during the policy period.

2. Concealment or Fraud. We do not provide coverage for any **insured** who has intentionally concealed or misrepresented any material fact or circumstance relating to this insurance.

3. Liberalization Clause. If we adopt any revision which would broaden the coverage under this policy without additional premium within 60 days prior to or during the policy period. the broadened coverage will immediately apply to this policy.

4. Waiver or Change of Policy Provisions. A waiver or change of any provision of this policy must be in writing by us to be valid. Our request for an appraisal or examination shall not waive any of our rights.

5. Cancellation.

a. You may cancel this policy at any time by returning it to us or by notifying us in writing of the date cancellation is to take effect.

b. We may cancel this policy only for the reasons stated in this condition by notifying you In writing of the date cancellation takes effect. This cancellation notice may be delivered to you. or mailed to you at your mailing address shown in the Declarations. Proof of mailing shall be sufficient proof of notice:

(1) When you have not paid the premium. whether payable to us or to our agent or under any finance or credit plan, we may cancel at any time by notifying you at least 10 days before the date cancellation takes effect.

(2) When this policy has been in effect for less than 60 days and is not a renewal with us. we may cancel for any reason by notifying you at least 10 days before the date cancellation takes effect.

(3) When this policy has been in effect for 60 days or more. or at any time if it is a renewal with us. we may cancel if there has been a material misrepresentation of fact which if known to us would have caused us not to issue the policy or if the risk has changed substantially since the policy was issued. This can be done by notifying you at least 30 days before the date cancellation takes effect.

(4) When this policy is written for a period longer than one year. we may cancel for any reason at anniversary by notifying you at least 30 days before the date cancellation takes effect.

c. When this policy is cancelled. the premium for the period from the date of cancellation to the expiration date will be refunded. When you request cancellation. the return premium will be based on our short rate table. When we cancel. the return premium will be pro rata.

d. If the return premium is not refunded with the notice of cancellation or when this policy is returned to us. we will refund it within a reasonable time after the date cancellation takes effect.

6. Non-Renewal. We may elect not to renew this policy. We may do so by delivery to you. or mailing to you at your mailing address shown in the Declarations. written notice at least 30 days before the expiration date of this policy. Proof of mailing shall be sufficient proof of notice.

7. Assignment. Assignment of this policy shall not be valid unless we give our written consent.

8. Subrogation. Any **insured** may waive in writing before a loss all rights of recovery against any person. If not waived. we may require an assignment of rights of recovery for a loss to the extent that payment is made by us.

If an assignment is sought. any **insured** shall sign and deliver all related papers and cooperate with us in any reasonable manner.

Subrogation does not apply under Section II to Medical Payments to Others or Damage to Property of Others.

9. Death. If any person named in the Declarations or the spouse. if a resident of the same household. dies:

a. we insure the legal representative of the deceased but only with respect to the premises and property of the deceased covered under the policy at the time of death:

b. **insured** includes:

(1) any member of your household who is an **insured** at the time of your death. but only while a resident of the **residence premises;** and

(2) with respect to your property. the person having proper temporary custody of the property until appointment and qualification of a legal representative.

HO-3 Ed. 7-77

AMENDATORY ENDORSEMENT
All Forms Except HO-1 and HO-8

Section I of this policy is amended as follows:

ADDITIONAL COVERAGES

The following Additional Coverage is added:

Collapse. We insure for risk of direct physical loss to covered property involving collapse of a building or any part of a building caused only by one or more of the following:

a. Perils Insured Against in Coverage C—Personal Property. These perils apply to covered building and personal property for loss insured by this Additional Coverage;

b. hidden decay;

c. hidden insect or vermin damage;

d. weight of contents, equipment, animals or people;

e. weight of rain which collects on a roof;

f. use of defective material or methods in construction, remodeling or renovation if the collapse occurs during the course of the construction, remodeling or renovation.

Loss to an awning, fence, patio, pavement, swimming pool, underground pipe, flue, drain, cesspool, septic tank, foundation, retaining wall, bulkhead, pier, wharf or dock is not included under items b, c, d, e and f unless the loss is a direct result of the collapse of a building.

Collapse does not include settling, cracking, shrinking, bulging or expansion.

This coverage does not increase the limit of liability applying to the damaged covered property.

For Form HO-5 the above Additional Coverage only applies to Coverages A and B and paragraph a. is revised as follows:

a. Perils Insured Against in Coverages A and B.

SECTION I—PERILS INSURED AGAINST

The peril **Collapse of a building or any part of a building** is deleted from all forms. In addition, the following exclusion is added to **HO-3 and HO-5** under Coverages A and B:

Collapse, other than as provided above in Additional Coverages—Collapse. However, any ensuing loss not excluded is covered.

Also, in **HO-3 and HO-5** the word "all" is deleted from the following sentence:

"We insure for all risks of. . . to the property described. . . except:"

SECTION I—EXCLUSIONS

The sentence:

"We do not cover loss resulting directly or indirectly from:"

is deleted and the following substituted:

A. We do not insure for loss caused directly or indirectly by any of the following. Such loss is excluded regardless of any other cause or event contributing concurrently or in any sequence to the loss.

Forms HO-3 and HO-5

The following exclusions are added:

B. We do not insure for loss to property described in Coverages A and B caused by any of the following. However, any ensuing loss not excluded is covered.

1. **Weather conditions.** However, this exclusion only applies if weather conditions contribute in any way with a cause or event excluded in paragraph A. above to produce the loss;

2. **Acts or decisions,** including the failure to act or decide, of any person, group, organization or governmental body;

3. **Faulty, inadequate or defective:**

   a) planning, zoning, development, surveying, siting;

   b) design, specifications, workmanship, repair, construction, renovation, remodeling, grading, compaction;

   c) materials used in repair, construction, renovation or remodeling; or

   d) maintenance;

   of part or all of any property whether on or off the **residence premises.**

All other provisions of this policy apply.

HO-330 (Ed. 9-83)
Page 2 of 2
Printed in U.S.A.
December 1983/60M/CC

Appendix

Appendix

State-by-State Listing of
Members of the NAIC

STATE	NAME AND TITLE	ADDRESS	TELEPHONE
Alabama	Michael DeBellis Commissioner of Insurance	135 S. Union Street #160 Montgomery 36130-3401	205/269-3550
Alaska	John L. George Director of Insurance	P.O. Box "D" Juneau 99811	907/465-2515
American Samoa	Afa Roberts Insurance Commissioner	Office of the Governor Pago Pago 96797	684/633-4116
Arizona	S. David Childers Director of Insurance	801 E. Jefferson, 2nd Floor Phoenix 85034	602/255-5400
Arkansas	Robt. M. Eubanks, III Insurance Commissioner	400 University Tower Bldg. 12th and University Streets Little Rock 72204	501/371-1325
California	Bruce A. Bunner Insurance Commissioner	600 South Commonwealth 14th Floor Los Angeles 90005	213/736-2551
Colorado	John Kezer Commissioner of Insurance	303 West Colfax Avenue 5th Floor Denver 80204	303/866-3201
Connecticut	Peter W. Gillies Insurance Commissioner	165 Capitol Avenue State Office Building Room 425 Hartford 06106	203/566-5275
Delaware	David N. Levinson Insurance Commissioner	21 The Green Dover 19901	302/736-4251
District of Columbia	Margurite C. Stokes Superintendent of Insurance	614 H Street, NW North Potomac Bldg. Suite 512 Washington 20001	202/727-7419
Florida	Bill Gunter Insurance Commissioner	Attention: Judy Lee State Capitol Plaza Level Eleven (11) Tallahassee 32301	904/488-3440
Georgia	Warren D. Evans Insurance Commissioner	2 Martin L. King, Jr. Dr. Floyd Memorial Building 704 West Tower Atlanta 30334	404/656-2056
Guam	Dave J. Santos Insurance Commissioner	P.O. Box 2796 011- Agana 96910	671/477-1040

STATE	NAME AND TITLE	ADDRESS	TELEPHONE
Hawaii	Mario R. Ramil Insurance Commissioner	P.O. Box 3614 Honolulu 96811	808/548-5450
Idaho	Wayne L. Soward Director of Insurance	700 West State Street Boise 83720	208/334-2250
Illinois	John E. Washburn Director of Insurance	320 West Washington Street 4th Floor Springfield 62767	217/782-4515
Indiana	Harry E. Eakin Commissioner of Insurance	509 State Office Building Indianapolis 46204	317/232-2386
Iowa	Bruce W. Foudree Commissioner of Insurance	Lucas State Office Building G23 Des Moines 50319	515/281-5705
Kansas	Fletcher Bell Commissioner of Insurance	420 S.W. 9th Street Topeka 66612	913/296-7801
Kentucky	Gil McCarty Insurance Commissioner	229 West Main Street P.O. Box 517 Frankfort 40602	502/564-3630
Louisiana	Sherman A. Bernard Commissioner of Insurance	P.O. Box 44214 Baton Rouge 70804 or 950 North 5th Street Baton Rouge 70801	504/342-5328
Maine	Theodore T. Briggs Superintendent of Insurance	State Office Building State House, Station 34 Augusta 04333	207/289-3101
Maryland	Edward J. Muhl Insurance Commissioner	501 St. Paul Place (Stanbalt Bldg.) 7th Floor-South Baltimore 21202	301/659-2520
Massachusetts	Peter Hiam Commissioner of Insurance	100 Cambridge Street Boston 02202	617/727-3333
Michigan	Herman W. Coleman Insurance Commissioner	P.O. Box 30220 Lansing 48909 or 611 West Ottawa Street 2nd Floor, North Lansing 48933	517/373-9273
Minnesota	Michael A. Hatch Commissioner of Commerce	500 Metro Square Building 5th Floor St. Paul 55101	612/296-6907

STATE	NAME AND TITLE	ADDRESS	TELEPHONE
Mississippi	George Dale Commissioner of Insurance	1804 Walter Sillers Bldg. P.O. Box 79 Jackson 39205	601/359-3569
Missouri	Lewis R. Crist Director of Insurance	301 W. High St. 6 North P.O. Box 690 Jefferson City 65102-0690	314/751-2451
Montana	Andrea "Andy" Bennett Commissioner of Insurance	126 North Sanders Mitchell Building Room 270, P.O. Box 4009 Helena 59601	406/444-2040
Nebraska	Michael J. Dugan Director of Insurance	301 Centennial Mall South State Capitol Bldg. P.O. Box 94699 Lincoln 68509	402/471-2201 Ext. 238
Nevada	David A. Gates Commissioner of Insurance	Nye Building 201 South Fall Street Carson City 89701	702/885-4270
New Hampshire	Louis E. Bergeron Insurance Commissioner	169 Manchester St. P.O. Box 2005 Concord 03301	603/271-2261
New Jersey	Hazel Frank Gluck Commissioner	201 East State St. CN325 Trenton 08625	609/292-5363
New Mexico	Vincente B. Jasso Superintendent of Insurance	PERA Bldg. P.O. Drawer 1269 Santa Fe 87504-1269	505/827-4535
New York	James P. Corcoran Superintendent of Insurance	160 West Broadway New York 10013	212/602-0429
North Carolina	James E. Long Commissioner of Insurance	Dobbs Bldg. P.O. Box 26387 Raleigh 27611	919/733-7343
North Dakota	Earl R. Pomeroy Commissioner of Insurance	Capitol Bldg. Fifth Floor Bismarck 58505	701/224-2440
Ohio	George Fabe Director of Insurance	2100 Stella Court Columbus 43266-0566	614/466-3584
Oklahoma	Gerald Grimes Insurance Commissioner	408 Will Rogers Memorial Bldg. Oklahoma City 73105	405/521-2828

STATE	NAME AND TITLE	ADDRESS	TELEPHONE
Oregon	Josephine M. Driscoll Insurance Commissioner	158-12th Street, NE Salem 97310	503/378-4271
Pennsylvania	George F. Grode Insurance Commissioner (Acting)	Strawberry Square 13th Floor Harrisburg 17120	717/787-5173
Puerto Rico	Juan Antonio Garcia Commissioner of Insurance	Fernandez Juncos Station P.O. Box 8330 Santurce, PR 00910	809/722-8686
Rhode Island	Clifton A. Moore Insurance Commissioner	100 North Main Street Providence 02903	401/277-2246
South Carolina	John G. Richards, V Chief Insurance Commissioner	2711 Middleburg Drive P.O. Box 4067 Columbia 29204	803/758-3266
South Dakota	Susan L. Walker Director of Insurance	Insurance Building 910 E. Sioux Avenue Pierre 57501	605/773-3563
Tennessee	William Inman Commissioner of Insurance	1808 West End Avenue 14th Floor Nashville 37219	615/741-2241
Texas	Lyndon L. Olson, Jr. Chairman-State Board of Insurance	1110 San Jacinto Blvd. Austin 78701-1998	512/463-6329
Texas	Catherine Brown Fryer David H. Thornberry Member-State Board of Insurance	1110 San Jacinto Blvd. Austin 78701-1998	512/463-6330
Texas	Doyce R. Lee Commissioner of Insurance	1110 San Jacinto Blvd. Austin 78701-1998	512/463-6464
Utah	Harold C. Yancey Commissioner of Insurance	P.O. Box 45803 Salt Lake City 84145	801/530-6400
Vermont	Thomas P. Menson Commissioner of Insurance	State Office Building Montpelier 05602	802/828-3301
Virginia	James M. Thomson Commissioner of Insurance	700 Jefferson Building P.O. Box 1157 Richmond 23209	804/786-3741

Appendix

STATE	NAME AND TITLE	ADDRESS	TELEPHONE
Virgin Islands	Julio A. Brady Commissioner of Insurance	P.O. Box 450 Charlotte Amalie St. Thomas 00801	809/774-2991
Washington	Richard G. (Dick) Marquardt Insurance Commissioner	Insurance Building AQ21 Olympia 98504	206/753-7301
West Virginia	Fred E. Wright Insurance Commissioner	2100 Washington Street, E Charleston 25305	304/348-3394
Wisconsin	Thomas P. Fox Commissioner of Insurance	P.O. Box 7873 Madison 53707 or 123 West Washington Ave. Madison 53702	608/266-0102
Wyoming	Monroe D. Lauer Acting Insurance Commissioner	Herschler Building 122 West 25th Street Cheyenne 82002	307/777-7401

Glossary of Health and Life Insurance Terms*

A

Accident. An event or occurrence that is unforeseen and unintended.

Accidental Bodily Injury. Injury to the body as the result of an accident.

Accidental Death Benefit. A benefit in addition to the face amount of a life insurance policy, payable if the insured dies as the result of an accident. Sometimes referred to as *double indemnity*.

Accumulation Period. A specified period of time, such as 90 days, during which the insured person must incur eligible medical expenses at least equal to the deductible amount to establish a benefit period under a major medical expense or comprehensive medical expense policy.

Actuary. A person professionally trained in the technical aspects of insurance and related fields, particularly in the mathematics of insurance, such as the calculation of premiums, reserves and other values.

Adjustable Life Insurance. A type of insurance that allows the policyholder to change the plan of insurance, raise or lower the face amount of the policy, increase or decrease the premium and lengthen or shorten the protection period.

Administrative Services Only (ASO) Plan. An arrangement under which an insurance carrier or an independent organization will, for a fee, handle the administration of claims, benefits and other administrative functions for a self-insured group.

Adverse Selection. The tendency of persons with poorer than average health expectations to apply for, or continue, insurance to a greater extent than do persons with average or better health expectations.

Age Limits. Stipulated minimum and maximum ages below and above which the company will not accept applications

---

*Used with permission of National Association of Consumer Agency Administrators

or may not renew insurance policies.

Agent. An insurance company representative licensed by the state who solicits and negotiates contracts of insurance, and provides service to the policyholder for the insurer. Insurance agents may also be called *underwriters*.

Aggregate Indemnity. The maximum dollar amount that may be collected for any disability or period of disability under the policy.

Allocated Benefits. Benefits for which the maximum amount payable for specific services is itemized in the contract

Amendment. A formal document changing the provisions of an insurance policy signed jointly by the insurance company officer and the policyholder or his or her authorized representative.

Annuitant. The person to whom an annuity is payable, usually the person to receive the annuity.

Annuity. A contract that provides a periodic income at regular intervals for a specified period of time, such as for a number of years or for life.

Annuity Certain. A contract that provides an income for a specified number of years, regardless of life or death.

Annuity Consideration. The payment, or one of the regular periodic payments, an annuitant makes for an annuity.

Application. A signed statement of facts requested by the company on the basis of which the company decides whether or not to issue the policy. This application may then become part of the insurance contract when the policy is issued.

Approval. Acceptance by an officer of the company of an offer from an applicant or policyholder in the form of a contract for new insurance, reinstatement of a terminated policy, request for a policy loan, etc.

Assignment. The signed transfer of benefits of a policy by the owner of the policy to a third party.

Assignment. The legal transfer of one person's interest in an insurance policy to another person.

Association Group. A group formed from members of a trade or a professional association for group insurance under one master health insurance contract.

B

Beneficiary. The person designated or provided for by the policy terms to receive the benefits of the policy.

Benefits. The amount payable by the insurance company to a claimant, assignee, or beneficiary under each coverage

Binding Receipt. A receipt given for a premium payment accompanying the application for insurance. If the policy is approved, this binds the company to make the policy effective from the date of the receipt.

Blanket Contract. A contract of health insurance affording benefits, such as accidental death and dismemberment, for all of a class of persons not individually identified. It is used for such groups as athletic teams, campers, travel policy for employees, etc.

Blanket Medical Expense. A provision that entitles the insured person to collect up to a maximum established in the policy for all hospital and medical expenses incurred, without any limitation on individual types of medical expenses.

Blue Cross. An independent, nonprofit membership corporation providing protection on a service basis against the cost of hospital care in a limited geographical area.

Blue Shield. An independent, nonprofit membership corporation providing protection on a service basis against the cost of surgical and medical care in a limited geographical area.

Broker. An insurance solicitor, licensed by the state, who places business with a variety of insurance companies.

Business Insurance. A policy that primarily provides coverage of benefits to a business as contrasted to an individual. It is issued to indemnify a business for the loss of services of a key employee or a partner who becomes disabled.

Business Life Insurance. Life insurance purchased by a

business enterprise on the life of a member of the firm. It is often bought by partnerships to protect the surviving partners against loss caused by the death of a partner, or by a corporation to reimburse it for loss caused by the death of a key employee.

C

Cash Surrender Value. The amount available in cash upon voluntary termination of a policy by its owner before it becomes payable by death or maturity.

Certificate. A statement issued to individuals insured under a group policy, setting forth the essential provisions relating to their coverage.

Certificate of Insurance. A statement of coverage issued to an individual insured under a group insurance contract, outlining the insurance benefits and principal provisions applicable to the member.

Claim. Notification to an insurance company that payment of an amount is due under the terms of a policy.

Claim. A demand to the insurer for the payment of benefits under the insurance contract.

Co-insurance. A policy provision frequently found in major medical insurance, by which both the insured person and the insurer share the covered loss under a policy in a specified ratio. For example, 80% is paid by the insurer and 20% is paid by the insured.

Comprehensive Major Medical Insurance. A policy designed to give the protection offered by both a basic and a major medical health insurance policy. It is characterized by a low deductible amount, a co-insurance feature and high maximum benefits.

Consideration. One of the elements for a binding contract. Consideration is acceptance by the insurance company of the payment of the premium and the statement made by the prospective policyholder in the application.

Conversion Privilege. A privilege granted in an insurance policy to convert to a different plan of insurance without providing evidence of insurability. The privilege granted by a group policy is to convert to an individual policy upon termination of group coverage.

Convertible Term Insurance. Term insurance which can be exchanged, at the option of the policyholder and without evidence of insurability, for another plan of insurance.

Coordination of Benefits (COB). The specific term used to designate the anti-duplication provision designed by the group health insurance industry through the Health Insurance Association of America (HIAA) to limit benefits for multiple group health insurance in a particular case to 100% of the expenses covered and to designate the order in which the multiple carriers are to pay benefits.

Covered Expenses. Hospital, medical, and miscellaneous health care expenses incurred by the insured that entitle him or her to a payment of benefits under a health insurance policy.

Credit Life Insurance. Term life insurance issued through a lender or lending agency to cover payment of a loan, installment purchase, or other obligation, in case of death.

D

Declination. The rejection by a life insurance company of an application for life insurance usually for reasons of the health or occupation of the applicant.

Deductible. The amount of covered charges incurred by the protected person that must be assumed or paid by the insured before benefits by the insurance company become payable. A deductible is most commonly used in major medical policies. However, it may also be incorporated in other policies.

Deferred Annuity. An annuity providing for the income payments to begin at some future date.

Deferred Group Annuity. A type of group annuity providing for the purchase each year of a paid-up deferred annuity for each member of the group, the total amount received by the member at retirement being the sum of these deferred annuities.

Deposit Administration Group Annuity. A type of group annuity providing for the accumulation of contributions in an undivided fund out of which annuities are purchased as the individual members of the group retire.

Deposit Term Insurance. A form of term insurance (not really involving a deposit) in which the first-year premium is larger than subsequent premiums. Typically, a partial endowment is paid at the end of the term period. In many cases the partial endowment can be applied toward the purchase of a new term policy or, perhaps, a whole life policy

Disability. Physical or mental handicap resulting from sickness or injury. It may be partial or total. (See also *Partial Disability; Total Disability*.)

Disability Benefit. A feature added to some life insurance policies providing for waiver of premium, and sometimes payment of monthly income, if the policyholder becomes totally and permanently disabled.

Disability Income Insurance. A form of health insurance that provides periodic payments to replace income when an insured person is unable to work as a result of illness, injury or disease.

Dismemberment. Loss of body members (limbs), or use thereof, or loss of sight due to injury.

Dividend. A return on part of the premium on participating insurance to reflect the difference between the premium charged and the combination of actual mortality, expenses and investment experience.

Dividend Addition. An amount of paid-up insurance purchased with a policy dividend and added to the face amount of the policy.

Double Indemnity. A policy provision usually associated with death that doubles payment of a designated benefit when certain kinds of accidents occur.

Dreaded Disease Insurance. Insurance providing an unallocated benefit, subject to a maximum amount, for expenses incurred in connection with the treatment of a specified disease, such as cancer, poliomyelitis, encephalitis, and spinal meningitis.

Duplication of Benefits. Overlapping or identical coverage of the same insured under two or more health plans, usually the result of contracts of different insurance companies, service organizations, or pre-payment plans. Also known as *multiple coverage.*

E

Effective Date. The date on which the insurance under a policy begins.

Eligibility Date. The date on which an individual member of a specified group becomes eligible to apply for insurance under the (group life or health) insurance plan.

Eligibility Period. A specified length of time, frequently 31 days, following the eligibility date during which an individual member of a particular group will remain eligible to apply for insurance under a group life or health insurance policy without evidence of insurability.

Eligible Employees. Those members of a group who have met the eligibility requirements under a group life or health insurance plan.

Elimination Period. A period of time between the period of disability and the start of disability income insurance benefits, during which no benefits are payable. (See also *Waiting Period.*)

Endowment. Life insurance payable to the policyholder if living, on the maturity date stated in the policy, or to a beneficiary if the insured dies prior to that date.

Enrollment Card. A document signed by an employee as notice of his or her desire to participate in the benefits of a group insurance plan.

Evidence of Insurability. Any statement of proof of a person's physical condition and/or other factual information affecting his or her acceptance for insurance.

Exclusions. Specific conditions or circumstances listed in the policy for which the policy will not provide benefit payments.

Expectation of Life. The average number of years of life remaining for a group of persons of a given age according to a particular mortality table.

Experience. A term used to describe the relationship, usually expressed as a percent or ratio, of premiums to claims for a plan, coverage, or benefits for a stated time period.

Experience Rating. The process of determining the premium rate for a group risk, wholly or partially on the basis of that group's experience.

Experience Refund. A provision in most group policies for the return of premium to the policyholder because of lower than anticipated claims.

Extended Term Insurance. A form of insurance available as a nonforfeiture option. It provides the original amount of insurance for a limited period of time.

F

Face Amount. The amount stated on the face of the policy that will be paid in case of death or at the maturity of the policy. It does not include additional amounts payable under accidental death or other special provisions, or acquired through the application of policy dividends.

Family Expense Policy. A policy that insures both the policyholder and his or her immediate dependents— usually spouse and children.

Family Income Policy. A life insurance policy, combining whole life and decreasing term insurance. The beneficiary receives income payments to the end of a specified period if the insured dies prior to the end of the period plus the face amount of the policy—either at the end of the period or at the death of the insured.

Family Policy. A life insurance policy providing insurance on all or several family members in one contract, generally whole life insurance on the principal breadwinner and smaller amounts of term insurance on the other spouse and children, including those born after the policy is issued.

Flat Schedule. A type of schedule in group insurance under which everyone is insured for the same benefits regardless of salary, position, or other circumstances.

Flexible Premium Policy or Annuity. A life insurance policy or annuity under which the policyholder or contract holder may vary the amounts or timing of premium payments.

Franchise Insurance. A form of insurance in which individual policies are issued to the employees of a common employer or the members of an association under an arrangement by which the employer or asssociation agrees to collect the premiums and remit them to the insurer.

Fraternal Insurance. A cooperative type of insurance provided by social organizations for their members.

Fraternal Life Insurance. Life insurance provided by fraternal orders or societies to their members.

G

Grace Period. A period, usually 30 to 31 days, following the premium date, during which an overdue premium may be paid without penalty. The insurance policy remains in force throughout this period.

Group Annuity. A pension plan providing annuities at retirement to a group of people under a master contract. It is usually issued to an employer for the benefit of employees. The individual members of the group hold certificates as evidence of their annuities.

Group Contract. A contract of insurance made with an employer or other entity that covers a group of persons identified as individuals by reference to their relationship to the entity.

Group Life Insurance. Life insurance provided, usually without medical examination, on a group of people under a master policy. It is typically issued to an employer for the benefit of employees, or to members of an association—a professional membership group, for example. The individual members of the group hold certificates as evidence of their insurance.

Guaranteed Renewable Contract. A contract that the insured person or entity has the right to continue in force by the timely payment of premiums for a substantial period of time. During this time, the insurer has no right to make unilaterally any change in any provision of the contract, while the contact is in force other than a change in the premium rate for classed of policyholders.

H
Health Insurance. Protection that provides payment of benefits for covered sickness or injury. Included under this heading are various types of insurance such as accident insurance, disability income insurance, medical expense insurance, and accidental death and dismemberment insurance.

Health Maintenance Organization (HMO). An organization that provides a wide range of comprehensive health care services for a specified group at a fixed periodic payment. The HMO can be sponsored by the government, medical schools, hospitals, employers, labor unions, consumer groups, insurance companies, and/or hospital-medical plans.

Hospital Expense Insurance. Health insurance protection against the cost of hospital care resulting from the illness or injury of the insured person.

Hospital Indemnity. A form of health insurance that provides a stipulated daily, weekly or monthly cash payment (indemnity) during hospital confinement. It is payable on an unallocated basis without regard to the actual expense of hospital confinement.

Hospital Medical Insurance. A term used to indicate protection that provides benefits for the cost of any or all of the numerous health care services normally covered under various health care plans.

I

Incontestable Clause. An optional clause that may be used in noncancellable or guaranteed renewable health insurance contracts providing that the insurer may not contest the validity of the contract after it has been in force for two, sometimes three, years.

Indemnity. Benefits paid in a predetermined amount in the event of a covered loss.

Individual Insurance. Policies that provide protection to the policyholder and/or his or her family. Sometimes called *Personal Insurance* as distinct from group and blanket insurance.

Industrial Life Insurance. Life insurance issued in small amounts, usually less than $1,000, with premiums payable on a weekly or monthly basis. The premiums are generally collected at the home by an agent of the company. Sometimes referred to as debit insurance.

Injury Independent Of All Other Means. An injury resulting from an accident, provided that the accident was not caused by an illness.

Insurability. Acceptability to the company of an applicant for insurance.

Insurance. Protection by written contract against the financial hazards (in whole or in part) of the happenings of specified events.

Insurance Examiner. The representative of a State Insurance Department assigned to participate in the official audit and examination of the affairs of an insurance company.

Insured or Insured Life. The person on whose life the policy is issued.

Insuring Clause. The clause that sets forth the type of loss being covered by the policy and the parties to the insurance contract

Integration. A coordination of the disability income insurance benefit with other disability income benefits, such as Social Security, through a specified formula to insure reasonable income replacement.

K

Key-Man or Key-Person Health Insurance. An individual or group insurance policy designed to protect a firm against the loss of income resulting from the disability of a key employee.

L

Lapsed Policy. A policy terminated for nonpayment of premiums.

Legal Reserve. The minimum reserve an insurance company must keep to meet future claims and obligations as they are calculated under the state insurance code.

Legal Reserve Life Insurance Company. A life insurance company operating under state insurance laws specifying the minimum basis for the reserves the company must maintain on its policies.

Level Premium. A premium that remains unchanged throughout the life of a policy.

Level Premium Life Insurance. Life insurance for which the premium remains the same from year to year. The premium is more than the actual cost of protection during the earlier years of the policy and less than the actual cost in the later years. The building of a reserve is a natural result of level premiums. The overpayments in the early years, together with the interest that is to be earned, serve to balance out the underpayments of the later years.

Life Annuity. A contract that provides an income for life.

Life Expectancy. The average number of years of life remaining for a group of persons of a given age according to a particular mortality table.

Life Insurance in Force. The sum of the face amounts, plus dividend additions, of life insurance policies outstanding at a given time. Additional amounts payable under accidental death or other special provisions are not included.

Lifetime Disability Benefit. A benefit to help replace income lost by an insured person as long as he or she is totally disabled, even for a lifetime.

Limited Payment Life Insurance. Whole life insurance on which premiums are payable for a specified number of years or until death, if death occurs before the end of the specified period.

Long-term Disability Income Insurance. Insurance issued to an employer (group) or individual to provide a reasonable replacement of a portion of an employee's earned income lost through serious and prolonged illness or injury during the normal work career. (See also *Integration*.)

M

Major Medical Insurance. Health insurance to finance the expense of major illness and injury. Characterized by large benefit maximums ranging up to $250,000 (or with no limit); the insurance, above an initial deductible, reimburses the major part of all charges for hospital, doctor, private nurses, medical appliances, prescribed out-of-hospital treatment, drugs and medicines. The insured person as co-insurer pays the remainder.

Master Policy. A policy issued to an employer or trustee, establishing a group insurance plan for designated members of an eligible group.

Medicaid. State programs of public assistance to persons regardless of age whose income and resources are insufficient to pay for health care. Title XIX of the Federal Social Security Act provides matching federal funds for financing state Medicaid programs, effective January 1, 1966.

Medicare. The hospital insurance system and the supplementary medical insurance for the aged created by the 1965 amendments to the Social Security Act and operated under the provisions of the Act.

Minimum Group. The least number of employees permitted under a state law to effect a group for insurance purposes. The purpose is to maintain some sort of proper division between individual policy insurance and the group forms.

Minimum Premium Plan. An arrangement under which an insurance carrier will, for a fee, handle the administration of claims and insure against large claims for a self-insured group.

Miscellaneous Expenses. Expenses in connection with hospital insurance. Hospital charges other than room and board, such as X-rays, drugs, laboratory fees and other ancillary charges. (Sometimes referred to as Ancillary Charges).

Morbidity. The incidence and severity of sicknesses and accidents in a well-defined class of persons.

Mortality. The incidence of deaths in a well-defined class of persons. The death rate.

Mortality Table. A statistical table showing the death rate at each age, usually expressed as so many per thousand.

Multiple Employer Trust (MET). A legal trust established by a plan sponsor that brings together a number of small, unrelated employers for the purpose of providing group medical coverage on an insured or self-funded basis.

Mutual Insurance Company. An insurance company that has no stockholders. It is managed by a board of directors, elected by its policyholders. Any earnings in excess of those necessary for the operation of the company are returned to the policyholders in the form of dividends. (See also *Stock Insurance Company.*)

N

National Association of Insurance Commissioners (NAIC). The association of insurance commissioners of various states formed to promote national uniformity in the regulation of insurance.

Noncancellable Guaranteed Renewable Policy. An individual policy that the insured person has the right to continue in force until a specified age, such as to age 65, by the timely payment of premiums. During this period, the insurer has no right to unilaterally make any changes in any provision of the policy while it is in force.

Nondisabling Injury. An injury that may require medical care, but does not result in loss of working time or income.

Nonforfeiture Option. One of the choices available if the policyholder discontinues premium payments on a policy with a cash value. It may be taken in cash, as extended term insurance or as reduced, paid-up insurance.

Nonmedical Limit. The maximum face value of a policy that a given company will issue without the applicant taking a medical examination.

Nonoccupational Policy. A contract that insures a person against off-the-job accident or sickness. It does not cover disability resulting from injury or sickness covered by Worker's Compensation. Group Accident and Sickness policies are frequently nonoccupational.

Nonparticpating Insurance. Plan of insurance under which the policyholder is not entitled to share in the dividend distribution of the company.

Nonparticipating Policy. A life insurance policy in which the company does not distribute to policyholders any part of its surplus. Note should be taken that premiums for nonparticipating policies are usually lower than for comparable participating policies. Note should also be taken that some nonparticipating policies have both a maximum premium and a current lower premium. The current premium reflects anticipated experience that is more favorable than the company is willing to guarantee, and it may be changed from time to time for the entire block of business to which the policy belongs. (See also *Participating Policy*.)

Nonprofit Insurers. Persons organized under special state laws to provide hospital, medical or dental insurance on a nonprofit basis. The laws exempt them from certain types of taxes.

O

Occupational Hazards. Dangers certain occupations expose to the insured.

Optionally Renewable Contract. A contract of health insurance in which the insurer reserves the right to terminate the coverage at any anniversary or, in some cases, at any premium due date, but does not have the right to terminate coverage between such dates.

Ordinary Life Insurance. Life insurance usually issued in amounts of $1,000 or more with premiums payable on an annual, semiannual, quarterly or monthly basis.

Overhead Insurance. A type of short-term disability income contract that reimburses the insured person for specified fixed, monthly expenses, normal and customary in the operation and conduct of his or her business or office.

P

Paid-up Insurance. Insurance on which all required premiums have been paid. The term is frequently used to mean the reduced paid-up insurance available as a nonforfeiture option.

Partial Disability. The result of an illness or injury that prevents an insured from performing one or more of the functions of his or her regular job.

Participating Insurance. Insurance issued by an insurance company providing participation in dividend distribution.

Participating Policy. A life insurance policy under which the company agrees to distribute to policyholders the part of its surplus that its Board of Directors determines is not needed at the end of the business year. Such distribution serves to reduce the premium the policyholder had paid. (See also *Policy Dividend; Nonparticipating Policy.*)

Permanent Life Insurance. A phrase used to cover any form of life insurance except term; generally insurance that accrues cash value, such as whole life or endowment.

Physician's Expense Insurance. Coverage that provides benefits toward the cost of such services as doctor's fees for nonsurgical care in the hospital, at home or in a physician's office, and X-rays or laboratory tests performed outside the hospital. (Also called Regular Medical Expense Insurance)

Policy. The legal document issued by the company to the policyholder that outlines the conditions and terms of the insurance; also called the policy contract or the contract.

Policy Dividend. A refund of part of the premium on a participating life insurance policy reflecting the difference between the premium charged and actual experience.

Policy Loan. A loan made by a life insurance company from its general funds to a policyholder on the security of the cash value of a policy.

Policy Reserves. The measure of the funds that a life insurance company holds specifically for fulfillment of its policy obligations. Reserves are required by law to be so calculated that, together with future premium payments and anticipated interest earnings, they will enable the company to pay all future claims.

Policy Term. That period for which an insurance policy provides coverage.

Policyholder. The person who owns a life insurance policy. This is usually the insured person, but it may also be a relative of the insured, a partnership or a corporation.

Premium. The payment, or one of the periodic payments, a policyholder agrees to make to keep an insurance policy in force.

Premium Loan. A policy loan made for the purpose of paying premiums.

Pre-existing Condition. A physical and/or mental condition of an insured that first manifested itself prior to the issuance of his or her policy or that existed prior to issuance and for which treatment was received.

Preferred Provider Organization (PPO). An arrangement whereby a third-party payor contracts with a group of medical care providers who furnish services at lower than usual fees in return for prompt payment and a certain volume of patients.

Pre-paid Group Practice Plan. A plan under which specified health services are rendered by participating physicians to an enrolled group of persons, with a fixed periodic payment in advance made by or on behalf of each person or family. If a health insurance carrier is involved, a contract to pay in advance for the full range of health services to which the insured is entitled under the terms of the health insurance contract. Such a plan is one form of health maintenance organization (HMO).

Principal Sum. The amount payable in one sum in the event of accidental death and in some cases accidental dismemberment.

Proration. The adjustment of benefits paid because of a mistake in the amount of the premiums paid or the existence of other insurance covering the same accident or disability.

Q

Qualified Impairment Insurance. A form of substandard or special class insurance that restricts benefits or the insured person's particular condition.

R

Rated Policy. Sometimes called an *extra-risk policy,* an insurance policy issued at a higher-than-standard premium rate to cover the extra risk where, for example, an insured has impaired health or a hazardous occupation.

Reasonable And Customary Charge. A charge for health care consistent with the going rate or charge in a certain geographical area for identical or similar services.

Recurring Clause. A provision in some health insurance policies that specifies a period of time during which the recurrence of a condition is considered a continuation of a prior period of disability or hospital confinement.

Reduced Paid-up Insurance. A form of insurance available as a nonforfeiture option. It provides for continuation of the original insurance plan, but for a reduced amount.

Rehabilitation. (1) Restoration of a totally disabled person to a meaningful occupation, (2) a provision in some long-term disability policies that provides for continuation of benefits or other financial assistance while a totally disabled insured is retraining or attempting to resume productive employment.

Reinstatement. The resumption of coverage under a policy that has lapsed.

Reinsurance. The acceptance by one or more insurers, called *reinsurers*, of a portion of the risk underwritten by another insurer who has contracted for the entire coverage.

Renewal. Continuance of coverage under a policy beyond its original term by the insurer's acceptance of the premium for a new policy term.

Renewable Term Insurance. Term insurance that can be renewed at the end of the term, at the option of the policyholder and without evidence of insurability, for a limited number of successive terms. The rates increase at each renewal as the age of the insured increases.

Reserve. The amount required to be carried as a liability in the financial statement of an insurer, to provide for future commitments under policies outstanding.

Residual Disability Benefits. A provision in an insurance policy that provides benefits in proportion to a reduction of earnings as a result of disability, as opposed to the inability to work full-time.

Rider. A special policy provision or group of provisions that may be added to a policy to expand or limit the benefits otherwise payable.

Risk. Any chance of loss.

Risk Classification. The process by which a company decides how its premium rates for life insurance should differ according to the risk characteristics of individuals insured (e.g., age, occupation, sex, state of health) and then applies the resulting rules to individual applications. (See also *Underwriting*.)

S

Self-administration. The procedure in which an employer maintains all records regarding the employees covered under a group insurance plan.

Self-insurance. A program for providing group insurance with benefits financed entirely by the employer in place of purchasing coverage from commercial carriers.

Senior Citizen Policies. Contracts insuring persons 65 years of age or over. In most cases these policies supplement the coverage afforded by the government under the Medicare program.

Separate Account. An asset account established by a life insurance company separate from other funds, used primarily for pension plans and variable life products. This arrangement permits wider latitude in the choice of investments, particularly in equities.

Settlement Options. The several ways, other than immediate payment in cash, that a policyholder or beneficiary may choose to have policy benefits paid. (See also *Supplementary Contracts*.)

Short-term Disability Income Insurance. The provision to pay benefits to a covered disabled person as long as he or she remains disabled up to a specified period not exceeding two years.

Special Risk Insurance. Coverage for risks or hazards of a special or unusual nature.

Standard Insurance. Insurance written on the basis of regular morbidity underwriting assumptions used by an insurance company and issued at normal rates.

Standard Risk. A person who, according to a company's underwriting standards, is entitled to insurance protection without extra rating or special restrictions.

State Disability Plan. A plan for accident and sickness, or disability insurance required by state legislation of those employers doing business in that particular state.

State Insurance Department. A department of a state government whose duty is to regulate the business of insurance and give the public information on insurance.

Stock Insurance Company. An insurance company owned and controlled by its stockholders, who share in the surplus earnings. (See also *Mutual Insurance Company*.)

Stock Life Insurance Company. A life insurance company owned by stockholders who elect a board to direct the company's management. Stock companies, in general, issue nonparticipating insurance, but may also issue participating insurance.

Straight Life Insurance. Whole life insurance on which premiums are payable for life.

Substandard Insurance. Insurance issued with an extra premium or special restriction to those persons who do not qualify for insurance at standard rates.

Supplementary Contract. An agreement between a life insurance company and a policyholder or beneficiary by which the company retains the cash sum payable under an insurance policy and makes payments in accordance with the settlement option chosen.

Surgical Expense Insurance. Health insurance policies that provide benefits towards the physician's or surgeon's operating fees. Benefits may consist of scheduled amounts for each surgical procedure.

Surgical Schedule. A list of cash allowances attached to the policy, that are payable for various types of surgery, with a maximum amount based upon the severity of the operation.

T

Term Insurance. Life insurance payable to a beneficiary only when an insured dies within a specified period.

Third Party Administration. Administration of a group insurance plan by some person or firm other than the insurer or the policyholder.

Time Limit. The period of time during which a notice of claim or proof of loss must be filed.

Total Disability. An illness or injury that prevents an insured person from continuously performing every duty pertaining to his or her occupation or engaging in any other type of work. (This wording varies among insurance companies).

Travel Accident Policy. A limited contract covering only accidents while an insured person is traveling, usually on a commercial carrier.

U

Unallocated Benefit. A policy provision providing reimbursement up to a maximum amount for the cost of all extra miscellaneous hosptial services, but not specifying how much will be paid for each type of service.

Underwriter. The term as generally used applies to either (a) a company that receives the premiums and accepts responsibility for the fulfillment of the policy contract; (b) the company employee who decides whether or not the company should assume a particular risk; (c) the agent who sells the policy.

Underwriting. The process by which a life insurance company determines whether it can accept an application for life insurance, and if so, on what basis.

Unearned Premium. That portion of the paid premium applying to the unexpired portion of the policy term; or that portion of the paid premium for which protection has not been received.

Uninsurable Risk. One not acceptable for insurance due to excessive risk.

Universal Life Insurance. A flexible premium life insurance policy under which the policyholder may change the death benefit from time to time (with satisfactory evidence of insurability for increases) and vary the amount or timing of premium payments. Premiums (less expense charges) are credited to a policy account from which mortality charges are deducted and to which interest is credited at rates which may change from time to time.

V

Variable Life Insurance. Life insurance under which the benefits relate to the value of assets behind the contract at the time the benefit is paid. The amount of death benefits payable would, under variable life policies that have been proposed, never be less than the initial death benefit payable under the policy.

W

Waiting Period. The length of time an employee must wait, from his or her date of employment or application for coverage, to the date his or her insurance is effective. (See also *Probationary Period*.)

Waiver. An agreement attached to a policy that exempts from coverage certain disabilities or injuries that are normally covered by the policy.

Waiver of Premium. A provision that under certain conditions an insurance policy will be kept in full force by the company without further payment of premiums. It is used most often in the event of total and permanent disability.

Whole Life Insurance. Life insurance payable to a beneficiary at the death of the insured, whenever that occurs. Premiums may be payable for a specified number of years (limited payment life) or for life (straight life).

Workers' Compensation. Insurance against liability imposed on certain employers to pay benefits and furnish care to employees injured, and to pay benefits to dependents of employees killed in the course of or arising out of their employment.

Index

Index

insurance,
  accidental death, 181
  applying for, 17
  auto, 157-204
  basics, 1-18
  basic health, 135
  credit, 186
  credit life, 186
  crime, 213
  disability, 100-130
  endowment, 36
  flood, 214
  health, 131-156
  homeowners, 205-242
  life, 19-99
  mail order, 64
  major medical, 135
  pure, 29
  savings bank life, 65
  single premium life, 37
  term, 20
  unisex, 44
  universal life, 33
  variable life, 35
  variable-universal life, 35
  whole life, 30
interest income, 61
IRA, 32, 126

J

Jeep Cherokee, 165

K

Kelley Blue Book, 159
Keogh, 32, 126

L

life income, 62
life insurance, 19-99
limited payment, 37
liquidity, 42
loss of use coverage, 207
lump sum, 61

M

mail order insurance, 64
major medical insurance,
  135-136
managing risk, 10
mature age discounts, 166

medical payments coverage,
  162, 181
Medicare, 146-153
  benefit period, 149
  supplement policies, 151
Medigap, 141, 150
model of auto, 171
mortgage, adjustable-rate, 126
motorists coverage,
  underinsured, 162
  uninsured, 163
multicar discount, 166
mutual company, 40

N

NADA Official Used Car
  Guide, 159
NAIC, 244
no-fault auto insurance, 164
non-forfeiture options, 50
non-participating, 51
non-smokers, 167

O

occupation classifications, 109
Official Used Car Guide, 159
overall injury loss, 172

P

P & C carriers, 10
par, 52
participating policy, 51-52
passenger vans, 174
passive income, 119
pension plans, 32
personal articles floater, 217
personal financial statement,
  24
Personal Injury Protection, 172
personal possessions, 216
Property and Casualty carriers,
  10
PIP, 172
policies,
  auto, 188-204
  dreaded disease, 142
  homeowners, 225-241
  hospital indemnity, 141
  switching, 63
  term, 67-84

275